TALES FROM THE TRACK

Stories from the early days of racing

J. Steve Strosnider

National Library of Canada Cataloguing in Publication

Strosnider, J. Steve
    Tales from the track / J. Steve Strosnider.
Includes index.
    1. Automobile racing drivers--United States--Biography. 2. Stock car racing--United States--History. I. Title.

GV1032.A1S86 2002   796.72'092'273   C2002-902043-3

Order this book online at www.trafford.com
or email orders@trafford.com

Most Trafford titles are also available at major online book retailers.

© Copyright 2002, 2007, 2011 J. Steve Strosnider.

All rights reserved. No part of this publication may be reproduced, stored in a retrieval system, or transmitted, in any form or by any means, electronic, mechanical, photocopying, recording, or otherwise, without the written prior permission of the author.

Printed in the United States of America.

ISBN: 978-1-5536-9509-7 (sc)
ISBN: 978-1-4122-4758-0 (e)

Trafford rev. 08/24/2011

 www.trafford.com

North America & international
toll-free: 1 888 232 4444 (USA & Canada)
phone: 250 383 6864 ♦ fax: 812 355 4082

Contents

Preface	2
Introduction	4
Acknowledgements	5
Tracks & Track Owners	
Eastside Speedway	6
Newspaper Advertisements of the Early Days of Racing	20
Early Action	24
Al Gore	27
Willie Wayne Gearhart	33
Drivers	
Bill Nalley	38
Junior Bowers	48
Smokey Stover	54
Clyde Harris	65
Cal Johnson	71
Tommy Irwin	80
Buddy Stinespring	87
Lewis Bocock	95
Dick Pappy Hansberger	103
Charlie Beeler	109
Al Grinnan	112
Earl Moran	115
Red Ninninger	119
Ray Dovel	123
Clem Lamaster	127
Roy Neff	132
Bob Dobyns	136
Jackie Clore	140
Avis Wyant	142
Short (Track) Stories	144
Summary of Personalities	148
Glossary of Terms	153
Index	156

Preface

Imagine the sugary aftertaste of a Dr. Pepper blended with the pungent taste of chopped onions from a lukewarm hot dog smothered in onions, the mustard stain still on my finger. Couple this with the smell of gasoline exhaust fumes and the faint, sweet smell of ether. I notice a trail of smoke drifting my way from a Lucky Strike cigarette held in the hand of a man with callused hands and dirty fingernails, no doubt a mechanic.

I am sitting on a rickety wooden grandstand with my mother and father. The grandstand is open beneath me. I see hotdog wrappers, what seems like thousands of cigarette butts, broken whiskey bottles, and Dr. Pepper and Pepsi bottles waiting to be retrieved for the two-cent deposit. A mechanic, bleeding profusely from the forehead, staggers across the track. His red blood turns black as it runs on his dark blue shirt. He collapses and is quickly attended by three men dressed in white. The obvious victim of a dispute settled by a tire iron, he is carted away in a 1949 Packard ambulance. Such violence is the exception, but danger at this place is the rule.

A scratchy record plays on a loud speaker, "Come along and be my party doll and I'll make love to you, to you. A white, a white, a white [the record skips], a white sport coat, and a pink carnation . . ."

It is July 1955. I am five and a half years old. It is a hot and humid evening in Waynesboro, Virginia. My father has paid a total of $3.50 admission for the three of us. I am intrigued by the shrill whistling sound of steam locomotives in the distance. Ahead of me are ten racecars sitting on a red clay track. Many of the fenders and bumpers are crumpled and dented, bearing witness to previous clashes with each other or the wooden fence that circles the track. The numbers are unusual, Car 501, Car 555, Car 292. Few, if any, are sponsored. The drivers look calm. Some are dressed in dirty white T-shirts, some in plaid short-sleeve shirts. No fireproof drivers' uniforms here. Their crash helmets look inadequate. I have learned now they are Cromwell Helmets. There is a hard cap, but what appears to be a leather side with a small visor at the top. Several wear goggles, many do not. One is smoking a cigar as he waits for the race to start. While the drivers sit in their cars loaded with methanol, one puffs on a cigarette. My heart rate rises as these cars emit a deep rumbling sound, reminding the onlookers of the danger that awaits. Anticipation rises as we await a parade lap or two and then the mad dash for the first turn at breakneck speed, often the most dangerous time of a race. This is a trophy race. In the 1950's, trophy races were a big deal. Drivers drove harder and took more risks to get a trophy back then. Now, a trophy is awarded every week.

On the night of July 2, 1955, Cal Johnson, a diminutive, popular journeyman driver from Ashland, Virginia, is driving Car 555, owned and built by Chuck Dedrick of Waynesboro, in the 30-lap amateur feature at Eastside Speedway in Waynesboro, Virginia. Coming off the fourth turn, he is hit on the left side by a spinning car driven by Otis Alfred, some say intentionally. Johnson continues to the first turn where his car, fueled with methanol and ether, explodes in a ball of flame. The car, a 1939 Ford Coupe with a Mercury overhead cam engine, is engulfed. Johnson jumps out of the car on the right side. Very few in the crowd see him, thinking he is no doubt burning alive. It is Johnson's small size that saves him in that it enables him to exit a small window. Johnson is burnt badly on his left arm and torso as well as his hands. He is carted away but will drive again five weeks later and will win the feature race at Lawrenceville, Virginia, over the legendary Wendell Scott. Chuck Dedrick will work long hours over the next week and have the Car 555 ready to race the following Saturday night.

I witnessed the car explode. I, too, thought the driver was burning inside the car. I was glad Johnson survived, but that event only made the danger of the sport more intriguing and exciting.

The races are over. My face and eyes feel gritty from the red clay dust of the races. I walk across the grass parking lot feeling the cool damp humidity of dew forming and smelling oil applied to the dirt roads to curtail the dust. I am tired, very tired. My ears ring from the noise.

I lay in the back seat of my father's 1950 Chevrolet. There are no seatbelts. I quickly fall asleep. I smell the rather moldy odor of the car seat. Two hours later we arrive at home in Woodstock, Virginia, after a brief stop at a late-night frozen custard stand in Harrisonburg, Virginia. I awaken long enough to consume raspberry frozen custard, but quickly fall asleep again. Upon arrival at my home, I am carried to bed by my father. I rest well, anxiously awaiting my next trip to the racetrack.

This book will chronicle the events of this night as well as many other nights of racing. Car 555's explosion has remained in the mind of the author for 47 years, but is representative of many memories that I have of that era of wrecks, wins, and culture of the 1950's stock car racers in the South.

Many of the tracks that operated then are defunct-- Keezeltown, Douglas, Fort Ashby, Red Banks, Royal, Devils Bowl, Starkey, Hilltop, Lynchburg, Pilot, Unionville, Craigsville, Charlottesville, Lawrenceville, Brookneal, Danville. Some continue--Eastside, Winchester, Hagerstown, Natural Bridge, South Boston. Some of the drivers are dead now. Many survive. This book will describe the lives of these very interesting men. These are men who for little pay and some recognition worked hard, spent money they did not have, and sacrificed a great deal for the glory of racing.

Stock car racing was a big part of my upbringing. I learned my numbers and ABC's from racecars. While most kids in the 1950's played with cowboys and Indians, I had toy racecars and had regular "races" with them. It is a wonder I did not grow up to be a hot-rodder or dare devil, but I didn't. I did not grow up to be a mechanic. I attended college and have a white-collar job, but my mind periodically travels back to that intriguing subculture of the 1950's which has now evolved into the multibillion dollar NASCAR.

The men described in this book never achieved the riches or fame of Dale Earnhardt, Jeff Gordon, Dale Jarrett, or Rusty Wallace; however, the men chronicled in this book are no doubt exemplary of thousands of men all across the country who risked life and limb and spent much to pursue racing. And while they were local stars and legends in their time, many have long since been forgotten, as have many of the tracks, which are now occupied by a mall, apartment complex, or serve as a host to grazing cattle.

In interviewing the racers and owners of that era, I found them all to be gentlemanly grandfather types who were more than willing to be of help. The respect and bond they established with each other then persists over the test of time and now overshadows the rivalries and controversies that often occurred. Their faces light when talking of past events and show sorrow when talking of the tragedies. These men, who were all extremely resourceful and mechanically inclined, often built fast racecars from junkyards. There was little safety equipment. They had guts. They are justifiably proud of what they accomplished. I admired them as a 5-year old and I admire them 47 years later.

INTRODUCTION

This book is the culmination of a year-long effort to locate and interview drivers, owners, and family members of the men involved in early stock car racing in the Shenandoah Valley of Virginia. In addition, information was garnered from The News Virginian of Waynesboro, Virginia, The Winchester Evening Star in Winchester, Virginia, the Staunton News Leader in Staunton, Virginia, The Richmond Times Dispatch, Richmond, Virginia, and the Madison County Eagle, Madison, Virginia.

This book is not intended to be a comprehensive history of racing in the Shenandoah Valley, but rather offers a series of glimpses into the life of the racing subculture of the era.

Apologies are made to those who could have contributed to this book but were not located by this author.

Individuals interviewed for this book include Al and Gary Gore, W. W. Gearhart, Clyde Harris, Bill, Sam, and Lorraine Nalley, Diane Bowers, Tommy and Bobby Campbell, Don Stover, Cal Johnson, Lewis and Jean Bocock, Buddy and Virginia Stinespring, P. C. Hansberger, Delores Hansberger Keagy, Tommy Irwin, Earl Moran, Red Ninninger, Ray Dovel, Roy and Hilda Neff, Clem and Doll Lamaster, Charlie Beeler, Al Grinnan, Bob and Joyce Dobyns, Avis Wyant, John Miller, Buddy Armel, Chuck Brannon, Marie Clore, Donnie Rodeffer, Chuck Dedrick, Ernest Claytor, and Mack Weaver.

The primary focus of this book will be on events that occurred at the two tracks that survive, Winchester Speedway and Eastside in Waynesboro, Virginia.

The author recognizes that readers unfamiliar with auto racing may have some difficulty understanding racing terminology. As such, a Glossary of Terms in order to enhance understanding is found at the end of the book.

The author further is aware that the reader may initially have some difficulty in placing names with events. To assist, a Summary of Personalities is also found at the end of the book.

Acknowledgements

This book is dedicated to my father, James A. Strosnider, Jr., who introduced me to stock car racing at the age of 4 at a race in Winchester, Virginia. He took me to and paid for dozens of racing events throughout the 50's and early 60's.

He also is an inspiration as an author, writing six books, including our family's genealogy which took untold hours of research and tenacity. His enjoyment of writing and his hard work will always be remembered.

This book is also dedicated to my wife, Robin R. Strosnider, whose patience and understanding of my passion for this project has been outstanding, and to my two special daughters, Becca and Mollie.

A very special thanks is extended to the many drivers, owners, and their families who allowed me in their homes and showed tremendous hospitality. Without their willingness to help, this project would not have been possible.

Thanks are also extended to Walker Nelms for expert photography services; to Melody Moore of Artistic Edit in Roanoke, Virginia, for expert transcription services; to Linda Cooper for painstaking editing; and to Steve McClintic for terrific graphic design.

Eastside Speedway

The Beginning

Eastside Speedway was originally built in 1953 by Eugene Kirby. It was a relatively flat one-fourth mile oval. Enticing racecars to come to the track was often a task indeed. The races were conducted on Saturday afternoons and as few as 12 cars would often appear for the races. At times, a car might be entered in as many as three heats during the afternoon. Kirby had installed lights and attempted to race at night with little luck. There were a number of other competing tracks at the time, namely Valley Speedway in Staunton, Douglas Speedway in Ruckersville, Hilltop Speedway in Zion's Crossroads, Cavalier Speedway in Charlottesville, 501 Speedway near Brookneal, Virginia, Lawrenceville, and Natural Bridge Speedway.

Claytor Buys the Track

In mid-summer 1954, Ulysses Prier (L. P.) Claytor and Ward Alford, who soon sold out, bought Eastside.

Under the direction of Claytor, the track was lengthened, widened, and the turns banked. Races occurred on Sundays and crowds approximated 500 fans, more than ever before.

In 1955, approximately 30,000 paid admissions were recorded for 20 nights of racing at Eastside.

The track, located on Route 340 one mile north of Waynesboro near the small town of Dooms, grossed nearly $50,000 in 1955. A total of $22,412 was divided among stock car drivers. The last race of 1954 yielded an amount of $1,725 in prize money to drivers. It is felt at the time to be the highest purses paid anywhere in the state of Virginia. The track at the time was labeled "the fastest outlaw track in the East" after it had been lengthened to four-tenths of a mile by Claytor in 1954. "Outlaw" sounded intriguing, but it simply meant that the speedway was not affiliated with the National Association of Stock Car Racing (NASCAR). It meant, too, that Eastside could make their own rules.

By 1955, Mr. Claytor had pretty well assembled his Eastside personnel. Leroy Radford of Stuart's Draft, a former stock car driver and hell driver with Joey Chitwood's Thrill Show, was track manager. Al Charles, a local radio personality was in charge of the general operation of the track and was the race announcer. Claytor watched over the equipment and concessions and counted the money.

The three had come to the conclusion that Saturday night was the best time to race stock cars. Claytor told The News Virginian, "Conditions are right. Fans usually have the time then as well as their entertainment dollar. Cars also appear to run faster at night. Sparks fly and they can be seen by the people, and the fans really eat up that sort of stuff."

Claytor was quoted in 1956 saying, "I went in debt to buy the track," admitting that he did not know a great deal about racing at the time, but added, "but I had men around me who did. However, I knew this much. The drivers have to be well paid. I want them to go away from here happy. In the beginning, I even took money out of my own pocket to see that they did." Claytor, who was a contractor by trade, said, "I've got $65,000 in this place. I've been offered $75,000. But I won't budge until I hear $100,000, and then I'll have to think about it."

Shortly before his death, Claytor was asked why he didn't put asphalt on the speedway. The answer was simple: he didn't want it. Though the argument, according to him, was that asphalt would solve the dust problem, dust, however, was no problem at Eastside according to Claytor.

He said that there were 500 loads of clay on the four-tenths of a mile oval. His workers started watering the track at 9:00 a.m. the day of the race until 5:00 p.m. non-stop. According to him, "A thick, heavy consistency forms and makes more traction. The surface becomes spongy, and by race time the track is setup 'just right.'"

In 1955, after all expenses had been made, Claytor made approximately $15,000, adding, "Practically all of it went back into the track."

As Claytor entered the 1956 season, his son Ernest assumed the role of track manager. The move was made to acquaint Ernest with the operation of the track in order for him to eventually inherit leadership of the track. Everett Cromer of Orange, Virginia, was the flagman and judges were Woody Huffman, Bill Grove, and Clarence Thompson. Their job was to enforce speedway regulations and to keep track of finishing order.

TRYING TO GET FANS

As a way of increasing fan support and attendance, Eastside offered door prizes to fans chosen at random. On Sunday, June 13, 1954, a 17-inch television was offered as the door prize. The ad read, "Eastside Speedway - thrilling, chilling, you'll love them."

On June 27, 1954, a $50 savings bond was offered as a fan incentive. The ad read, "You don't have to sit in the sun. There's a roof over the bleachers."

On Sunday, July 4, 1954, Eastside offered a $75 savings bond and a week later on July 11, 1954, a $25 bond was offered.

On July 18, 1954, a radio and two irons were door prizes.

On Friday, September 4, 1954, the door prizes were an electric iron and electric mixer.

DEATH AT EASTSIDE

L. P. Claytor had a history of heart trouble. On the night of April 28, 1956 at Eastside Speedway, before the second race of the 1956 season, Claytor had talked of his future plans for the track in an interview with Charlie Burtner, a feature writer for the Waynesboro News Virginian.

Claytor said, "My health is not what it used to be. My heart has gone back on me, but I plan to be around to run the track a couple more years. Then I'll turn it over to Mary (his wife) and Ernest (his son). It will be a good business for them," he added. "Where else can they make $15,000 in such a short period of time?"

Approximately an hour and a half after he made these statements, Claytor collapsed while counting money in the concession stand and the announcer called for a doctor in the house. Ernest, who was sitting atop the grandstand watching the races, instinctively knew that his father in trouble. He quickly jumped off his perch and ran to the concession stand. He took off his father's jacket, placed him on the floor, and loosened his tie and shirt. A Dr. Smith soon arrived. Claytor died on the way to the hospital with Ernest by his side in the ambulance.

The following Saturday night, everyone in attendance at Eastside stood in silence for half a minute before the playing of the national anthem. The account in The News Virginian continues,

The silent tribute climaxed in pre-race ceremonies observing the death of Mr. L. P. Claytor, owner and operator of the Eastside Speedway.

After the stock cars had been lined up on the front stretch for the first heat race of the evening, the drivers stood beside their cars with the flagman facing them at attention, holding the green and checkered flags in a cross position in front of him. From the public address system came the story of how this man was responsible for making stock car racing in this area such a huge spectator attraction. Those present were informed that Mr. Claytor realized very little monetary return on his huge investment in the track. It was explained he was satisfied in the knowledge that he was presenting the best racing ever offered in this area.

It was pointed out that during the past two years, Mr. Claytor had continued to invest heavily in the racing plant in order to bring it to its present efficient operating condition. Ernest Claytor (his son) will continue to operate the speedway in the same manner it has been run in the past. The staff will remain the same. Members of the family express sincere appreciation for the kindness shown in the past week. The staff pledged continued effort to operate the track in the same manner to the best of its ability. During the tribute, absolute silence reigned over the area where noise usually is a predominant factor.

Notables racing that night were Bill Nalley, John Strickland, Junior Bowers, Bob Dobyns, Rod Harris, Smokey Stover, Tommy Irwin, Al Grinnan, Cal Johnson, Gip Gibson, Chuck Saul, Charlie Sipe, Harry Rodeffer, and Robert Peer. Feature races that evening were won by Gip Gibson and Rod Harris.

CLAYTOR TEACHES A LESSON

On the night of April 21, 1956, a week before his death, L. P. Claytor caught two youngsters climbing into the speedway by scaling the outside fence. Seeing them, he yelled at them in his rough, deep voice.

Both ran, but Claytor caught one of them by the seat of the pants and said to the youngster, "Look here, boy, by the time you're 21 years old you'll be in jail somewhere if you keep on pulling stunts like this.

"If you come down here to the races and have got 50¢, come to see me and I'll let you in free. But I don't want to see anymore of this coming over the fence and trying to sneak in."

The youngster wanted to know if his buddy, who had gotten away, could come under the same deal Claytor had made with him.

"Hell, yes," L. P. bellowed, "but I doubt if you can catch him. He's probably halfway through the next county by now."

Claytor is quoted saying that his job was the "most dangerous." "I have the most dangerous job at Eastside. You know why? It falls on my shoulders to try and keep everybody happy.

"Stop a minute and look around. There are a lot of people. Count them--drivers, fans, and my own employees here at the track. Just try pleasing everybody sometime and you'll see what I mean."

Ernest Claytor Takes Over

L. P. Claytor's son, Ernest Claytor, currently lives outside Waynesboro in a well-decorated ranch home with impeccable grooming. A three-car garage sits behind his home and houses many momentos from the Eastside era.

Ernest is an extremely talented man who can make just about anything from wood. He is terrific at whittling and carving items from wood, and can also make figures from different pieces of wood, often using hundreds of different of pieces with different colors to produce a figure.

He took over Eastside after his father's death. He provides additional insight into what it was like to run Eastside Speedway in 1956. Each night, approximately 200 cartons of Coca-Cola were on hand for spectators sold at 50¢ a piece. A total of 2,400 hotdogs would usually be on hand, also sold at 50¢ a piece. The track had its own specially made chili, which added to its flavor, usually with chopped onions and mustard.

Ernest paid the announcer, Al Charles, $200 per race, which eventually increased to $500 a race. There was also a $500 fee that had to be paid every evening for racing insurance.

Ernest is Ousted

The next year (1957) in the midst of a dispute, Ernest's stepmother Mary, who had been willed the track by her husband L. P., said to Ernest, "I don't need you down here anymore." Ernest says now, "I never thought she'd do what she did. My dad wanted me to run the track and I got run off." He seldom has returned to the track.

Selected Events from the Past

The following are excerpts from the 1954 and 1955 seasons under the direction of L. P. Claytor:

L.P. and Earnest Claytor walk Eastside Speedway. Notice the fence missing, taken out the night before by a wayward racecar.

On April 8, 1954, an ad in The News Virginian headed *"Racing Fans of Eastside Speedway - The Following Drivers Are Expected to Participate in the Upcoming Race on April 11th:"*

Bob Cook   *Leroy Radford*
J. D. Dillon   *Jeff Steel*
Ed Hockman   *Smokey Stover*
Chester Stanley   *Earl Moran*
Doug Batten   *Maynard Hockman*

On May 28, 1954, an ad in The News Virginian advertised racing at Natural Bridge Speedway on May 30, 1954, competing with Eastside. According to the ad, *"An electric mixer will be given to the lucky contestant."*

On June 10, 1954, at Eastside, amateur heats were won by Smokey Stover and Earl Brooks of Lynchburg. Sportsman heats were won by Cotton Shiflett of Richmond and Gip Gibson of Charlottesville. The amateur feature was won by John Coffman from Craigsville, Virginia, and Cotton Shiflett won the sportsman feature.

On July 18, 1954, at Eastside, Gip Gibson won the sportsman feature with Smokey Stover winning the amateur feature. Other notables racing that day Wendell Scott, Bill Nalley, Junior Bowers, Charlie Propst, and Paul Cauley.

In August 1954, Eastside began racing on Friday nights. Winners of the last Sunday race, which was held on August 5, 1954, saw Claude Baldwin winning the feature race over Smokey Stover and Earl Brooks.

The first Friday night race at Eastside on August 13, 1954 was won by Claude Baldwin over Charles Sipe and Smokey Stover.

On September 3, 1954, Smokey Stover's wife Ruby won a powder puff race at Eastside. Bill Nalley won the sportsman feature race over Claude Baldwin and Cotton Shiflett. A participant in that race was Tommy Stinespring, older brother of Buddy Stinespring, who was later killed in a boating accident in Florida.

The 1955 season saw Eastside start racing each Saturday night. An article in The News Virginian dated April 9, 1955 boasts:

The old Eastside plant has undergone a face lifting since last year. The track has been rebuilt and enlarged to four-tenths of a mile. L. P. Claytor who manages the speedway maintains now that Eastside is the fastest outlaw track in the East.

Notable drivers on hand for the inaugural event of the 1955 season include Claude Baldwin, Charlie Propst, Chester Stanley, Lewis Bocock, Harry Rodeffer, Bill Nalley, John Strickland, Gip Gibson, Cal Johnson, Bob Dobyns, and Paul Cauley, among others. The sportsman feature that evening was won by Claude Baldwin in front of a turnout of 955 fans who braved threatening weather.

On April 30, 1955, crowd favorite Claude Baldwin flipped his Car 703 end over end and then rolled over three complete times. He came to rest on all four wheels and was rushed to the hospital for minor cuts and bruises. He was later released, not seriously injured.

On May 7, 1955, 1,268 fans saw Junior Bowers and Bill Nalley tangle on the front stretch. Bowers' car

L.P. Claytor points over the grounds of Eastside Speedway to son, Earnest saying, "This will be yours one day." It was not to be.

went skidding down the front stretch on its side, resulting in only slight damage. Neither driver was hurt. The race was eventually won by Gip Gibson.

On May 29, 1955, 1,948 spectators saw Mrs. Ruby Stover (Smokey Stover's wife) win a powder puff race over second place Mrs. Junior Bowers.

The sportsman feature was won by Paul Cauley, who won the sportsman feature with an average speed of 66.8 miles per hour for 50 laps.

The amateur feature that evening was won by Ray Chandler of Staunton with a speed of 62.4 miles per hour for 40 laps.

On May 21, 1955, Kuda Bux, "the man with x-ray eyes", appeared at Eastside.

On June 18, 1955, some 1,316 fans were on hand to witness a total of 17 cars go over the banks at Eastside. No one was hurt.

An article in the August 1, 1955 edition of The News Virginian has this to say about recent improvements at Eastside:

The important project facing the track now is the public address system. A considerable amount of time, effort, and money has been spent in an attempt to improve the sound system. To date it has not been successful. Heads will be together again this week to see what can be done about the problem. The P.A. setup has been one of the sore spots of the season at the Eastside racing plant. Officials feel confident that an improvement will be made in the near future.

The article continues,

Speedway owner, L. P. Claytor, has announced that the nine officials, who have charge of the judges' stands and the pits and direct running of the races, will attend the Southern 500-Mile Stock Car Classic at Darlington, SC on Labor Day. The Eastside owner has purchased reserved seats for the group. Plans include a get-together with Russ Catlin, Press Relations Director of the Darlington International Raceway.

On July 2, 1955, Cal Johnson is seriously injured

Sign at Eastside Speedway. circa 1956.

when his car explodes.

On August 27, 1955, Lewis Bocock won the amateur feature over Claude Baldwin and Earl Moran. The sportsman feature was won by John Strickland of Orange, followed by Paul Cauley and Bill Nalley.

On August 20, 1955, in the running of the second

amateur 10-lap heat, Car 35A, driven by Earl Moran, and Car P38, owned by Roy Neff, but driven that night by Bob Crosen of Winchester, finished fender to fender as the checkered flag dropped. It was ruled a dead heat.

The following excerpt from the August 22, 1955 edition of The News Virginian was found related to Eastside:

Track officials cracked down on the rules regarding admission to the pits and infield this week. It had become evident that something had to be done to limit the number of people inside the working area of the track in order to insure the safety of everyone and to allow officials and mechanics to do their work more efficiently. The result was one of the best-run races of the season. Even with a huge field of cars, the action was completed before 10:30 p.m.

Throughout the 1955 season, there had been a great deal of competition between Paul Cauley and Claude Baldwin. In the end, Cauley was declared the track point champion, receiving $200 for first place. Baldwin finished in second place and received $175. John Strickland was third and received $125, with Bill Nalley fourth, receiving $100.

Swallowing a Cigar

Superstitions develop in any sport; however, in the early days of racing, several strong superstitions had developed among most drivers by 1956. Peanuts in the pits, green cars, black cats, and cameras before races were superstitions shared by many drivers. Cotton Shiflett speaks of a superstition he once had, but abandoned. In 1956 he said, "I used to smoke a cigar in every race I drove. One day in upper Marlboro a year or two ago, I was hanging pretty close to the inside rail. My front wheel caught a post and my car rolled over three times.

"I swallowed my cigar, fire and all, and I haven't smoked one during a race since then. Before that, I was never without one when I drove."

More Events at Eastside

The 1957 season at Eastside opened with a convincing win by Bill Nalley over second place Cal Johnson. Also racing that night were Gip Gibson, Al Grinnan, and Wendell Scott. This race occurred on April 22, 1957.

On April 27, 1957, Nalley won again over second place Tommy Irwin, Cal Johnson and Robert Peer.

On May 21, 1957, the North American Thrill Drivers, which featured both automobile and motorcycle drivers, appeared at Eastside.

Al Gore buys Eastside in 1958.

At the opening race of the 1958 season on April 28, rain halted action after four events. The News Virginian has this account:

Thirty cars were on hand for the opening night races, and stock jockeys found the superbly groomed clay oval at Eastside to their liking. The track has been improved by Eastside officials and is considered to be in the best condition of the five years that the track has been in existence.

On July 7, 1958, Tommy Irwin won the sportsman feature over second place Smokey Stover and third place Lewis Bocock. Bill Nalley missed the race due to the death of his mother. 1,672 race fans were on hand.

On September 1, 1958, Bill Nalley won a hotly contested sportsman feature over Smokey Stover. The amateur feature was won by Dick Pappy Hansberger.

On September 15, 1958, Gip Gibson won both the amateur feature and his heat race, but was disqualified when it was discovered that he did not meet amateur qualifications. Buddy Stinespring picked up the money for the heat race, and Car 555, owned by Chuck Dedrick of Waynesboro and driven by Herb Breeden of Orange, was awarded the feature money. On this particular night, Bill Nalley won the sportsman feature, followed by second place Junior Bowers, third place Lewis Bocock, and fourth place Smokey Stover.

On May 3, 1959, over 1,000 racing fans ushered in the 1955 stock car season at Eastside, seeing once again a victory by Bill Nalley in the sportsman feature.

On July 4, 1959, 2,150 fans were described as "lucky enough to get tickets" as part of a first "turn away crowd in the history of the track." It is said that over 100 more fans had to be turned away as there was simply no more room.

Approximately $1,700 in purse money was up for grabs, which was also described as the largest purse ever paid at the speedway.

The News Virginian carries this account:

Track officials and many fans agreed that it was the finest show the speedway has offered. There was something to suit the taste of every racing fan. Three cars rolled over; there were numerous flips off the banks; collisions galore; hard, fast racing; and many tight battles down to the wire.

But in the final analysis, the favorites ran true to form. Bullet Bill Nalley of Winchester won the 50-lap sportsman trophy in the Car S3. He picked up the checkered flag, the gold trophy, and $202 for his efforts. Jack Denison of Arlington piloting Car B82 won the 40-lap amateur trophy feature. He also took home a gold trophy and $135. Both cars won by wide margins.

The second place in the sportsman feature went to Car 5, driven by Ray Dovel of Elkton, while Smokey Stover of Staunton in Car 306 romped home in third place.

On July 18, 1959, Smokey Stover won the 25-lap sportsman feature at Eastside under threatening skies, topping Ray Dovel of Elkton in second place and Bill Nalley in third.

In this particular race, Nalley claimed after the race that he used almost five quarts of oil during the event and could not have competed for two or three more laps. The newspaper account says, "It looks like as if Car S3 is due for a major overhaul in the near future."

Earl Moran won the 20-lap amateur feature that evening.

On July 25, 1959, track officials announced that, because of the lack of sportsman cars at Eastside, the division had been cancelled and the hobby cars along with amateurs would run a full cart of events for the remainder of the season.

This particular night, a total of five cars--four hobby and one amateur--rolled over. Jim Harris, a driver from Staunton, Virginia, was injured and taken to the hospital. It was later determined that Harris was not seriously injured.

On August 15, 1959, the light poles at Eastside took a beating. There was enough damage to the lights that the feature race was deferred to the following week because of the length of time estimated to repair the lights.

On this night, Chuck Dedrick of Waynesboro, driving the Car 555, in the seventh lap of the amateur heat started a chain of events which led to the lighting difficulties, when his seat came loose, tossing him into the floor. He was attempting to steer from this position and keep the car under control when it careened across the track into the path of Car 404 driven by Tucker Thomas of Staunton. After meeting Dedrick's car broadside, Thomas' car swerved into the infield, striking the light pole and disconnecting the lights.

Electricians came to the rescue and made the necessary repairs and the race was completed.

On the 19th lap of the hobby feature, three cars went out of control with one car again hitting a light pole and putting out the lights. At this, racing ended for the night.

The final event of the 1959 racing season held on September 7, 1959, saw a record-breaking field of 64 amateur and hobby stock cars in action. The season had been deemed a success, however, the sportsman cars being discontinued because of a lack of participation was a significant development.

No races were held during the 1960 season until August 14, 1960. The season opened with the once again modified and sportsman cars racing in the same feature because of a lack of modified cars.

1,100 fans were in attendance for the first race of 1960. Smokey Stover won the 20-lap feature race, which found the modifieds pitted against the sportsmen in open competition. Second place went to Lewis Bocock, with Jackie Clore in third, and Wendell Scott fourth. Clore's car, however, was a sportsman and received money for being the top finishing sportsman racer. This race was held on a Sunday afternoon and it was delayed approximately for one hour due to dust. According to The News Virginian,

The dirt had pulverized during the long layoff of racing and the rains of Saturday and the many loads of water just soaked in and dried fast. "This won't happen again," Al Gore said as he promised in the future that dust would not be present.

In 1960, the sportsman division became known as the modified division. The amateur division became known as the sportsman division. The word amateur was eliminated. This change was seen at Eastside, Devil's Bowl, and Winchester.

A third division, hobby class, first known as jalopy class, was added in 1959.

On August 28, 1960, more than 1,000 fans showed up on a Sunday afternoon at Eastside to see Smokey Stover win his third consecutive feature at Eastside in the modified division. He won despite stiff competition from Lewis Bocock, Bill Nalley, and Red Ninninger who finished in that order.

The News Virginian has this account of Wendell Scott's participation in this race:

Also finishing high on the list was Wendell Scott of Danville, a Negro race driver for NASCAR. He ran into tough trouble in the early rounds, but finished gamely to rank high on the list.

The final race of the 1960 season occurred on October 2, 1960 with approximately 500 persons in attendance at Eastside. The 25-lap sportsman feature was won by Jackie Clore.

On April 12, 1961, The News Virginian had this account of recent events at Eastside:

Renovations Are Underway at Eastside
Work is continuing on the renovation of Eastside Speedway for the opening of the 1961 stock car racing season on Saturday, April 22nd.

Al Gore, promoter, observed that all efforts are

being made to have the track in top shape for the first event, which will begin at 8:30 p.m. next Saturday.

"Jalopies, sportsmen, and modifieds will be included on the program for the opening night. Heats and features in each will be run if sufficient cars are on hand," Gore said.

The main items being renovated at the track this year include moving the fence back from the track on the far side, giving the drivers more room to swing wide in coming off the second turn. The pit area also is being enlarged. More and new lights are being installed for the convenience of racing fans. New clay is being placed on the oval.

The 1961 season opened at Eastside with more than 900 racing fans in attendance. On this night, Charles Atwell of Lynchburg was injured in the first sportsman heat when his car failed to negotiate the first turn, went over the embankment, and then flipped end-over-end through the wooden fence, coming to a rest outside the park. Atwell was taken to the hospital and later released.

The modified feature this night was won by Smokey Stover. Bill Nalley, driving in the sportsman division, won that feature.

FLAGMAN KILLED

On April 29, 1961, 49-year old Bob Cook, standing next to promoter and flagman Al Gore, was killed. Two cars, driven by Bobby Parker of Lynchburg and Earl Matheny of Waynesboro, overturned into the infield on the front stretch in front of 500 horrified fans, crushing Cook and narrowly missing Gore. A more detailed account is found in the chapter on Al Gore.

MORE STORIES

On May 1, 1962, the 1962 season at Eastside started. The April 30, 1962 edition of The News Virginian had this account:

Big Program is Scheduled at Eastside
Stock car drivers will have an added incentive for a bigger pot at the end of the season at Eastside Speedway.

The added incentive this year is a point system, which will build up during the year. The more points piled up by the driver, the more chance he will have of collecting a bigger pot at the end of the year.

One of the ways in which points can be added is promptness in responding to a call for appearance on the track for any given heat or race. If the driver has his car on the track within the required time, he will be given points. If he is not on the track within the required time, he will not be given points. If he is not on the track within a certain period, the gate will be closed and he will miss the heat or feature. This will be a loss of points.

The timing of entrance onto the track will also tend to speed up the program, which at some times last year proved to be dragging in the time element. Besides allowing points for the drivers, this system will also benefit the fans since the races will go off on schedule rather than lagging.

On June 2, 1962, Smokey Stover won the modified feature and Buddy Stinespring won the sportsman feature. It was a wild night as The News Virginian recounts:

The night was not without incident. Fences around the dirt oval at Eastside were constantly in for a banging, as were the various stock cars. The action began early in the evening with Lynchburg's William Shipp smashing the fence in front of the grandstand in the first hobby heat. In the finale, the modified feature, Stover's vehicle was banged up somewhat in a collision, but not enough to keep the veteran driver from winning.

Lewis Bocock finished second to Stover, with third place going to Buddy Stinespring driving Lewis Bocock's second car.

On June 16, 1962, Buddy Stinespring's dominance in the sportsman division was broken by Buck Shipp of Troy, Virginia, who battled with Stinespring the majority of the race. During the race, the two of them had collided with Stinespring sliding into the infield. This incident kept Stinespring from challenging Shipp the rest of the way.

Earl Moran won the modified feature, which was interrupted for 15 minutes when tempers of some of the participants got out of hand following a three-car pileup on the fourth turn. Al Grinnan finished second to Moran.

On July 1, 1962, Smokey Stover crashed into a pole at Eastside, taking out the lights. He was not injured. The features that night were won by Buddy Stinespring in the sportsman division and Lewis Bocock in the modified division.

On July 7, 1962, more than 1,200 persons were on hand at Eastside for the Dr. Pepper Trophy Night.

Larry Williams of Staunton, driving a modified racer, was admitted to Waynesboro Community Hospital after his car went out of control on the first turn and crashed through the board fence, coming to rest outside the park. He was described as having lung and brain injuries.

Winners of trophies that night were Avis Wyant in the hobby feature, Buck Shipp in the sportsman class, and Smokey Stover in the modified division.

The 1963 season at Eastside began on May 12, 1963 with over 1,000 spectators in attendance and a rather controversial wreck in the modified feature. Earl Moran and Car 88, driven by Earl McCrary of Staunton, were involved in an accident along with Bill Nalley. While McCrary and Moran were out of the race, Nalley was able to finish but was not competitive.

The three-car crash came on the fourth lap of the feature in full view of the stands. The car driven by McCrary spun into the path of Moran and Nalley as all three were battling for the lead. Although damage was severe, none of the drivers sustained injuries.

Just prior to the three-car pileup, Smokey Stover had gone over the embankment off the first turn. This allowed Stover to start at the rear of the field, re-enter the lineup, and then win the feature, finishing ahead of Lewis Bocock in Car 500.

A wild night of racing occurred on May 18, 1963 at Eastside. Over 1,100 fans witnessed 18 crashes involving one to nine cars and was described as "nerve shaking" by The News Virginian which had this account:

It took five starts to move the 21-car sportsman feature and the red flag was out so often that speedway officials will put a new plan into effect next Saturday. By adding a third sportsman heat, the speedway can qualify the five finishers in each and send 15 speedsters into the feature, a far better number toward fewer re-starts.

At the end of the fence-busting event, it was Winchester's Charlie Beeler flashing past the checkered flag in near record time for his second big win of the season. The dark haired youngster put on enough of a show to line himself up for the modified competition next season.

In the classic 35-lap modified feature, Staunton's Smokey Stover gained a step over Winchester's Bill Nalley with his second major purse of the season.

From the clean start, this feature had all the appearance of a four-way duel between the two veterans and Lewis Bocock of Greenville and Earl McCrary of Staunton.

But Stover won it going away after a remarkable recovery from a ninth lap spinout. With Nalley's S3 developing carburetor trouble after slipping into a 100-yard lead, it was just a question of time before Stover and then Bocock passed the ace driver. Staunton's pride went past on the 15th lap and Bocock the 30th, leaving Nalley in third about 250 yards in front of McCrary. The other starters were never in contention.

Dick Pappy Hansberger of Mount Jackson opened the night's racing with an easy victory in the first sportsman heat.

On June 1, 1963, an exciting race occurred between Bill Nalley and Smokey Stover before 1,500 fans at Eastside. Stover led the first 9 laps of the 50-lap modified feature and then was overtaken by Nalley, who led until the 47th lap when he spun onto the infield. Through a masterful display of driving, Nalley returned to the track only 50 yards behind Stover. Stover held on for the win.

Earlier in the race, Stover came close to a major accident when he got too close to Bill Nalley, who was leading and slipped sideways. He had to fight his Car 306 all the way to keep control and lost about 100 yards in the process.

Buddy Stinespring came from behind to win over Charlie Beeler in the sportsman feature. Beeler took the checkered flag only an instant before hitting a loose wheel on the track and skidding off the clay surface into the fence in front of the East grandstand.

According to The Virginia News Leader,

Lumber was cheap at the speedway on Saturday as the fence smashing crew in the sportsman division continued the weekly assault on the woodwork. In five racing dates, the sportsman drivers have sent their speedsters through, over, and into the fences with complete lack of interest in repair work. An effort was made to cut down on the number of accidents by limiting the feature race to 15 cars, qualifying only 5 cars from each heat and another 5 from a consolation.

On June 15, 1963, the assault on the fence continued as 15 feet of fencing on the number two turn disappeared when Car 409 driven by Gene Garrison of Staunton was heading for the pit area when a front wheel snapped free and slammed into the tall fence. No one was injured with the wheel taking the fence section with it into the woods beyond.

On July 13, 1963, the surprise winner, Bobby Hite of Waynesboro, who had won the 25-lap sportsman feature race, was protested by Charlie Beeler who posted $25 to have Hite's motor examined. It was determined that his motor measured 314 cubic inches, considerably above the 290 cubic inch limit. The disqualification gave Beeler the feature win, with Buddy Stinespring finishing second. Interestingly, track owner Al Gore's partner, Clyde Trenary, presented Hite with $50 of his own money to soften the loss.

The following week on July 20, 1963, Hite, who had finished third to Beeler and Buddy Stinespring, posted the $25 to have Beeler's car torn down. Track management posted an equal amount to have Stinespring examined. Despite Hite's hopes to vindicate himself from the previous week, both Beeler and Stinespring were felt to be legal. Adding insult to injury was that Hite lost the $25 that he had posted to initiate the protest.

On August 3, 1963, Pete Mack, driving a 1953 Studebaker, won a destruction derby at Eastside

Speedway.

On August 17, 1963, Tommy Hudson of Lynchburg, a skydiver, jumped from 420 feet into Eastside Speedway. He barely missed the 15-foot target. He had planned to drop from 1,200 feet, making it the longest jump in Augusta County history, but high winds forced him to jump from the lower altitude. The jump was deemed to be especially difficult because of the numerous overhead wires at the track.

On September 1, 1963, 1,500 stock car fans at Eastside saw Bobby Shipe narrowly escape death. Shipe, driving a new freshly painted car, was on the tail end of a three-car collision. What looked like a modest head-on collision became a shocking scene as flames enveloped Shipe's car. Clyde Harris, a scorer at Eastside and good friend of Shipe, raced from the judge's stand with a fire extinguisher to kill the flames. Shipe, who was slightly injured by the shoulder harness upon impact, dove through the window to safety, suffering additional bruises in his headfirst dive to the ground.

NALLEY AND STOVER COME CLOSE TO BLOWS

The rivalry between Bill Nalley and Smokey Stover during the 1963 season was intense. The two tangled frequently and on September 7, 1963, the rivals had a major confrontation. The News Virginian has this account:

There was a tossup at Waynesboro's Eastside Speedway on Saturday night between stock car races and a mass footrace. The latter was an unplanned dash across the track at the close of the final event by hundreds of stirred up fans.

In the modified feature, Smokey Stover of Staunton took the lead away from Brunswick, MD Bill Nalley after crashing into S3 and demolishing its rear section. The wreck, thought by many fans to be unavoidable because of the superior brake control and driving ability of Stover, sent Nalley to the pit area, through for the night.

There were few among the fans who weren't aware of the long-standing feud existing between the two top flight drivers, and it's a matter of history that Nalley usually comes up on the short end when the two cars tangle. One accident, a number of weeks ago at Winchester, was quite similar and sent S3 end-over-end four times and put Nalley in the hospital with cracked ribs.

The explosive crash Saturday began when Nalley spun on the sharp number four turn with 306 close behind. Car number 12, driven by Winchester's Clem Lamaster, did his best to avoid the twisting S3 and lost too much ground to remain a threat to Stover over the 35-lap course.

It had started as a wild race when Nalley spun on the number four turn on the first start and touched off a wild melee between six cars. None had to leave the race, but it set the stage for later action after the restart. This time, Nalley was leading by a cool margin again when up popped the number four turn.

As for the footrace across the infield, the fans who were anxious to see Stover take his licks from Nalley were due for a disappointment. Although Nalley was as angry as the mild-mannered man ever gets and called the accident inexcusable, he controlled his temper and stuck with his crippled racer rather than confront Smokey. Once before the two exchanged "pleasantries" in a one-punch bout which left Stover flat, but Nalley stated he'd rather spend the night at home than in jail on an assault and battery charge.

As for Smokey, he was just as sure the wreck couldn't have been avoided as Nalley was the other way.

Since most speedway fans are about evenly divided

into two camps, Nalley's ability to control his anger probably avoided serious trouble.

Just the night before, Stover had won at Winchester's Airport Speedway, capturing the silver bowl for winning the Langhorn Entry Race.

MORE STORIES

Another wild night at Eastside occurred on September 14, 1963 when Dave Alexander of Hyattsville, Maryland, driving for the first time at Eastside, sailed his brand new racer over the number four turn fence without touching a board and landed over the turn banking.

Later, Gene Garrison, driving in the modified division, drove his car through the third turn fence, "posts and boards flying in all directions."

Later that evening, Bobby Hite of Waynesboro spun his car through the infield, stepped from his car, and collapsed. He was later taken to the hospital for observation and released.

On this night, Charlie Beeler's car, which had won the sportsman feature, was torn down once again. But once again he was found to be legal.

The 1964 season at Eastside started before a crowd of 1,500 on April 18, 1964. The modified feature was won by Bill Nalley, with a surprising 40 cars on hand for opening night.

Racing that evening had been delayed by 45 minutes because of a muddy track. As the weather had been predicted to be clear and dry, track officials had dumped tons of water on the newly added 100 truckloads of red clay to the track. Close to race time, an unexpected shower went through the area, rendering the track too muddy to race. Every available racecar was asked to drive around the track and compact the mud, which eventually led to the track being race-worthy.

The 1964 season once again saw a paucity of cars in the modified division and had already seen Bill Nalley win most of the races as Smokey Stover had retired. As a result, in July 1964, the modifieds were discontinued and the hobby cars were added. Hobby cars were essentially completely stock cars with only safety equipment added.

On the Memorial Day race in 1964, Smokey Stover, coming out of retirement to drive a car built and owned by Clyde Harris and Earl McCrary, sustained a severe leg injury. Accounts of this event are found in the chapters on Clyde Harris and Smokey Stover.

On July 18, 1964, Louie Newland of Woodstock was the surprise winner at Eastside in the sportsman division when Charlie Beeler's car developed motor trouble. Buddy Stinespring was second.

On August 15, 1964, Lee Vest of Grottoes suffered a fractured vertebrae in two places when his sportsman car hit the fence at Eastside.

In the sportsman feature, Louie Newland won his third sportsman feature in four weeks over Buck Shipp. Charlie Beeler, who had been dominating the season, lost a wheel in the 18th lap of the feature, went out of control, and crashed.

One week later, Newland won again in the sportsman feature at Eastside and survived a protest by second place winner Buck Shipp of Troy.

— Newspaper Advertisements from the Early Days of Racing —

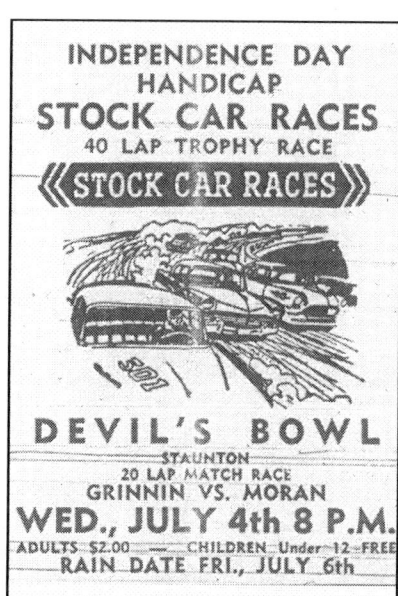

circa. 1961

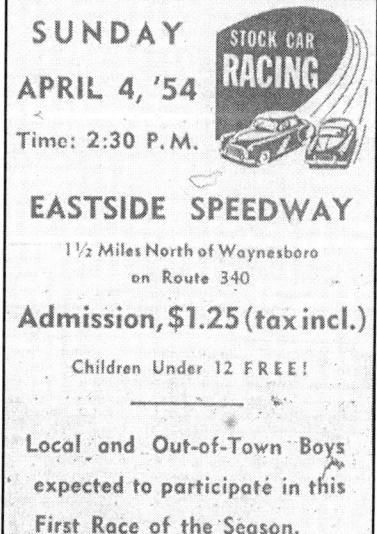

circa. 1960

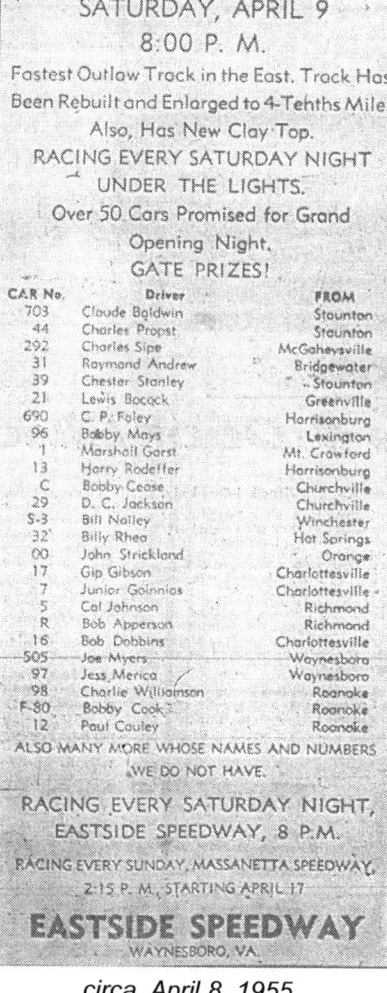

circa. April 8, 1955

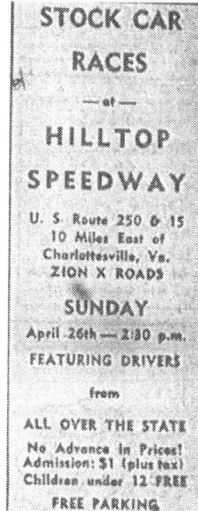

circa. 1954

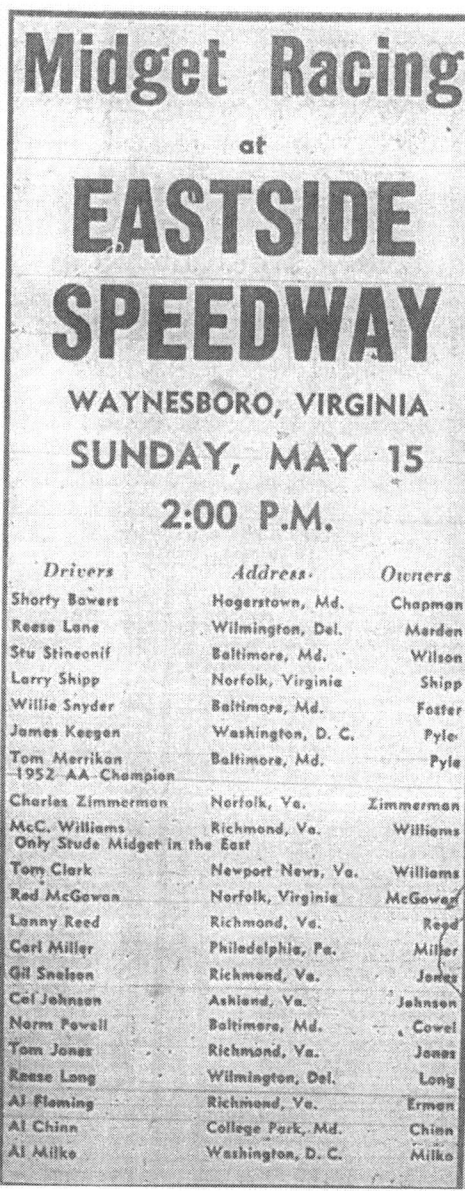

circa. May 14, 1955

Date unknown

circa. 1961

circa. June 17, 1961

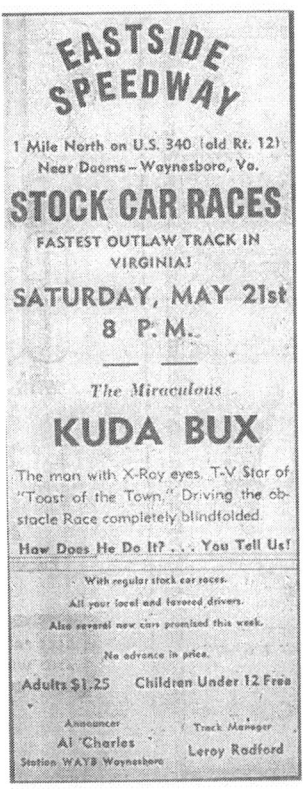

circa. May 28, 1954

circa. May 20, 1955

circa. June 3, 1955

RACING RULES FOR 1960 AT DEVIL'S BOWL SPEEDWAY, STAUNTON

MODIFIED CLASS

Any type of enclosed passenger car body and frame combination. Any make or model of engine of American manufacture with no limit on displacement. No restrictions on carburation except that superchargers and fuel injection may be used only on flatheads or six cylinder engines. Safety features must comply with rules outlined below. No dog clutches.

SPORTSMAN CLASS

ANY TYPE of enclosed passenger car body and frame combination. Restricted to any flathead eight cylinder or any six cylinder engine of American manufacture with displacement limited to 302 cu. inches. If displacement is questioned a protest bond of $25 must be posted by a representative of car protesting and if the car undergoing teardown is found to be within limits this bond shall go to its car owner. One carburetor of any stock type is all that is allowed in Sportsman Class. Safety features as listed below.

JALOPY CLASS

All equipment must be common to the make, model and year of the basic body. Only exceptions to this are:

All glass except windshield must be removed.
Interior may be stripped.
Rear end may be "locked".
Wheels on right side may be strengthened and offset.

Teardown protest fee in this class is $5.00 which shall go to owner of car torn down if it is found to comply with specs. Safety features as outlined below.

SAFETY FEATURES REQUIRED

Roll bars minimum O.D. 1-3/4 inches both at front and just back of seat and connected by bracing at top. Safety belts must be of adequate strength and fastened securely to the frame. Crash helmets must be of a type manufactured specifically for racing. There must be a firewall on all cars located so as to separate the driver from the fuel tank.

Racing at Devil's Bowl is scheduled to start on Saturday, April 30th and will continue on every Saturday night thru October 8th, weather permitting. Normally track will be ready for warmup laps at 7:15 and first race will be started promptly at 8:15 P.M.

A lineup and five minute warning will be given before each race and any cars not on the track ready for pace lap will be positioned at rear of field.

To be eligible for trophies in championship events, both car and driver must have participated in at least two of the four preceding race programs, though not necessarily driving the same car.

The starter shall have full authority on the track and his signals are to be obeyed at all times. All protests must be made on completion of the particular race involved and must be made to the track manager. After he has consulted with the parties or officials involved, his decision will be final. Any violence against any official is punishable by the offending party being barred from the track for the balance of the season.

A guaranteed purse of $600.00 against 40% of gate after taxes will be paid for the first four race meets at which time it may be re-evaluated based on previous attendance. For the opening program $100 will be paid to Jalopy Class and $250 each to Sportsman and Modified Classes.

Sportsman Payoff: In two heats 1st - $10; 2nd - $5
In feature 1st - $85; 2nd - $60; 3rd - $40
4th - $25; 5th - $10
All other cars competing in this class will receive minimum of $3

Modified Payoff: In feature: 1st - $100; 2nd - $70; 3rd - $45; 4th - $25; 5th - $10 and all other cars $5

Note: After opening program if above payoff is unfair to number of entrants in one of above classes, the ratio will be changed in favor of such class for future programs.

Jalopy payoff still to be determined.

Entry fee of $3.00 shall entitle each car to up to four admissions either for gate or pits and insurance similar to 1959 will be in force on pit and racing personnel, providing track release form is signed. No children, ladies or alcoholic beverages allowed in pits during racing program.

BILL LYDLE
TRACK MGR.

Early Action

Staunton's Valley Speedway. circa. 1953

Lewis Bocock at Valley Speedway.

Valley Speedway. circa. 1953

*Valley Speedway. circa. 1954.
Note car #39 driven by Chester Stanley on the pole.*

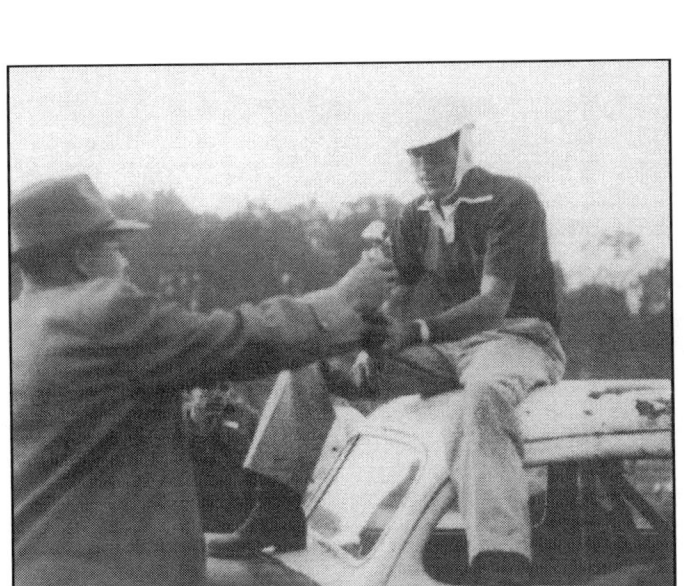

Chester Stanley dominated in early racing at Valley Speedway.

Massanutten Speedway during the early 1950s.

Winchester (Airport Speedway). circa. 1954.

Al Gore

Of the many men and women who owned and operated stock car tracks during the 50's, 60's, and 70's, only Al Gore has the distinction of having been successful from 1952 to the present.

In 1949, Gore was a construction superintendent in northern Virginia who was involved in replacing the roof on the House and Senate buildings in Washington, D.C. In 1952, he bought Longview Speedway in Manassas, Virginia, which was originally built by Johnny Counts in 1947 as a dirt track. At that time, it was mostly a racetrack for roadsters.

Gore Gets Going

Gore, along with five other partners, completely rebuilt the track in April 1952. It was enlarged from a quarter of a mile to a three-eighth mile oval with high banks, rebuilt grandstands, and a paved track. This was all done in approximately six to seven weeks. It was renamed Old Dominion Speedway. Gore says, "I took off from work to do it and opened it with roadsters. The first race was won by Dick Frazier, an Indianapolis car driver." Charging $1.50 per adult, Gore was able to fill his limited grandstand for the first race.

After the 1953 season, his other five partners wanted out of the venture and offered to sell the track to Gore; however, according to Gore, "I didn't have any money. I'd borrowed already against my home. One of the other guys took a liking to me and bought the rest of them out. He came up with a lease price and I couldn't pay it. He said, 'Just take it, take it, forget it.' His name was Harold Nesbeth."

Gore says, "I told him to take it. He said, 'You take it.'"

At that, Gore assumed sole responsibility for the operation of the Manassas track. He then sold his home to obtain enough money to operate the track. This was a major decision for him and reflected his passion to be successful in the racing business. When talking of his home, he says, "I had built this home myself. It had seven bedrooms. I had four sons. My wife didn't like it, but she didn't complain." Gore continues to speak of his late wife, "She was a real good woman. I was trying to support a family and a racetrack at the same time. I took every job I could and worked 16 to 17 hours a day."

As the track at Manassas continued to struggle, Nesbeth eventually stopped charging rent to Gore. He then told Gore to repay him for the track when he could. According to Gore, "Twenty-five years later I paid him off. I never paid a nickel for it for the first 20 years."

Gore Buys Eastside

In 1958, Al Gore bought Eastside Speedway in Waynesboro, Virginia and its land for $6,000 from the widow of L. P. Claytor. She had not reopened the track for the 1958 season. Gore describes Eastside at the time, "It was nothing to it. It was grown up with weeds." Gore continues, "We were running short of cars at Manassas. These Staunton and Waynesboro drivers said to me, 'Look, if you open up Eastside, we'll go to Manassas and run both tracks.' After I bought Eastside, though, they didn't want to run Manassas but ran Eastside and Winchester instead."

Gore opened Eastside with no guaranteed purse to the drivers, offering 60 percent of the gate to the drivers.

Initially at Eastside, Gore had a partner by the name of Clyde Trenary; however, the two of them had a disagreement and Gore eventually bought out

Trenary.

Several years into the Eastside venture, Gore found himself $20,000 in debt and creditors were threatening to file suit. On the threat of suit, Gore threatened bankruptcy. In the midst of controversy, he got a call from his friend Nesbeth who said, "I want to talk to you." Gore continues, "So I went to northern Virginia and Nesbeth says, 'I understand you're in another mess.' I said, 'How did you know?' He said, 'It doesn't matter, but I know it. What's it going to take to get out of this one?' I said, '$20,000.' He said, 'Well, see me Friday.'" That Friday, Nesbeth gave Gore a check for $20,000, which saved Eastside Speedway.

Gore's friendship with Nesbeth continued over the years. They regularly had lunch together. The two of them had planned on building another racetrack around Nokesville, Virginia. Nesbeth intended to finance the venture and Gore planned to manage the track. Three days before the two of them were to sign papers, Nesbeth suddenly died. Gore still owns the land earmarked for the racetrack; however, at this time there are no concrete plans to build a track.

Gore started having races on Sunday afternoons at Eastside. As he had only promoted an asphalt track at Manassas, he had a great deal to learn about operating a dirt track. He later moved races to Saturday nights.

GORE ON CONTROVERSY

Gore acknowledges that operating a racetrack often involves dealing with owners and drivers who are caught in the moment of emotion. Gore says, "My policy always was I don't care what happens today. It's done today. You don't take it to tomorrow. If you and I had a hell of a fight, we'd kick the heck out of each other, and that would be the end of it. It's done. Don't carry your grudges."

During the summer of 1960, Gore had his hands full promoting Winchester Airport Speedway, Eastside Speedway, Old Dominion Speedway, and a racetrack in Marlboro, Maryland. He was the promoter at Winchester Airport Speedway the day Junior Bowers was killed.

Gore talks of the importance of building and maintaining a field of cars whose drivers would regularly come to your track. According to Gore, "Without the cars, you don't have a race."

Gore did not hire private security. During the early days of racing at Eastside, he had not gotten the support of the local sheriff. Gore was forced, therefore, to police his own track. He was not shy about barring unruly drivers from participation, and had rules for drivers' wives and girlfriends. A posted sign read, "All drivers must keep their wives and girlfriends separated in the grandstands or you may be barred from the track."

Gore also knew when not to intervene. He tells this story of an altercation that occurred in the stands. He says, "One night there was a fight on the backstretch. Bob Dobyns, Otis Alfred, and Lionel Johnson got into a fight. They had a heck of a fight. I was sitting over here on the front stretch on a fence post watching on the backstretch. There was a state trooper in the stands who came up to me and said, 'What are you going to do about that fight over there?' I said, 'Nothing, just let them fight. They'll get tired, they'll quit.'

"The trooper said, 'I'm going to close this damn place.' Gore said, 'No you're not going to close it.' I said, 'Just go on home and forget about it. When they get through fighting, they'll stop. And when the race is over, they'll sit out here on their trailers and drink beer together.' And that's what they did. You just don't stick your nose in something like that. It's already going bad enough as it is. As long as they're not hurting each other, forget it. Just don't pick on somebody

who has nothing in it. Then I'll get involved."
When Gore reflects on the heydays of the 50's and 60's at Eastside, he remembers the names Smokey Stover, Bill Nalley, Gip Gibson, Ray Dovel, Earl Moran, and Lewis Bocock. He considers Ray Dovel to be the best driver who ever raced at Eastside. He says of Bill Nalley, "He was one hell of a driver."

FOOD AT EASTSIDE

Al Gore is quite proud of the food served at Eastside. He has never sold frozen hamburger in the 33 years the track has operated under his leadership. He says that 700 pounds of hamburger are purchased each weekend for the Saturday night show and Sunday afternoon drag races. He also estimates that 400 pounds of hotdogs are purchased. At one time, Gore insisted that all hamburgers be made by hand. He did not want them to be thin like "cardboard." He conveniently sets his food prices so that the sales tax will end with a round dollar figure.

FINANCIAL SUCCESS

In 1963, Gore borrowed $15,000 to rebuild the grandstands at Eastside, performing much of the work himself.

Gore credits his financial success in racing to building drag strips at both Manassas and Eastside. He opened the first drag strip east of the Mississippi at Manassas in 1954. It was a dirt track for the first two years of its existence. "Big Daddy" (Don) Garlits raced there. He opened the drag strip at Eastside in 1965.

NHRA HALL OF FAME

In 1997, Gore was inducted into the National Hotrod Association (NHRA) Hall of Fame when he once again saw Garlits many years later who reminded him of visiting Manassas. On that day, Gore was one of 12 along with Garlits who were inducted into the Hall of Fame.

Gore says that at one time there were 2,300 short dirt tracks in the United States. He says now there are approximately 1,100 and adds, "You'd be surprised how many of those are for sale now."

GORE GIVES ADVICE

Gore talks of the night that Clyde Harris and his wife Ann came to Eastside and visited Gore, asking him about operating a track. According to Gore, Harris said, "I want you to tell me all the pitfalls and things that can happen on a racetrack because we're think-

Al Gore at Eastside. Notice the paved dragstrip in the foreground with clay oval track in the background.

ing about opening a track at Craigsville." Gore replied, "Clyde, why don't you do yourself a favor and forget it?" Harris said, "I don't want to forget it. I want to build it." Gore continues, "So I told him everything that could happen and told him how maybe it would work."

After he closed the Craigsville track, Harris and his

wife came back to Gore. She said, "Remember the night we came down here and asked you about having a track? After we left, Clyde told me, 'Don't listen to that SOB, he wouldn't tell you the truth.' But you know, everything you told us would happen, happened." Gore replied, "I wasn't going to lie to you. You asked me and I told you."

Gore says that on one occasion he was offered the Natural Bridge, Virginia Speedway. Gore says that he almost bought the track with the sole intent of destroying the track to put it out of competition. According to Gore, "This Valley would not support two tracks. The reason we get by at our tracks is that we do our own work ourselves."

Gore Narrowly Escapes

Tragedy and near death occurred at Eastside on April 29, 1961. Bob Cook, who had been a flagman for Gore at Eastside, came to Gore the week before and said, "My wife's afraid I'm going to get hurt and she wants me to quit, so this is my last night." Gore said, "I said, 'That's okay, fine. I don't want you doing anything she's not comfortable with.' So I flagged myself. We were flagging at that time from the infield behind a fence."

The following week, Gore says, "I was out there flagging and I felt somebody touch me on the shoulder. I turned around and it was Cook. He says, 'I saw you out here. I thought I'd give you some pointers.'" Gore says, "He distracted me. I look up and here's a car right on top of us, through the infield right on us. I grabbed Cook by the shoulders and started to push him out of the way, and the car flipped and landed on him and was right up against my leg and stopped. Everybody thought I was under the car, too, but I wasn't in it. It mashed him. He died later that night in Charlottesville."

Gore attended Cook's funeral in Buena Vista, Virginia, but got a rude reception from Cook's family as they apparently blamed Cook's death on Gore, according to Gore.

Gore was asked about the emotional effect of having had such a close call. He replies, "I've had so many close calls in my life that it didn't really bother me."

When asked to recount the worst accident at Eastside, he recalls a driver in the 1970's by the name of David Repass, who was severely burned when his car went over the fourth turn and caught on fire. Gore continues, "I should have honored a bunch of guys who went to help Repass when they got over there and moved the car as hot as it was. The gas tank was out of the car burning and the car was laying on it. These guys picked up the car off the gas tank. It burned many of their hands and burned 33 percent of Repass's body. I went to see Repass over at Charlottesville. After he recovered, he came back to the track a few times but drifted away."

Gore and the Motorcycle Gang

In the 1970's, Gore promoted a motorcycle race at Eastside. According to him, "Approximately 30 to 40 members of a motorcycle gang arrived and announced they were 'taking over' the track. Someone called the law and when the officers arrived, I dismissed the officers, saying I would take care of the situation myself." Gore went inside, came out with a shotgun, and, as he cocked his weapon, saw one of the motorcycle gang members reach for a handgun. Gore said, "I wouldn't do it, if you don't want to get cut in two." Gore then announced, "You can stay here if each one of you pay half price and sit in that grandstand," pointing to some bleachers. "I'm not going to tolerate any trouble from you, though." According to Gore, the gang members brought him the money and sat politely without altercation through the rest of the motorcycle races that day. Gore says they never came back.

Gore and NASCAR

Throughout the years, Gore has had the opportunity to interface with many notables of stock car racing. He remembers the late Wendell Scott racing at Eastside and how other drivers often helped him by giving him tires, gas, and oil.

From 1953 to 1967, he promoted NASCAR-sanctioned races at Manassas. He remembers Lee Petty, Richard Petty, Bobby Allison, Buck Baker, Tiny Lund, Curtis Turner, and Joe Weatherly, among others who drove at the track. According to Gore, Ned Jarrett won a race there; he also remembers Junior Johnson lapping the entire field twice in route to his victory. In the late 50's, NASCAR ran convertible races at Manassas. Gore says, however, that he had to make deals with each driver. "It got so the deal money and the purse were greater than your gate. That's when it was time for me to quit." Gore says that deal money means that he had to guarantee appearance money for many of the prominent drivers. In those days, it was approximately $100 to $150 per race. This was over and above anything the driver won from the purse.

When asked about his favorite NASCAR drivers, Gore replies, "Lee Petty was the only guy on the Grand National Circuit that didn't make me pay appearance money. I said to him one time, "Lee, how come you don't want my money? He said, 'Because I started with nothing and you started with nothing. I don't want your money. I know how hard it is to get started.'" Gore continues, "He was the only one. Richard Petty was always real nice. I really enjoyed Buck Baker and Fonty Flock. Flock was a real comedian."

Gore continues, "Fonty Flock raced at Manassas and his wife had a baby that night. They called him and told him he was a boy, and after the race he got as drunk as a skunk."

On one occasion he was in Hanover, Pennsylvania for a race. Ned Jarrett was there and was standing outside with a rather forlorn look. Gore continues, "I was getting ready to come home. Ned said, 'Boy, I'm in a pickle. I need to get to Washington Airport and I don't have a ride.'" Gore said, "Yes, you do. Get right in that car there. I'll take you to the airport." Gore delivered Jarrett in time to the airport.

Gore also speaks affectionately of Marvin Panch and Johnny Parsons, who each spent a week at Gore's house as Gore's guest. He does say that Fireball Roberts, "wouldn't even talk to you."

On another occasion at Manassas, Tiny Lund, who had been contacted by Gore prior to the race and received no answer, appeared at the track. At that time he demanded appearance money. Gore refused, saying, "I'm not going to do it. I didn't use your name for this race."

At that, Lund and his crew went outside to the track and attempted to lead a boycott of other arriving NASCAR drivers. When the Pettys did not honor Lund's boycott, most of the other drivers raced.

Gore says with some sadness that he's had ten fatalities in all his years of racing, both on drag strips and oval tracks.

GORE'S SONS

Gore has transitioned his Manassas track to his son Dicky, who also has a position within NASCAR on its Discipline Appeals Committee. Gore transitioned Eastside to son Gary in 1973 and says, "I'm here all the time, but if Gary makes a decision and I get a lot of squawking about it, I'll look into it. If I think it's wrong, I'll tell him, but I won't ever overrule him. I figure that's up to him, but I will explain to him where I think he's wrong, but I won't overrule him."

Gary stays in living quarters that are located in the tower at the track. For the past seventeen years, Al has had a house trailer he occupies when at

Eastside.

Both he and Gary live in the Warrenton, Virginia area, but spend an average of two to three days each week tending to business at Eastside.

Al was interviewed in his house trailer at Eastside Speedway. He's an outgoing, energetic man who is opinionated and philosophical. It is quite apparent that his tenacity, willingness to take risks, and innovation have served him well in terms of succeeding as a track promoter. He is no doubt a tough cookie who over the years has had to periodically deal with controversy at times with an iron fist, but also with an eye toward the difficult task of pleasing both fans and drivers.

When the author exited Gore's house trailer at Eastside, the track was dark and quiet. It was something to which the author was not accustomed at a racetrack. As Eastside was a big part of the author's upbringing, a few moments savoring the experience of being at the track in silence, knowing all the events that have occurred there over the years, was initially eerie; but as the reflection continued, the sense of being at one with a sense of history and intrigue was almost spiritual in nature. I also had the realization that I had just spent three hours with one of the most influential men of early stock car racing in Virginia.

Willie Wayne (W.W.) Gearhart

Willie Wayne (W. W.) Gearhart opened a garage outside Pilot, Virginia, between Christiansburg and Floyd, Virginia, in 1948. In the early 50's he raced on a number of local dirt tracks, which according to him were rapidly closing. He ran at tracks such as Hillsville, Pulaski, and Starkey, Virginia. Gearhart continues, "Pee Wee Martin, Tody Noland, Paul Radford, and I got together and decided we'd build a quarter-mile or three-eighth mile dirt track. The problem was that it was almost impossible to get land where people would allow us to build a racetrack, so we decided that we'd build it on our own property."

A Track is Built

Gearhart constructed a quarter mile dirt track in a valley on his property behind his garage and began racing in 1958. While Gearhart had constructed, built, and raced a hobby car with a Flathead engine, he stopped racing when he built the track. He closed the Pilot track in 1970.

In the twelve years he operated the track, Gearhart said his attendance ranged from 3,000 to 12,000. At times he had skydivers, motorcycles, and go-carts from a racing club in North Carolina to draw a bigger crowd. His admission started at $2.50 and then went $3.50 in the early 60's. He charged $5.50 for a championship race. According to him, "We made enough to pay for the track." He had 38 acres for parking.

Gearhart paid K&K Racing Insurance $250 per night, which eventually was increased to $300 per night.

Gearhart says, "When we started racing, there wasn't anything like a life-saving crew. We'd have an ambulance from a funeral home, which cost us $50 a night. We gave the Sheriff Department $100 and they furnished four men. The drivers received 60 percent of the gate. We ran usually on Saturday nights."

In the twelve years of racing at Pilot, there was only one claim for K&K Racing Insurance. A fan sustained a broken leg in a fight in the parking lot after another fan kicked him in the leg.

He mentioned that there were quite a few fights, but how did Gearhart deal with them? "We had a bunch of 'He' men guys working for me. They could all take care of themselves and they took care of any trouble that happened. The announcer was a pretty good guy, too, Bosconi. He'd have a race going before it even started. The announcer was paid $25 a race and eventually this was increased to $100."

Trouble from Floyd County

Despite the success of the speedway, Gearhart says he received ongoing resistance from Floyd County. According to him, "They didn't want us to put billboards up on Route 221 advertising the track. After we quit and all the local businesses saw the loss of revenue, and the county didn't get that tax money, they said, 'Well, what does it take to get it going again?' I told them, 'You didn't want me when I was in it, now you can forget about it.' They did absolutely nothing to help the Pilot Speedway. They got 5 cents on the dollar and the state got 10 cents on the dollar for taxes."

Concessions

Gearhart's wife was responsible for the concession stand, which was quite profitable. Gearhart's father had a secret recipe for his chili. According to Gearhart, "This made our hotdogs first class. We bought our hotdogs from Valleydale and they gave us a good price because they liked racing. We got our hamburger from them, too.

"Valleydale would deliver the meat on Fridays and we'd keep them in coolers. We had a restaurant license but it could only operate on Saturday night. My wife would get nervous and say that she'd have cold chills running down her spine because she had to feed that many people."

Gearhart relates that some fans, out of love for racing and like for Gearhart, would bring Cokes and bread for them to sell at the concession stand. Local farmers saw the food being delivered and said, "There ain't no way you're going to sell all that. It's going to go bad. I'd like to feed it to my pigs." Gearhart adds with a laugh, "We never had a lot left over."

Rainouts

When Gearhart was asked about rainouts, he replied, "It was a bad thing. That's when you lost your money. K&K Racing Insurance would give us credit for another race, but all that stuff you prepared was on the line. We'd only have a couple a year, but when a dirt track is wet, it's no drying out like an asphalt track. With all the chloride we added to the track to maintain the moisture, it held the moisture. It's not going to dry quickly."

Designing Restrooms

Gearhart had four outdoor restrooms. He was especially proud of a urinal he designed for the men's restroom. He built a urinal out of stainless steel. He built a pipe at the top of the urinal with holes through which water constantly ran. He says he had never before seen this design and, even though it appears to be in common practice now, he says the idea was originally his.

Trash at the Track

When asked about trash clean up at the track, Gearhart says, "That was a terrible thing there." He says that there were mostly bottles, which at that time were returnable for deposit. He would allow a "Coke guy" and his wife to pick up the bottles and they could keep the deposit money. In return, they bought items for his concession stand.

Gearhart designed a stick with a sharp welding rod inserted that he used to pick up loose paper. It took approximately four people about a half a day to clean up the parking lot.

Robberies

Gearhart carried a gun and was surrounded by men he describes as "big and rough." These men also served as scorers, and this apparently prevented scoring controversies.

There were three attempts to rob Gearhart of money after the races. Since the drivers received their money in checks, Gearhart had a great deal of cash in his possession.

On one occasion, several men dressed in ski masks ambushed Gearhart and several of his men who were leaving the track in a pickup truck. One of Gearhart's helpers brandished two unloaded guns and got out of the pickup, deterring the robbers. The robbers ran. A similar outcome occurred on a second occasion, and on a third occasion, several men in ski masks showed up at his garage banging on the door. Gearhart said, "We told them they had five minutes to leave or they'd be picking up their bodies. They left."

Legal Troubles

Gearhart's track was originally a quarter of a mile.

At the beginning of each season, drivers paid a $25 entry fee for the season. This gave them the right to vote in matters related to the track. The drivers voted to enlarge the track.

Gearhart tells what happened next. "When we tore down the rail and started working on it to enlarge the track, the guy that owned the property next to it got a court order to stop us. He said it was on his property. We fought that battle for about a year and it seemed we weren't going to be able to race. We couldn't do anything. At the same time, the Pulaski Speedway had folded and the drivers wanted to go to Pulaski, so I bought the lease there. We then closed Pilot."

GEARHART TRIES PULASKI

Gearhart operated Pulaski Speedway for three years; however, it was not a pleasant experience. Gearhart continues, "The first year we had run four or five races and then came a flood. The water got as high as 20 feet inside the infield. There were 10,000 bales of hay washed in there that belonged to Valleydale Farms. There was a Mr. Smith who owned the property at that time and he couldn't understand why that happened. We tried to get him to drain a pond above the track, but he didn't want to because he couldn't supply water for his cattle.

"We built it back the next winter and started the next year racing three or four races and it flooded again. At that point it looked like we were going to go broke, but we got some help from the drivers and we decided to build it back again. The owner still wouldn't drain the pond and when it took us out a third time, we went bankrupt."

Pulaski Speedway was closed until the 1980's when it was reopened as New River Valley Speedway by a man named Steve McMurray. Gearhart's lease was still active when McMurray wanted to open the track. Gearhart continues, "My wife and I signed the lease over to McMurray. We told him, 'If you don't drain that pond, you're throwing your money away.' He bought the property so he could get the pond drained. He reopened the track as New River Valley Speedway and cut it down to three-eighths of a mile from a half-mile and also paved it. He lost his tail--over a million dollars."

Gearhart regrets leaving the Pilot track for Pulaski. He says, "We'd probably still be racing if we hadn't tried to enlarge the track. Before we could get it settled, we'd gotten involved at Pulaski and went broke."

With regard to the dispute at Pilot, the suit was eventually dropped when several years later it was revealed that the man who was disputing the enlargement of the track did not in fact own the property after all. Shortly after the suit ended, the man bringing the suit died in a chainsaw accident.

PREPARING PILOT SPEEDWAY

Gearhart was very proud of the banking at Pilot Speedway. His brother, who worked for a construction company, used a bulldozer to fill dirt behind the turns to give the track a great deal of banking. The banking was so high that the water truck, attempting to water the track before the race and carrying 2,000 gallons of water, couldn't get to the top of the track. Gearhart was innovative in that he designed a pump that sprayed water from the truck upward. This truck also doubled as a fire truck for the races. Gearhart also reveals that small grooves were placed in the track surface where chloride was inserted. The track was then smoothed over again and watered. The chloride helped retain moisture and retard dust.

DRUNK DRIVERS

Gearhart had to periodically deal with race drivers who were drunk. Once again, Gearhart's "muscle guys" would keep drunk drivers from racing. Every driver was checked for the smell of alcohol on his breath before each race.

STINESPRING DOMINATES PILOT

By far the dominant driver at Pilot Speedway was Buddy Stinespring. Stinespring, who first came to Pilot in the sportsman division, not only dominated that division but also the modified division while driving a sportsman car. Gearhart says of Stinespring, "In the twelve years we raced, he was one of the best sports, but there were a lot of problems because he had this car that nobody wanted to race against. We put him in the modified to build the sportsman division back up, and then we started losing modified drivers because he won all of those races. Nobody could beat him. He had a 6-cylinder GMC truck engine. Nobody could figure out how he was so good, but he was."

Because of Stinespring's domination, Gearhart put a bounty on him, offering extra money to any driver who could defeat him without Stinespring having mechanical problems or wrecking. This eventually grew to $8,000. No one ever claimed the bounty even though Earl Moran from Staunton came close one night. Drivers came from all over to try to beat Stinespring.

"POP" STINESPRING

Stinespring was always accompanied to the races by his father, "Pop." Gearhart continues, "Pop Stinespring was one of the nicest people I ever came upon in the racing business. Nobody that we ever fooled with had a car that could outrun the 501 (Stinespring's car), and we never had anybody who was a better sport than them. They'd give their winnings to another driver who had bad luck. As a matter of fact, they very seldom took the winnings. Stinespring's father is quoted as saying, 'Wayne, I don't need the money. I just love to race.' We became really good friends."

Gearhart tells the story of Pop Stinespring's risking serious injury one night during hobby car warm-ups at Pilot Speedway. A wheel had come off a car and was bouncing toward the pits. Gearhart continues, "Pop saw it coming and went out there like a dummy and tried to grab it. It would have killed him if he hadn't been in shape, but he kept it off this guy's car."

Gearhart adds, "After a race, if there was any controversy or any ill feelings, Pop would come up to the stand and grab the microphone and say, 'Anybody thinks that Buddy done wrong or bumped or cheated anybody, we'll forfeit our place.' That's the reason I can truthfully say he was an excellent sport, good people. He wanted to win but he wanted the track to live, too, and I appreciated that."

"I never knew Pop Stinespring's name. He always signed his signature 'Pop.'"

DEATHBED CONFESSION

Gearhart speaks of the night he was in Staunton at approximately 2:00 to 3:00 in the morning several years after he had closed Pilot Speedway. He had driven his wrecker to pick up a car and was lost when he came upon Buddy Stinespring. Gearhart tells the story, "Buddy got me out of the wrecker and said, 'You've got to see my dad. Dad wants to talk to you bad. He's in bad shape.'

"I went with Buddy to this house. Pop was in bad shape. This was 3:00 in the morning. I hated to go in the house where he was. I wasn't what you'd say filthy dirty, but I'd been out hooking to a truck. I wasn't clean, that's for sure.

"He was lying in bed there. He looked up and hugged my neck and really got with me and told me he loved me. He said, 'I'll never forget you. I want to tell you what I did to that motor to get us to win so many races.' I said, 'I know what you've done.' He said, 'You did?' I says, 'I knew all the time but I wasn't going to tell on you.' I said, 'I love you and Buddy both. I wasn't going to tell on you.' He said, 'What do you think?' And I told him. Pop Stinespring said, 'Buddy told you that.'" Gearhart said that he could barely talk. Gearhart replied, "No he didn't. I know what you done."

Pop Stinespring's secret will not be revealed by this author. Pop Stinespring died shortly thereafter. The Pilot track is now host to over 700 junked cars and dozens of pine trees. The roar of engines there will never be heard again.

W. W. Gearhart was interviewed on the porch of his ranch home overlooking his garage and within a half-mile of the old Pilot track. He's a dignified gentleman who is friendly, warm, and interactive. While he has fond memories of his racing days, evident also is the pain and bitterness of the financial disaster from the failure of the Pulaski Speedway.

Pilot Speedway owner W.W. Gearhart circa 2001.

Bill Nalley

By far the preeminent driver of this era was William (Bill) Nalley. He dominated at almost every track he raced.

Nalley began racing in 1952 at Winchester Airport Speedway. He had his own car, a Ford Coupe number N-2. In those days, the owner of the car had to put the initial of his last name first followed by a number. The first race he ever drove, however, was when he was working in the pits for Red Ninninger at Unionville Speedway outside of Orange, Virginia. Red wasn't feeling well and Nalley said, "Well, I'll drive it. I opened my big mouth and I did. That hooked me on racing." He drove his own car until approximately 1955 when he blew an engine in Winchester. He says, "I was going to quit racing. Someone went to Lee Stultz and said, 'You ought to get Nalley to drive for you. He's a good driver, he's just had bad luck.' Stultz said, 'Hell no. He's torn up too much stuff.'" Nalley continues, "But we got together. I never drove for anybody else after that."

Nalley and Stultz Become a Team

Bill Nalley and Lee Stultz.

Lee Stultz was a mechanic at B&M Chevrolet in Winchester, Virginia. He was a meticulous man who became known as one of the premier car owners and mechanics of the era.

Nalley continues, "Lee and I were together fourteen years and we never had a cross word between us. Some man he was. He could talk to you and ask you questions about your car and you wouldn't realize it 'til he walked away. He had a sense of getting the right people to talk to."

Nalley began driving for Stultz receiving 50 percent of the prize money with Nalley retaining all of any point money. Later, as expenses got higher, Stultz renegotiated the arrangement so that Nalley got 40 percent of the prize money. Even though Nalley and Stultz won most of the time, fans came to them at times and simply give them money as a gesture of gratitude.

When Bill Nalley started with his own car, he wore a leather football helmet to race. Charlie Armel, the flagman at Winchester Speedway, took up a collection and bought him his first helmet, a Cromwell helmet.

Nalley was known for his hard driving style. On many occasions, he drove in both the modified and sportsman classes and won both features and all heats in both divisions. Eventually, tracks outlawed drivers driving in both divisions. On one Sunday in Winchester, he won four trophies.

Nalley and the Ambulance Tire

Lee Stultz bought used ambulance tires from an ambulance company in Washington, D.C., for $5 a piece. They were wide and heavy tires, which Stultz used on the Car S-3 which Nalley drove, until 1961 when they began to purchase manufactured racing tires.

Bill Nalley poses with an ambulance tire on which he won 27 features.

Nalley has a story of a particular ambulance tire that, out of superstitious belief, he kept on the car for some time during which he won a total of 27 features. According to him, Stultz removed the tire four or five times, but every time Nalley would tell him to put the tire back on. According to Nalley, "Stultz would put a new tire on. I'd drive it and that bastard would go to the fence. I said, 'Lee, put my tire on.' He'd put the tire back on and I'd win."

BILL'S WIFE

Bill's wife Lorraine very seldom watched him race. She went to the races and took care of their three children, however, would not watch the races. She notes that the first time she saw him race, Nalley went in the air flipping and several cars ran under him. Because of that she did not like to watch what happened in races and avoided them.

Lorraine says that she was often with Red Ninninger's wife. She describes a typical day at the race. "Red's wife and I would take food, wet rags, and drinks and we'd sit in the car and the kids would play beside the car and we'd talk. We'd look once in a while, but never watched the race. After it was over, we'd clean the kids up and go over in the pits." She continues, "The races were fun but things changed. There was a lot of squabbling. That was no fun."

Later, when her son Sam Nalley became a racing star, she never saw him race.

CONTROVERSIES

Nalley says that he never liked to argue and that he tried not to be controversial; however, his frequent winning made him an easy target for controversy.

On one occasion, the crew of Car J-5 threw rocks, bricks, and a piece of a 2x6 board at Nalley as he circled the track after a racing incident with Ray Dovel. On another occasion at Waynesboro, an unknown assailant hit Lee Stultz in the mouth.

Nalley becomes sad when relating controversy with Smokey Stover. He prefaces this story by saying that one Sunday at Winchester, "I was running with Smokey. I was passing him and he ran his right front wheel up behind my left front wheel and put me in the fence. I had him passed and backed off to keep from hitting him. And he just hit me." He continues, "Several weeks later at Eastside, boy, there's a sad story here. Smokey tried to ram me in the side down at Waynesboro. I had him passed and I was getting ready to lap him and went in the corner. He hit his brakes and I didn't spin him out. He went to the starting line and sat on the inside. As I came by, he tried to ram me on the side and didn't hit me.

"After the race, I walked over and started to ask him what was the matter with him and he said something to me. I don't know what it was. I don't know whatever made me do it, but it's the worst thing I've ever done in my life. I hauled off and hit him. I busted his mouth all up and knocked some teeth out.

"It was terrible. Nobody stepped in. They took him to the hospital and sewed his mouth up. That really hurt me. I didn't want to do that. I never liked that kind of living, but it just happened. I wasn't raised that way.

"After that Smokey and I just didn't speak to each other for a long time, and I was down at Daytona one day and saw him walking down the street. We got to talking and made up. It was never mentioned after that. I went to his house the next year in Staunton. He took me and showed me his basement where he had his trophies. It was a beautiful place. That was really the worst thing I've ever done. I wasn't brought up that way."

His wife Lorraine says, "I was shocked that Bill hit Smokey. He was upset that he did it. When he came home that night he was disturbed. Smokey, however, was cocky. He was 'king of the roost'."

NALLEY GOES NORTH

Nalley claims that the most controversial track he ever raced was Everett, Pennsylvania. According to him, "They didn't like foreigners. They called us foreigners. They'd beat, bang, and carry on. I was winning a lot there and the money was good. One time I passed all the cars on the first lap. On the restart, they threw the black flag and said my motor was 'too new.' They didn't allow me to race. The owner, however, gave me $100."

NALLEY AND WENDELL SCOTT

Nalley speaks with affection about the late Wendell Scott. According to him, after a race at Hagerstown, Scott had won the feature; and when it came time for him to be paid, he was paid only $6, the apparent victim of racism. Scott, who didn't like to create controversy, came to Nalley and told him that he didn't have enough money to get home to Danville, Virginia. Nalley continues, "I brought him home and we fed him. I gave him money to get home and fixed his radiator on his tow vehicle. He really was appreciative of that.

"I asked him what the promoter at Hagerstown had told him. According to Scott, he was told that there wasn't enough money to pay him for the feature besides the $6." Nalley continues, "I felt so sorry for him, but he never forgot it. I can tell you that."

NALLEY AND PATSY CLINE

Nalley said he had a close relationship with the late Patsy Cline, who would often appear at Winchester Speedway. He notes that his wife Lorraine went to Patsy's funeral saying, "That was a big affair, I'll tell you." According to Nalley, the last time he saw Patsy Cline was at the track. She wore a blue suit with tassels on her boots. Nalley continues, "She was in the grandstand, she waved, and I went up and talked to her about ten minutes. She presented the trophy that day, but I broke down or something. Cal Johnson won it."

INNOVATION

The Bill Nalley/Lee Stultz's S-3 was an attractive car painted in yellow and blue. They were the first racing team in the area to utilize a trailer to haul the car. This negated the need to remove the axles while towing. After Smokey Stover's pit crew began to wear red uniforms, Bill Battle, one of the owners of B&M Chevrolet, bought Nalley's crew uniforms.

NALLEY REMEMBERS

When asked to name his favorite track, Nalley says, "I liked all of them." He goes on to say that he felt he had a knack for getting the feel of different tracks and could drive each track differently, mostly going wide open.

He talks of racing at South Boston, Virginia. He says he won four of five features there and finished second in the other. It was the first time that he had raced against cars using alcohol for fuel. He describes what it was like. "When they'd let off the gas," he says, "a stream of fire would fly off. I thought, 'What in the world are we into?'" It is noteworthy that Nalley, despite his success, never used alcohol in his racers. Nalley often joked, "Where I come from, we drink alcohol, not burn it in our cars!"

Nalley speaks affectionately of the late Charlie Armel, who was the colorful flagman at Winchester. Nalley says, "He'd stand in the track and put his boot out and I'd run over his toes. He'd get a big kick out of that. He had more faith in me than I had in myself."

Nelley wins at Winchester. Note the leather football helmet and snow tires.

The most Nalley says he ever won in a race was $500. Nalley lost track of how many features he won, but he does know that in 1964 he won a total of 42 features, winning track championships at Winchester and Hagerstown, along with teammate Charlie Beeler.

When speaking of his driving style, Nalley says, "I drove the car the way it was. You'd have five different cars and have to drive all five differently."

PROTESTS

Nalley says that on numerous occasions, his car was protested and torn down. He says, "Oh, my God, in Everett, Pennsylvania, every time we'd win a feature we were torn down. We were always legal, but they said if we had to tear it down we might miss something putting it back together." Nalley and Stultz split 50-50 the protest fee they received.

UNUSUAL WINNINGS

Nalley remembers a track at Condon, Maryland, the track where driver Red Matthews was later killed. He says that on one occasion, he won two heats, the consolation and the feature. His prize was a bushel of corn and a six-pack of beer. On another occasion, he finished second and won $6, but the promoter couldn't pay him until the following week. On another occasion he won a bushel of potatoes. According to him, the track was in the middle of a cornfield. He says that once he saw a driver go off the track into the cornfield and got lost. You could see the car running through the cornfield, tearing down the cornstalks. He says, "You could see the corn flopping everywhere. The farmer wanted us to pay for it."

NALLEY ON FAVORITE DRIVERS

Nalley has the following comments about other drivers and racing notables.

Buddy Armel--"One of the most raw talented drivers I've ever seen. He'd get it all out of a car."

Jackie Clore--"'Little Humpty-Dumpty.' The blue and white number 1. It was spotless. It sounded different than any other car. He was an alcohol burner."

Winchester track owner Kermit Batt--"Batt used to lie to us a lot. We'd get people to do the count at the track and see. Never did work out. Drivers got 40 percent of the gate. He made so many special deals and let some people in free. The drivers suffered as a result."

Lewis Bocock--"When the track got hard, you couldn't touch that Crosly."

Buddy Stinespring--"In the 501 with the chrome grill. Man, that thing would glisten."

Shorty Bowers--"I got along well with him, but one time he and I got in an argument. I told him, 'I'll trade you cars and still beat you.' I was just running off at the mouth to aggravate him."

Roy Neff--"What a character. Ran racecars with chains and dual wheels."

Of Clem Lamaster, Nalley speaks of the 1965 accident that ended Lamaster's career. "He had built a new car," says Nalley. Stultz and I were standing there talking and Clem came off the second turn down the backstretch. I said, 'Clem's done fixed something to kill himself.' He was wobbling all over the place. He was standing on it. Between two and three he went up in the air. Oh man, he was in bad shape. Very little space between his head and the roof. He messed his speech up."

Nalley himself was injured on several occasions. He broke several ribs when he did seven end-over-ends and rolled four times at Winchester in 1963.

NALLEY DOMINATES

As Nalley became more of a legend at almost every track he raced, various nicknames emerged such as "Bullet Bill," "Brunswick Bullet," and "The Brunswick Ace."

In 1959, Nalley was so dominant at Winchester that there was often a bounty placed on him with extra money to the driver who could defeat him.

As of May 1959, no one else had won the sportsman feature race at Winchester for approximately ten months. Dave Mader of Morgantown, West Virginia was brought in to challenge Nalley. On May

Nalley's car at the Apple Blossom Festival in Winchester, Va. The lady sitting to the left is Delores Hansberger, daughter of fellow driver, Dick "Pappy" Hansberger.

10, 1959, Mader raced at Winchester and dominated a 10-lap heat, almost lapping Nalley. This was very unusual because at that time, no one was challenging Nalley at Winchester. In the feature, however, Mader went out of the race with a burnt universal joint, ending any chance of defeating Nalley.

The next week, Mader returned and defeated Nalley in the feature after Mader was knocked unconscious in a heat race and had to have his car repaired in order to make the feature.

In 1959, Lorraine Nalley won her second powder puff race. She then promptly retired from powder puff racing.

In 1954, Nalley won the opening race at Winchester Airport Speedway in front of approximately 500 fans who turned out despite threatening weather. Nalley had won the 1953 finale at Winchester, a 100-lap feature. On opening day 1954, he captured both heats and the 30-lap feature, winning all by wide margins.

Nalley raced on an asphalt track on only one occasion at Langley Speedway in Tidewater, Virginia. When he wore out all four tires warming up, car owner Lee Stultz said, "The hell with this place. We're going home." And they did.

On October 2, 1955, Bill Nalley won $325 when he won the 100-lap sportsman feature at Eastside before a crowd of over 2,500 fans. Part of Nalley's purse included $100 for finishing fourth in the point standings for his performance at the speedway during the 1955 season.

On September 22, 1956, Bill Nalley clinched the point championship at Eastside by winning a heat in the Class A sportsman division and finishing second in the feature to Al Grinnan.

The final rundown in point standings for 1956 at Eastside were as follows: Bill Nalley, Car S-3, 573 points; Tommy Irwin, Car 41, 556 points; Junior Bowers, Car 1/2, 547 points; John Strickland, Car 00, 537 points; Robert Peer, Car Z01, 536 points; Gip Gibson, Car 29, 516 points.

Bill Nalley, then 32 years old, won the first L. P. Claytor Memorial Race at Eastside in 1956. This race was in memory of track owner L. P. Claytor, who had died earlier that year.

In this race, Nalley won $200 and received another $10 for qualifying as one of the top five cars in his class. It swelled his earnings at Eastside for the 1956 season to $1,461. He also received a trophy for the L. P. Claytor event. It was the fifth trophy Nalley received at Eastside that year.

Finishing second was Cal Johnson, who won after a struggle with Al Grinnan.

On June 30, 1957 at Winchester, an epic race occurred between Nalley and Tommy Irwin. The newspaper account is as follows:

Irwin Fails to Catch Nalley in Best Sportsman Feature

Purcellville's Tommy Irwin had the fans on their feet and screaming their heads off at the Winchester Airport Speedway Sunday as he closed in on Bill Nalley of Brunswick at the finish line of the Sportsman feature.

But the Marylander held off just enough to win by less than half a car length over the late starting Irwin. For as far back as it was possible to be and still be in the race, Irwin began to creep up on the speedway's champion until he pulled up along side heading into the stretch just in front of the grandstand. What was electrifying as much as anything was what happened on the lap before when Irwin jammed his bright red and white number 6 into a turn sideways and couldn't come out as fast as Nalley. If the Virginian had rammed into the fancy Chevy then, he would have come out of the turn in position to move into the lead. As it was, he was 30 feet behind with a lap and a half to go. The job was much too much, but everyone in the place knew that Nalley's domination of the Speedway was being threatened hard.

On September 1, 1957, Bill Nalley won a trophy race at Eastside with an average speed of approximately 70 miles an hour around the four-tenth mile clay oval in the 50-lap feature. He also won his heat race and walked away from the track with $234. Another $25 went to Nalley as a result of a protest by the second place car driven by Al Grinnan of Fredricksburg. Grinnan filed a protest fee of $25. The engine inspection of Nalley's car proved the car to be within the rules, and the $25 went to Nalley.

Third place in the race went to Tommy Irwin, followed by Cal Johnson and Wendell Scott.

On May 6, 1958, at Eastside, Nalley and Smokey Stover had one of their first controversial battles. The News Virginian has this account:

Bill Nalley of Winchester and Smokey Stover of Staunton roared along fender to fender with second place at stake. Stover in Car 306 and Nalley in S-3 finally hooked wheels on the next to last lap and both spun into the infield. However, Nalley recovered to get back on the track and take fourth place.

On June 1, 1958, Bill Nalley won the 50-lap trophy race sportsman feature at Eastside in front of 1,600 fans. He won easily because Tommy Irwin went out of the race with engine trouble. Lewis Bocock was third and Smokey Stover was fourth. Nalley picked up $213 for his win.
On June 7, 1958, Nalley won an exciting race over Junior Bowers. The News Virginian has this account:

Nalley Wins Sportsman Feature with Come-From-Behind Finish

Bill Nalley did it again. The lanky pilot of S-3 still has a virtual stranglehold on the sportsman feature at Eastside Speedway.

It looked for awhile as if Junior Bowers of Staunton in the Car 1/2 was going to be the fair-headed boy to stop the Nalley run. Bowers opened a big lead in the feature, but the Winchester driver closed the gap and took over one lap from the checkered flag.

When Nalley in S-3 collared Car 1/2 in the number three turn, he wrapped up his fourth feature win of the 1958 season. Bowers looked to be a sure winner, and Eastside fans wouldn't have given a plug nickel for Nalley's chances with only five laps remaining.

The Staunton driver was roaring along with a comfortable lead that looked insurmountable, but the lanky lead foot from up the Valley just kept coming. Nalley gained consistently in the number three turn and was running on Bowers' tailpipe with only two laps remaining.

Bullet Bill Nalley did it the hard way as he took Car 1/2 on the outside going into the number three turn on the 24th lap. He came out of the number four turn with a car length lead and stretched it to two by the time he took the checkered flag.

The Winchester pilot's tremendous driving feat is even more remarkable as he tangled with Car 500 of Lewis Bocock coming out of the number two turn on the fourth lap and was bumped temporarily off the track. However, Nalley kept the S-3 under control and set sail after the field.
On August 16, 1958, at Eastside, it took Nalley just five laps, starting at the rear of the field, to take the lead in the 25-lap sportsman feature and win over Ray Dovel, Smokey Stover, and Junior Bowers in that order.

On April 14, 1962, Nalley won the modified feature

at Winchester Speedway, winning the Easter Trophy Race over Jackie Clore, Clem Lamaster, and Red Ninninger.

On October 6, 1962, Bill Nalley won the 25-lap modified feature at Eastside. He took the lead early and lapped all vehicles in the race except second place finisher, Ray Dovel of Elton. Finishing third was Lewis Bocock, with Earl Moran fourth. Smokey Stover did not run in this race because of mechanical difficulties.

On May 6, 1963, the inaugural event of the 1963 season at Eastside, Nalley won the 25-lap modified feature in front of over 800 fans. He took the lead at about the 1/3 mark of the race and held on for the victory, walking away from the field at the end. Lewis Bocock was second and Smokey Stover was third.

The Nalley and Stover duels became legendary during the 1963 season. The May 17, 1963, edition of The News Virginian has this account of their rivalry:

Nalley and Stover Headed for Rough Duel at Speedway

Ordinarily, this would be too early in the stock car season to have a red hot duel shaping up, but there's a sizzler in the making at Eastside Speedway for tomorrow night between Staunton's Smokey Stover and Winchester's Bill Nalley. Each has won a modified feature and each is dead set on taking the 35-lap climax race this time around. There will be the usual threats from other cars, but early indications point to a two-auto scrap right now to the final line.

Nalley got the big money on opening night two weeks before 800 fans, and then Stover bounced back with the lion's share last Saturday before 1,200 fans. The increased size of the crowd was due for the most part to the large turnout of speedsters in both the sportsman and modified classes, and it could reach 1,400 tomorrow with the odds split even on Stover and Nalley.

Both drivers are veterans of the winner circle at many tracks, but their personal duel has never been settled. Aside from not seeing eye-to-eye on many phases of racing, Nalley and Stover have one thing in common--expert crews. This could be a large percentage of their success over the years, but the main factor is their ability to weave through congested traffic like a Keystone Cop movie.

Nalley won the first three features in the modified division at Eastside during the 1964 season. On May 2, 1964, he overcame Winchester's Chuck Brannon on the fourth lap of the feature and held on the rest of the way. The race was so one-sided that it is said that the sparse crowd in attendance turned their attention to the second place battle between Brannon and Earl Moran. Moran finished second and Brannon third.

On April 25, 1964, Nalley won the 25-lap modified race at Eastside, lapping the entire field.

On July 1, 1956, The Winchester Star has this account of Nalley's sportsmanship on the track:

In the fourth heat--the most exciting of the afternoon--Bill Nalley showed fine sportsmanship when he braked up to let Robert Peer's Z01 out of a hole when the Star Tannery driver's car skidded and ran up the edge of the infield. Nalley's quick action, when a bump might have flipped Peer's racer or certainly put him out of competition, allowed Z01 to get back on the track and finally copped the winner's flag. It was nip and tuck in the final laps between Peer and Nalley.

On July 20, 1958, Bill Nalley won the 50-lap modified feature at Winchester when Tommy Irwin's car, the front runner, was involved in an accident.

On July 13, 1958, the Winchester Speedway presented midget racing. After the regular midget races, Bill Nalley, driving a midget, won a special three-way race over Doug Bailey and Al Grinnan. None had ever before driven a midget.

Fights

On June 27, 1959, Lee Stultz was beaten up at Waynesboro. The July 3, 1959, edition of The Winchester Star has this account:

In last Saturday's events at Waynesboro, S-3 owner Lee Stultz was right thoroughly beaten up during the running of the modified feature. Far away from his own crew, Stultz tangled with one of the other crew members and then found himself being hit by three at the same time. The uneven fight sent Stultz to the hospital, but he was back at the Winchester Speedway on Sunday to keep his car and the money.

The Winchester Star continues,

That fight, as well as a near fight here and another which developed between Stover and Nalley several weeks ago at Waynesboro, has caused a rule at the track. The management will not allow any driver or member of his crew to appear at the speedway again this year if he provokes a fight.

Incidentally, Nalley's bout with Stover was a one-punch affair, with Smokey taking the full count, but it was at least a man-against-man bout.

In the fall of 1958, Nalley set a track record at Winchester with a lap of 20.2 seconds.

On August 17, 1958, Bill Nalley won the Class A feature at Winchester when Junior Bowers, who was dominating the race, blew an engine on the 24th lap. Nalley won the 30-lap feature when, over the last six laps, he passed Ray Dovel to take the lead.

Lee Stultz Dies

Lee Stultz died of congestive heart failure on May 29, 1987, at the age of 72 after 35 years of auto racing. Pallbearers included Sam Nalley, Bill Nalley, Red Ninninger, Ray Dovel, and Charlie Beeler, all former drivers for Stultz.

Nalley retired from racing after the 1964 season because of heart problems. He reveals in the year 2001 that he's had several heart by-pass operations.

Bill and Sam Nalley were interviewed along with Bill's wife, Lorraine, at their pleasant home in a somewhat rural setting outside Knoxville, Maryland. Outside is a fully equipped garage and racing shop.

Nalley, originally from Brunswick, Maryland, was a 42-year veteran of the B&O Railroad, now known as CSX. He also owned a trucking business in 1959 and 1960. He started with the railroad as a laborer in 1939 at 21¢ per hour and eventually moved to the role of machinist. He was laid off in 1952 because of the influx of diesel locomotives as steam locomotives were being discontinued. He then went to the railroad yard as a welder and later operated a crane. For the last 15 years of his service with the railroad, he was a foreman. He retired in 1982.

Sam Nalley

Nalley's son, Sam, began racing late model cars in 1967 and retired in 1986. He raced regularly at Winchester and Hagerstown and won track championships at both. He also participated at St. Thomas and Everett, Pennsylvania, and Eastside. Everett, Pennsylvania was Sam's favorite track. Bill Nalley helped prepare Sam's cars. On one occasion Sam drove for Lee Stultz in the S-3 and won the race. All told, Sam won 96 features and only rolled his car once at Everett.

In 1980, Sam won the Virginia is for Lovers 200-lap

modified race at Waynesboro. The flagman for this event was Smokey Stover.

Sam only occasionally goes to races now and Bill does not attend races. They both, however, watch NASCAR races on TV and Sam has a Harley-Davidson motorcycle which he takes regularly to Daytona's Bike Week. Sam is a supervisor of the boiler shop at a local school system near Knoxville, Maryland.

Bill is a tall and friendly man who has a good sense of humor and obviously enjoys talking of his racing career. Despite his success, he is quite modest and quick to give credit to Lee Stultz for much of his success. In the view of this author, however, this one quote by Nalley says it best in terms of his success. "I could make two laps on a track and I know how to drive it. It was something natural, I guess."

Bill, Sam and Lorraine Nalley. Circa. 2001.

JUNIOR BOWERS

The death of Andrew C. "Junior" Bowers on August 3, 1960, from injuries he received in a stock car racing accident at Winchester on July 24, 1960, shattered the innocence of local drivers and reminded them of the danger of the sport. Bowers was a popular driver, a regular at Devil's Bowl, Eastside, and Winchester. His car was distinctive. It was a black Ford Coupe with a yellow star with the number 1/2 emblazoned in the middle.

BOWERS' BIGGEST WIN

He was respected and well liked by all. Bowers' biggest victory was winning the L. P. Claytor Memorial Race at Eastside Speedway on September 28, 1957. The prize was $285.

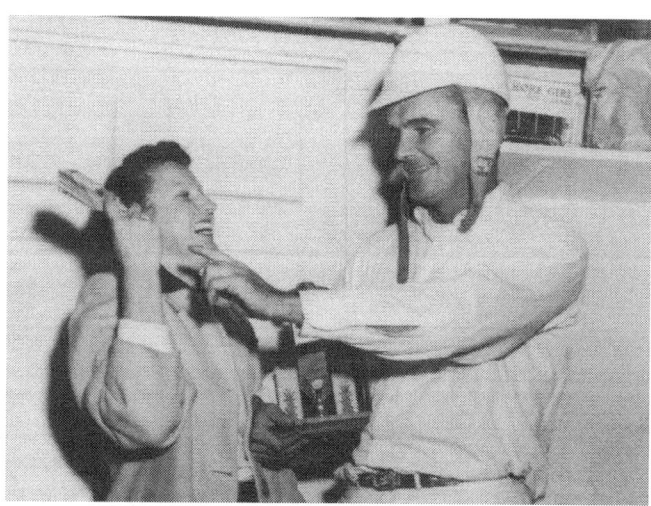

Happy times! Junior Bowers and wife, Helen banter with his winnings of $285 on September 28, 1957.

Bowers, who feared at one time that he would miss the Claytor race due to job commitments, started on the outside position in the front row. On the second lap of the 40-mile event, he tangled with Bill Nalley who lost ground to Bowers and fell back to second place. Later in the race, Nalley threatened to overtake Bowers when he tangled with Al Grinnan, who was having mechanical trouble with his car. Nalley never threatened again and Bowers won.

TRAGEDY

On July 24, 1960, the then 37-year old Bowers suffered a fractured skull as well as burns, bruises, and abrasions in a spectacular crash. In the second lap of the modified feature race at Winchester, Bowers' car, which was running near the center of the pack, catapulted into the air, turning over approximately

Car in which Junior Bowers was killed.

nine times and rising 75 feet in the air. When the car stopped, the engine burst into flames.

It was unclear how the accident occurred, but it appears that Bowers' wheel went over the wheel of another car, which launched his car into the air. The Winchester Star newspaper account of the wreck describes the aftermath:

Everyone on the infield converged on the scene. The flames were near the injured driver when the first rescuers, including Clifton Wilson and Mitchell Heironimous who were go-cart drivers, started freeing Bowers. The fire was doused by hand extinguishers, including one from the Allegheny Freight Lines wrecker at the truck.
Bowers was rushed to the hospital in the Friendship

Fire Company ambulance. The side of his face and head appeared to have taken a terrible blow.

The race was delayed for 30 minutes and won by Lewis Bocock of Staunton.

Bowers was employed by Smith Transfer Company as a truck driver and dock worker. He was a member of the Staunton Volunteer Fire Department and was a veteran of World War II. He left behind a wife and two daughters.

Active pallbearers at his funeral were Smokey Stover, Claude Baldwin, Lewis Bocock, Earl Moran, Buddy Stinespring, Carl Bridgeforth, Charlie Almond, and Bill Nalley. All were racecar drivers. Almond was the flagman at Winchester Speedway.

Honorary pallbearers included Bobby Campbell of the 306 car, Lee Stultz, mechanic and owner of the S-3 car, Charlie Propst, local driver, Tommy

On July 30, 1960, a go-cart race was held at Winchester Speedway to support the family of Junior Bowers. Bowers' daughters, Diane (left) and Cindy (right) present trophies to winners.

Campbell of the 306 car, Al Gore, owner of Eastside Speedway, Roy Neff, race driver, and Donald Stover, brother of Smokey Stover.

Bowers is buried in Thorn Rose Cemetery in Staunton, Virginia. His tombstone is reputed to be the first black marble tombstone in that cemetery. His wife Helen took a picture of his racecar and had it carved into the monument.

HIS DAUGHTER REMEMBERS

An interview was conducted with Diane Bowers, daughter of Junior Bowers. Her perspective is unique in that she is able to recount the effects of Bowers' death on her family and describe how it was for a nine-year-old child (her age at that time) to experience her father's death.

Bowers' daughter, Diane, poses with his trophies in 2001.

She remembers her father racing from the age of five. She remembers that Chester Stanley, Earl Moran, and a mechanic and truck driver by the name of Austin Snell would often help her father build and service his racecars in the basement of his home on Beverly Street in Staunton.

She remembers going to the races as a regular part of her life. Her mother would fry chicken and make sandwiches and according to her, "Off to the track we'd go. We'd have a slab of cheese on crackers. We ate on the road." Bowers' racecar was towed behind the family car.

She describes herself as "Daddy's girl." He called her "Toady" because she was allegedly pudgy for her age.

Diane Bowers continues, "I was close to Daddy.

When he had a screwdriver in his hand, I had a screwdriver. The way he died has been a lot of the stress in my life because no one will ever take my father's place."

Diane still likes to work on cars. She adds, "It reminds me of my dad. He will always be missed." Continuing to describe her relationship with her father, Diane says, "Daddy worked the midnight shift on the dock at Smith Transfer so he could sleep during the day and be up by the time I got home from school, and then we'd both work on the racecar 'til it was time for him to go to work that evening. We worked on the car in the basement. As a child, I never missed a race. My dad would also take me along to the Volunteer Fire Department with him."

Diane Bowers said that her father had a bookshelf made for the trophies he won in races. As a superstitious gesture, Diane Bowers says, "If there was a trophy race he was going to, he'd clean off a spot for it hoping he'd win it."

She admires her father's even temper and gains solace in the fact that her father had no enemies. She remembers fights at the racetrack after races and adds, "A lot of people gathered around the fight. When that would happen, Daddy would shake his head and say, 'Let's go. We're going home.'"

Diane's life changed the day of her father's accident. She goes on to describe what happened. "I can remember the car up in the air flipping. I still dream about it. It went up in the air nine times and came back on the ground and went up in flames. My mother, sister, and I were sitting in the grandstand. We had a dog named Pretty Boy. Mom must have just pitched the dog because some spectator had the dog and brought it to the hospital afterwards. Mom, Cindy (her sister), and I ran over to a gate. Some guy said, 'You can't go there.' Well, between Mom and I, he moved. We got onto the track and rode with him in the ambulance to the hospital. I remember him lying motionless in the ambulance. I remember being scared. His helmet was split and the attendants were talking about taking it off. His head was bleeding. Once we got to the hospital, they wouldn't let any of us see him."

Bowers continues, "We spent several days at the home of a man by the name of Harry Pingley. They were very nice. He owned a dry cleaning business.

"While Dad was in a coma, they had a go-cart race at Airport (Winchester) Speedway to raise money for Dad and our family. My sister Cindy and I presented the trophies."

Diane Bowers, at the age of nine, was not told directly about her father's death. Instead, she was told that she was being taken back to Staunton for some new clothes, but when they arrived at the home there were flowers at the door. Diane is still bitter about the way she learned of her father's death.

She remembers Winchester Speedway sending flowers to the family with the one-half logo, which was on his car. She remembers receiving approximately 150 sympathy cards. A heavy rain fell the day of the funeral and she continues, "You wouldn't believe the flowers. There wasn't a flower left in Staunton."

Track owner Al Gore came to the house several times after her father died. He told her, "Any time you ever want to go to the races, no matter how old you are, you can get in for free." According to Diane, however, she has never been back to the local tracks and has never set foot in Winchester since her father's death.

Bowers' Racing Highlights

On June 20, 1954, Junior Bowers won the amateur feature at Eastside Speedway with Smokey Stover finishing second.

One June 26, 1954, Junior Bowers won the amateur feature at Eastside driving his 1940 Studebaker V-8, once again edging Smokey Stover for the win.

On May 21, 1955, before a gathering of 1,248 fans at Eastside, Junior Bowers, with a speed of 62.4 miles per hour, was the winner in the amateur feature over Gip Gibson and Russell Breedan.
At the first race of the 1956 season at Eastside Speedway before 1200 spectators, Bowers won the first heat in a Class A sportsman division. He also won the feature, winning over John Strickland of Orange, Virginia. Tommy Irwin finished third.

When the race was completed, Strickland protested Bowers and posted a $25 protest fee. Bowers' car was found to be legal. He stepped to the payoff office, received the $25 protest fee, $35 for first place in the heat race, and $110 for his feature win as well as a trophy, making his total winnings of the evening $170.

On June 23, 1956, Bowers won the Class A feature race at Eastside. The News Virginian account on June 25, 1956 is as follows:

The Class A feature was a wild affair. For the first 10 laps all eyes were on Car 7 driven by Al Grinnan and Car S-3 driven by Bill Nalley. Grinnan held the lead for nine laps and then gave way to Nalley. The two were still fighting it out when Car 1/2, driven by Junior Bowers, began to close in. Bowers who won the first trophy race of the season has developed a very definite plan of attack. In the feature events, he lays back for about the first 10 laps and then begins to make his bid. The strategy paid off for him again Saturday night as he won his second feature. Bowers passed Nalley at about the 20-lap mark and finished the race in front of S-3. Al Grinnan took third place money.
The News Virginian gives the following account of Junior Bowers' running in the Class A sportsman feature at Eastside on August 18, 1956:

Probably the most exciting bit of driving was done by Junior Bowers of Staunton in Car 1/2. Bowers, who lost a lap in his early scramble in the lower turn, made it all up and roared home in third place.

On October 4, 1958, the L. P. Claytor Memorial Grand Championship 100-lap feature race at Eastside became quite controversial. The News Virginian has this account:

It appeared that Junior Bowers of Staunton, a rank outsider at race time, had successfully defended his Grand Championship and could claim the fat share of a $1,000 purse.

That was when the bomb was thrown. Bowers' victory was protested by second place driver Lewis Bocock of Greenville. This is his right under Eastside rules and the track mechanic was called to inspect Car 1/2. To the surprise of most observers, Car 1/2 was found to be over Eastside engine specifications and was disqualified, with Car 500 and Lewis Bocock being declared the winner.

The protest was the first successful one of its kind in three seasons at Eastside.

Bowers and Car 1/2 bested Bocock in a great battle over the last 15 laps, but the protest disqualified Bowers completely and pushed Bocock with Car 500 into first place.

This is the protest which is lamented to this day by Lewis Bocock, and it is described in the chapter dedicated to Lewis Bocock.

On June 28, 1959, Junior Bowers won a lengthened modified feature at Winchester, which required two pit stops changing all four tires. Second place went to Chester Stanley driving Bowers' second car. Ray

Dovel was third and Bill Nalley fourth.

Just one week before Bowers' fatal accident in 1960, Bowers experienced a close call at Winchester. The Winchester Star has this account:

Disaster nearly struck one of the drivers, Junior Bowers of Staunton, yesterday as his racer went into a solid sheet of flame just after crossing the finish line. Before the car had even started to slow down, Bowers was flying out the window. If he hadn't thought quickly, it is doubtful if he could have lived through the seared heat generated by the flames, but Bowers had his safety belt off fast and headed for open spaces.

The Friday following this near miss and preceding the accident that would be fatal, The Winchester Star had this to say about Bowers:

Junior Bowers, whose racer went up in a sheet of flames last Sunday as he hit the silk just in time, says he will be back and running this week. He may not have his racer rewired and ready, but he wants to drive something and get in on that fat purse.

CAR 1/2 RACES AGAIN

Approximately two months after her husband's fatal accident, Bowers' widow had the Car 1/2 completely rebuilt to race. Leroy Radford of Waynesboro was driving the car at Winchester for the first time. The Winchester Star tells what happened,

A near tragedy marred the start of the 50-lapper as the roaring pack went past a green flag for the first time. Running on the outside, Leroy Radford of Waynesboro had his wheels lock and his car sped in a straight line through the fence of the number one turn.

Visible to everyone in the grandstand and on the backstretch, Car 1/2 brought back the jolting memory of the racetrack's only fatality a couple of months ago when Junior Bowers of Staunton was piloting the same racer.

However, Radford came out of the jarring wreckage unhurt, but the car was demolished again. Mrs. Bowers, who's had a personal ambition to prove that she could do it, had paid for the rebuilding of 1/2.

Bowers' tombstone with replica of his car, 1/2.

No one could have felt any worse than Mrs. Bowers when the racer slammed through the heavy timbers, but finding Radford unhurt was a lifesaver for the plucky widow. Will this car ever race again is a matter between Mrs. Bowers and her ambition to show the racing world it can be done.

To those who don't understand Mrs. Bowers and her ambition, let's just say she is determined not to let the sport which took the life of her husband lick her and the car he loves so much.

Before sailing through the wall, Radford won the third heat of the day, so Mrs. Bowers had her one moment of triumph anyway, even though it came to an end on a sad note.

Mrs. Bowers did not rebuild the car.
It is unfortunate that after her father's death, Diane's

family began to disintegrate. Her mother had an alcohol problem and she became distant from her mother and sister Cindy. Diane failed that year of school, dealing with her father's death. She spent most of her time with her grandmother. The grandmother and others couldn't convince her mother to get help for her alcohol problem. Her mother remarried and moved to Tidewater, Virginia.

Sadly, Bowers' wife, Helen Argenbright Bowers, died on May 3, 1968 at the age of 42 of alcohol related disease. She is buried beside Junior in Thorn Rose Cemetery, Staunton, Virginia.

Diane Bowers was interviewed in her comfortable home in Staunton. She is a branch bank manager. Her continued love and affection for her father is striking, and the pain of what happened to her family after her father's death lingers to this day.

Millard "Smokey" Stover

One of the most successful and colorful drivers in the Shenandoah Valley was Millard "Smokey" Stover.

Born in Augusta County on December 27, 1936, he was a World War II veteran of the 101st Airborne Division, serving in the Pacific where he was injured. He also served two years during the Korean War.

He was a tool and dye maker and drove racecars from 1953 until September 22, 1968, when he suffered a near-fatal accident at Hagerstown Raceway, resulting in severe burns and a subsequent 16-month hospitalization.

Stover raced in the first-ever event held at Eastside Speedway in 1953 in his #15 Flathead Ford, and eventually went on to win over 200 feature races and numerous track championships at Eastside. He drove a variety of cars from 1953 to 1957, but saw his greatest success in the Car 306 owned by Tommy and Bobby Campbell of Staunton, Virginia, from 1957 to 1963.

Stover's brother Don owns Stover Store in Dooms, Virginia, just a half-mile from the track at Eastside. He's quoted as saying, "Smokey loved the tough competition of championship racing. He was born with a love for speed and a touch for danger. He loved to have fun."

Stover's quest for speed apparently started when he was in high school, when he took up flying and earned his pilot's license before he graduated. Colorblindness kept him from flying in the war, so he served as a paratrooper. After World War II, he couldn't find a car to buy, so he bought a motorcycle. The cycle gave him another outlet for his love of speed. He soon entered local hill climbs in and around Augusta County, and did stunt riding on his motorcycle at local speedways before going

306 car owners Tommy (left) and Bobby (right) in 2001. Note the wall hanging with car 306 in the background.

back into the service in 1951 because of the Korean War.

After returning from the Korean War, he bought a 1939 Ford Coupe and began racing at local tracks, including Craigsville (John's Speedway), Zion's Crossroads, Charlottesville, Lynchburg, Brookneal, Lawrenceville, and Valley Speedway in Staunton. He was quite successful at Eastside, Winchester, Hagerstown, and Natural Bridge. In 1962, he won 24 of 26 features at Eastside.

The author spent several hours interviewing Bobby and Tommy Campbell, owners of the 306 car driven by Stover. These two men are now in fragile health but have vivid memories of the years of the 306 car and Smokey Stover.

Tommy Campbell had started building racecars and racing on a limited basis in 1955 at Eastside and Valley Speedway. When his brother Bobby was discharged from military service in November '55, the two bought their first car from Roy Neff from Toms Brook, Virginia. The Car 306 was built in 1957, which they ran until 1963 and thereafter owned a late model racecar for two years.

Drunk Driver Gives Ride to Smokey

Bobby Campbell talks about how their racing career began with Smokey Stover. "When we built the modified, we knew it was going to run pretty good," says Campbell. Tommy and I disagreed over Smokey Stover and Cotton Shifflet as to who was going to drive the car. Shifflet was a wild, throw-the-tail-around crazy kind of guy. I wanted Smokey because he was a gutsy kind of guy. We went over to the speedway in Waynesboro to talk to Cotton about running our car and he was drunk. So we started talking to Smokey Stover."

Campbell continued, "Smokey was there. He had just gotten a cast off his leg that he had broken in a softball game. He was driving Car 55, a six-cylinder coupe, and he didn't have it ready yet. Smokey stepped in and drove it the rest of the time.

Stover's first win for the Campbell brothers was a 4th of July race at Eastside in 1957.

Stover retired from Car 306 in 1963 because of an ulcer; however, he received numerous requests to drive and did so on a sporadic basis.

Junior Bowers' Memorial Race

In 1960 when Junior Bowers was killed, Stover was very affected by the loss of his friend. Just a week after his death, a Junior Bowers' Memorial Race was held at Winchester. Both Stover and Lewis Bocock had vowed that if they could win the race, they would give the trophy to Bowers' widow, Helen. Stover, driving the #306 car owned by Bobby and Tommy Campbell of Staunton, won the race when Bocock experienced mechanical difficulties. Stover gave the trophy to Helen Bowers.

Smokey Severely Burned

On Sunday afternoon, September 22, 1968, driving in a sprint car race at Hagerstown, Maryland Raceway, Stover blew a brand new tire and brought the car to a stop on the back straightaway. He was hit in the rear by Johnny Crum. Stover's car was burning alcohol, which when ignited has an invisible flame. Smokey, sensing that the car was on fire, unbuckled and rolled in what he thought was water standing along the infield of the dirt track. Unfortunately, it was alcohol from his car, which was indeed aflame. He was severely burned and spent the next 16 months hospitalized, undergoing numerous operations.

Having learned that their friend had been burned, the Campbells drove the four-hour trip to Hagerstown, Maryland, from Staunton, Virginia, that Sunday night to visit Stover. Campbell continues, "I looked straight at his face. He was burned on over 75% of his body. You couldn't see his ears he was swollen that much. When I got there, he looked more swollen than anything else, but before I left the skin was starting to peel off and his blisters were popping on their own. The doctors didn't think he was going to make it, and they said the crucial part was mental toughness to deal with the pain and the after effects. But shit, he didn't know Smokey."

Stover survived, but never raced again.

Soft Clay at Lawrenceville

Campbell speaks of running at the Speedway in Lawrenceville, Virginia. "It was the most beautiful clay track you've ever seen," he says. "When we arrived, you could see cars just really running fast. I thought, 'My God, are we ever in the wrong place.' Then I saw the Triple Nickel (Car 555) and I thought, 'Well, we beat him over here (Eastside) with no trouble.' But that track was so fast, we just didn't realize how fast we could go there."

Bobby Campbell had the job of warming up the Car 306 and continues, "So I warmed it up. I always warmed the 306 up just playing with it. Smokey took it out there and he was motioning for me to come and talk to him. I went over and he said, 'You can run this track all the way around without backing off.' I said, 'Bull shit.' He said, 'Well, get in here.' It was a funny thing about Smokey. He flew an airplane and I always trusted him. I should never have trusted him, I realized as I got older. I squatted down and grabbed a rollbar. Sure enough he went into the turn wide open. Smokey scared the crap out of me that day. I was so glad when he stopped the car. But with that surface, you could stand on it and your feet would sink in it about half an inch. After you stepped away, there'd be no footprints. It was a beautiful track. I've never seen anything like it. Just a quarter of a mile."

Racing at Devil's Bowl

The Campbells were pipe fitters. Despite the fact that they were from Staunton, they did not particularly enjoy racing at Devil's Bowl. The track was often operated unprofessionally, according to them. There was often controversy about how much money was due the drivers. On several occasions winning a feature at Devil's Bowl only brought $25 to the Campbells.

When talking about Devil's Bowl, Campbell continues, "There were not a lot of cars there. It would seem like they would have a good crowd but something always seemed to happen to the money."

First Win for 306

The Campbells mention that they won $246 for the first win, which was a 4th of July Pepsi Cola Trophy Race in 1957 at Eastside.

On that day, Campbell continues, "We won the heat and the feature. That's when Smokey finally realized he knew how to drive. From that day on, we were pretty much a threat to win. We dominated the tracks we ran."

Smokey Stover and car 306.

Rick Mast

Bobby Campbell has fond memories of driving a young Rick Mast, currently a NASCAR driver, around the track at Eastside. According to Campbell, "He was just a kid then."

Smokey Holds Back

The 306 car was so dominant that often owners and other drivers would attempt to negotiate financial deals "designed to create the illusion of a close race."

Bobby continues, "The only time I remember Tommy getting upset with Smokey was when Al Gore came to Smokey and I one night and said, 'If you guys will let somebody stay close, it will be good. You know people are getting disinterested in this.'

"Well, Lewis Bocock was running about as close as anybody to us at that time, but he seldom would beat us.

"Gore said, 'I'll pay both of you for first place if you just let him stay close.'

"So we told Bocock we'd keep it close, but you just make damn sure Smokey wins because if you're not, we're going to run the way we usually do.'

"Man, there was a hell of a race and people in the stands were standing. Smokey won, it was close, and we didn't tell Tommy that Smokey was backing off. You're talking about a hot son-of-a-gun now!"

Going North

Bobby Campbell speaks fondly of the racing days saying, "The most fun we ever had. We'd get calls from tracks up north to run Chambersburg, Pennsylvania. We'd carry a big Rebel flag with us, and once we got above the Mason Dixon Line, we'd run the flag up the pole and we'd all wear Rebel hats. We were called the Rebel Chevy. They would play Dixie when we'd cross the track to go in the infield. People really enjoyed it. It was all in fun. I've seen Smokey sign autographs up there in Pennsylvania for hours."

Campbell continues, "We were in Hagerstown one night and fans came and asked us to go to Williams Grove, Pennsylvania, the next day. We had won the race, but the car locked up afterwards and we lost a rear end. We stayed at a truck stop that had a garage. We worked all night to fix the car at the truck stop, went up there, and won. The most we ever won was $600 in Chambersburg."

Booed by Locals

At the same time, however, Campbell says that the Car 306 and Smokey were controversial and often were booed by local fans because they won "too much." According to Campbell, "Even my own kids rooted for other people. We had no fans. We'd go to the concession stands and people would throw things at you. Mostly it was good fun, but some of it wasn't."

Dueling with Nalley

Some of the most memorable encounters occurred between Stover and Bill Nalley. Each accused the other of causing serious accidents. On one occasion in 1963, Nalley is alleged to have caused an accident, flipping the 306 on a Saturday night at Waynesboro. Then on the following Sunday at Winchester, Stover allegedly flipped Nalley, which resulted in injured ribs for Nalley.

Campbell continues, "I really liked Bill. He was a class guy. I guess he was the biggest competition we had. A good, clean competitor, but like Smokey, neither one of them wanted to get off the throttle. It was sort of a personal thing between the two when they were racing. They both started in the rear and both tried to get to the front first and take all kind of chances. Boy, it was competition there."

Campbell goes on to say that the Car 306's chief competition besides Nalley included Ray Dovel, Earl Moran, Gip Gibson, Al Grinnan, and Lewis Bocock.

Campbells Work on 306

Bobby Campbell was responsible for the painting of the car, which was bright red and white. The

Campbells were the first pit crew to wear coordinated red shirts, and Stover was the first driver to wear a uniform, usually wearing a white helmet with red letters, red shirt, white pants, and red gloves.

Tommy Campbell was responsible for the motor work. It is said that he was a genius in working with race motors; however, he is somewhat modest when questioned. The Campbells were also quite innovative in that they were the first in the area to experiment with radio communication between pit and driver.

Tommy Campbell is proud of the fact that only one engine was lost during their racing career. In this case, they had drained the oil, forgot about it, and started the engine for just a few minutes, long enough to doom the engine. They were apparently distracted by fans who had stopped by their race shop to talk. Campbell says, "There was always people coming around wanting to hear the car run."

Campbell describes losing the motor. "At Waynesboro that Saturday night, Smokey had a hell of a lead," he says. "He came down the front stretch gesturing that the car was overheating. I had noted that he had kept getting slower and slower. Finally it just locked up on him on the front stretch."

Tommy Campbell says that the motor bearings in Car 306 were changed at mid-season every year. They did not burn alcohol but used a special mixture of Sunoco gas with 93 octane. They experimented with airplane fuel on one occasion; however, it "plugged up the lines." They used a basic stock 327 cubic inch Chevy engine that was never deemed to be illegal in numerous protests. Later, the Campbells ran a 427 cubic inch Ford.
In the 50's and 60's it was not politically incorrect to display the Rebel flag, and the 306 car had prominent Rebel flags painted on the body. The Campbells often flew a Rebel flag in the pits where they serviced the car.

Tommy Campbell got most of his engines from junkyards and rebuilt them. However, the 327 cubic inch Chevrolet, which was the most successful, was bought new from the factory. Stover bought a new Ford with a 427 cubic inch motor in 1962, driving the car from the dealership to his home where he parked the car with just a few miles on it, taking the motor to install in the racecar. He later put the motor back in his private car.

Bobby Campbell is proud that he brokered the sale of the Eastside Speedway's track in 1958 from L. P. Claytor's widow and her relative, Al Charles, to promoter Al Gore. Campbell took Gore to Charles' house where a deal was made and closed in an afternoon.

BIRTHDAY CAKE AND MOONSHINE

One night at Eastside, a birthday party was planned for Bobby Campbell. The plan was to enjoy cake and moonshine after the race. A fan had brought a sheet cake with the #306 on it, colored red and white. The cake was set on the ground when Ray Dovel drove into the pits, angry over an incident on the track. Dovel came to a stop, angrily put his car in reverse, and backed over the cake! According to Campbell, "We ate the cake around the tire tracks, drank the moonshine, and had a great time!"

SERIOUS INJURY IN 1964

Stover's most serious injuries came after he had "retired" in 1963 and was driving cars for owners other than the Campbells. His 1968 accident at Hagerstown has been previously described. The first accident occurred in 1964 when Stover drove a car owned by Clyde Harris at the request of Al Gore, the promoter and owner of Eastside Speedway. The car is described by Bobby Campbell as a "stainless steel car." It was nicknamed "The Flying

Rollbar." Campbell continues, "I didn't think much of it. The car really didn't look safe. I told Al Gore and he asked us to work on the car so we did. The car had a drive shaft running right between the driver's legs. We put a cover on the drive shaft and changed the accelerator so he could control it with a stirrup.

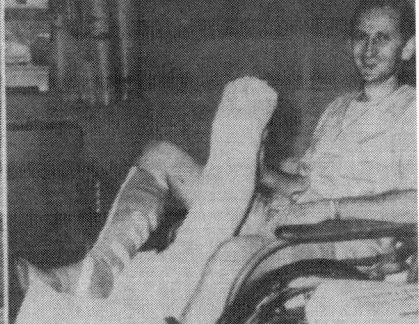

Smokey Stover recuperates in Waynesboro Hospital after serious injury to leg in 1964.

"On that day, they had put Nalley and Stover in the rear and advertised it for two weeks, so there were probably about 18 cars ahead of them.

"Going into the turn, somebody lost it and the cars were stacking up. Smokey just seemed to bump a car in front of him. It didn't seem like much."

Stover was famous for quickly exiting the car after an accident. Campbell continues, "He got his head and shoulder out of the window. He was motioning for me to come down there and I took off running. When I got there, he had just got his right leg out. He complained of awful pain, but at first you couldn't see anything and he was pointing under his leg. He held his leg up and then you could see the skin hanging down with all the blood running. Also on the track with Stover was car owner Clyde Harris and Stover's wife Ruby.

"He had just bumped that car in front of him and the drive shaft came out with the transmission turning, and that stainless steel gear shift lever tore a knob off and that jagged metal end cut Smokey in the calf and pulled the whole calf muscle out. Pulled all the tendons out of his leg, ankle, and knee.

"That was 1964. So they gave him a couple shots of morphine and he was happy as he could be. He didn't have any idea of how badly he was hurt or what was going on.

"It took a lot of therapy and a lot of work, but he never got much muscle back in that leg. For a little fellow, Smokey was the toughest man I've ever seen."

JUNIOR BOWERS' DEATH

The Campbells recall the day Junior Bowers was killed at Winchester Speedway in 1960. The 306 car had raced the night before at Manassas, but had cracked the bell housing, rendering it unable to race the next day in Winchester. Nevertheless, the Campbells and Stover met Junior Bowers and his entourage at an icehouse close to the speedway and accompanied them to the race. They all witnessed the crash that ended Bowers' life and ran to his assistance when the race was red flagged. Bobby Campbell still has a photograph of the mangled car Bowers was driving when he was killed.

Tommy Campbell recounts going to Bowers' aid. "The car flipped five or six times," he says. "I saw Junior. He wasn't cut anywhere, but he was making noises. It looked like somebody had sewn a finger in his forehead. He had a long knot. His Cromwell helmet wasn't cracked that I saw. We all knew it was bad, however."

SELECTED EVENTS

On Saturday, September 16, 1961, Stover's wife Ruby drove a car to win in the so-called "Petticoat

Derby" as well as Smokey in the modified feature at Eastside.

The Tuesday, September 19, 1961, of The Waynesboro News Virginian has this account of Smokey Stover and his wife winning features the previous Saturday night:

A husband and wife join hands in the winner's circle at Eastside Speedway Saturday night after they had taken wins in their respective feature races. Smokey Stover, the modified stock car racer from Staunton, piloted the Car #306 to win in the modified feature and then sat back to watch his wife Ruby drive to a victory in the Petticoat Derby.

The win by the male member of the Stover family was not the easiest for the Staunton driver. Smokey had to battle all the way before he took the checkered flag. The battle was fought with Earl Moran in 35A with Smokey taking the lead for the first time on the 18th lap of the 20-lap feature. Moran held the lead for the majority of the race, although he was involved in a crash on the 8th lap and almost flipped his vehicle.

Ruby Stover's victory was gained after she took the lead on the 3rd lap and never let up. Ten cars were in the field for the Petticoat Derby.

On September 9, 1961, nearly 800 race fans saw Smokey Stover win over Jackie Clore and Lewis Bocock at Eastside.

On April 19, 1954, Smokey Stover won $55 as the winner of the amateur's feature at Eastside.

On September 10, 1955, driving in the amateur division, Smokey Stover won his first checkered flag of the 1955 season and a gold trophy as he drove Car #55 owned by Hugh Batten of Waynesboro at Eastside. He took the lead on the first lap and was never threatened seriously. Over 1,400 spectators saw the race.

On July 4, 1957, Smokey Stover won his first race for the Campbell brothers in the #306 car. The following is the account of The News Virginian:

Stover Captures Stock Car Feature at Eastside Oval

Millard "Smokey" Stover survived accidents, heavy traffic, mechanical difficulty, and unsound rubber at Eastside Speedway Saturday night to win the 20-mile Fourth of July Gold Trophy Race for Sportsman Stock Cars.

The win was the first trophy sweepstakes the 30-year old machinist from Staunton has earned this year. It was worth $234 for him and it swelled his total earnings for the season to more than $500. He piloted Car #306 to a decisive victory over 14 other rivals in a field that was chock full of the top names in stock car racing in the state.

Stover steered the car, owned by Tommy and Bob Campbell of Staunton, into victory lane and said, "I finished on borrowed time." He then pointed to his right rear tire, which contained a wide slit about 8 inches long.

"Boy, somebody meant for me to win this one tonight in more ways than one," he mused.

In Stover's qualifying heat, he collided with John Strickland, who was runner up in the feature event, but managed to haul down top money. The Staunton driver guessed that the brief sideswiping episode had accounted for the deep cut in the tire.

The happy winner said #306 still has some "bugs" in it. "It has run as good on other occasions," Stover quipped, "but not for as long as it did tonight."

The Stover-Campbell team ran into mechanical trouble prior to the race. Three fan belts were lost before they could find one that would stay in place. It was borrowed from a tow car owned by Tommy Irwin.

Number 306 was built by the Campbell brothers last winter. They estimate their cash investment into the automobile at $1200. It has a 1955 Chevrolet engine with a displacement of 283 cubic inches. The entire car is made up of Chevrolet parts.

On May 16, 1959, Stover won a close race over Bill Nalley in the inaugural event of the 1959 season at Eastside. The News Virginian stated that Stover received a "tremendous ovation from the crowd of 600 diehard racing fans who braved unseasonably cold weather to witness the action."

On June 20, 1959, Smokey Stover won his second feature of the year at Eastside. Stover's win was significant considering that he rolled his car on the number four turn during warm-up laps.

On July 11, 1959, Smokey Stover won the 25-lap sportsman feature at Eastside over Bill Nalley. The following is an account from The News Virginian:

The 25-lap sportsman event saw Smokey Stover of Staunton in Car #306 and Bill Nalley of Winchester in S3 come up from the back of the pack and ride bumper to bumper all the way. Nalley was never able to get in front of Stover, and they crossed the finish line less than a car length apart.

On August 20, 1960, Smokey Stover won the 50-lap modified feature at Eastside Speedway after a close battle with Lewis Bocock. The newspaper described the race as a "bumper to bumper thrill show."

On September 4, 1960, in the 25-lap modified/sportsman feature, Stover won a very exciting race over Bocock at Eastside. The News Virginian has this account:

Stover's Sunday triumph in the sportsman feature did not follow the script for Stover, as had been the case the prior three Sundays. In the previous features, he stayed back in the field until about midway to the finish. Then he would come on in fine style to take the lead. Sunday, he was fourth on the first lap, advancing to second on the next lap, and taking the lead on the third lap as he came past the starter. All the time Bocock was next to Stover. From the third lap to the finish, the two men staged a blistering duel.

Going into the turns Bocock would seem to get the best of Stover, but as they would come out, Stover would nudge again into the lead. This proved to be the story for the last 20 more laps. Stover would gain the lead on the straightaways, which Bocock could not completely overcome.

This possibly was the race described earlier by Bobby Campbell in which promoter Al Gore had requested the two to run a "close race."

On May 6, 1961, Smokey Stover won the sportsman/modified feature at Eastside over Earl Moran and Buddy Stinespring, who was driving a sportsman vehicle.

On July 29, 1961, Smokey Stover was unable to drive because of cracked ribs sustained in the incident two weeks earlier at Eastside when he prematurely exited the car and was hit in the rear by another car. According to accounts, "His ribs were too sore to drive." The Car 306 did run with Earl Moore driving in the heat and Chester Stanley in the feature; however, that night at Eastside the Car 306 was no factor in these races.

On August 12, 1961, nearly 1,000 fans witnessed Stover edge Lewis Bocock in the 25-lap modified/sportsman feature at Eastside. Bocock led from the start of the race until the fourth turn on the last lap of the feature. At this point Stover edged in front of Bocock to gain the checkered flag.

Earlier that night, Stover had won a similarly close heat race against Earl Moran. These wins were remarkable because of serious engine difficulties encountered by Stover prior to the race. The News Virginian has this:

The wins by Stover Saturday night were a result of teamwork by the pit crew, the driver, and other interested persons. Prior to the start of the race program, motor trouble developed in 306. Helping hands joined in to mend the vehicle.

An article in the April 27, 1962, edition of The News Virginian gives this account of Stover's participation in the 1962 season:

Stover Will Test 306 Once Again

Does competitive spirit make for a better stock car racing program? The answer is a definite yes.

Smokey Stover, a Staunton driver who last year lost only five races at Eastside Speedway, has this spirit and will be out to redeem himself this week. He was shut out last week by another Staunton driver, Earl Moran, in the modified class.

The majority of the trouble last week was due to overheating in his entirely rebuilt 306 which Smokey drives. After the race, Smokey vowed to "get the bugs out" during this week and will be raring to go Saturday night when another racing card is presented at Eastside Speedway.

During the winter months, Smokey tore down 306 and rebuilt the vehicle. Last Saturday night was the first time he had an opportunity to put it to a test. The test failed as the vehicle continued to overheat. This week, the vehicle's heating system was overhauled.

On May 11, 1962, Smokey Stover won the modified feature at Devil's Bowl Speedway in Staunton. Earl Moran was second, followed by Buddy Stinespring and Lewis Bocock in that order.

On May 19, 1962, Stover won the 25-lap modified race at Eastside with this account given in The News Virginian:

A switch in motors brought victory to the veteran stock car driver at Eastside Speedway here Saturday night. The veteran, Smokey Stover of Staunton, once again proved to be a crowd pleaser when he changed motors prior to the start of the regular Saturday night race and then piloted the Car 306 to a win in the modified feature before a crowd in excess of 700 persons.

Prior to Saturday night, Stover had been having trouble with 306. He rebuilt the vehicle from the ground up before the start of the 1962 season. Then he decided that a switch in the motors, going back to last year's number, could bring better results. The switch was made, and by the way the car ran Saturday night, it revealed that he was right. Finishing second to Stover in the feature was Earl Moran of Staunton in Car 35A.

On October 13, 1962, a demolition derby was held at Eastside Speedway. Although Stover was entered, the contest was won by Wes Right of Lynchburg, Virginia, who pocketed $150, out-dueling Stover in the fading moments of the derby. The final blow came when Right shoved his vehicle in reverse and backed into the front of Stover's car, rendering it useless for the evening.

During the 1963 season, one of Smokey Stover's chief threats was Clem Lamaster. The July 1, 1963 edition of The News Virginian proclaims,

The King Has Regained His Throne!

In a manner of speaking, Staunton ace Smokey Stover has informed Winchester speedster Clem Lamaster that he just isn't ready to relinquish his modified racing crown. Stover's "message" came in the form of a thorough drubbing for the daring Lamaster during racing here at Eastside Speedway Saturday night. Not only in the 35-lap modified feature but in an 8-lap heat as well.

Determined to regain his lost luster from nemesis Lamaster, Stover jumped to the lead of the tangled 35-lap feature race (which required four restarts as cars tangled on the slick clay oval) on lap five. And when he picked up the checkered silk on his final circle, he was a full lap ahead of Lamaster.

Lamaster overtook third place Lewis Bocock of Greenville in the seventh lap of the feature and held onto second place. But he just wasn't able to gain ground on the Staunton ace Stover who ran all alone for the major portion of the race. The two wins over Lamaster Saturday night gave Stover a solid total of four in two races. He also outdistanced the Apple Capital Speedster at two heats at Winchester's Airport Speedway on Friday.

Stover this past week went from 9 1/2 to 11 inch tires, an inch and a half difference. He feels that made up the margin of difference.

Lamaster, though, isn't going to be outdone by the Staunton ace who has dominated racing circles in the area for a number of years. He already has purchased a set of big 11-inch rubber. He's searching his bag of tricks for another gimmick to spring in races this week.

Although the continuing duel between Stover and Lamaster is just what the crowd ordered, it may prove costly to both drivers in the coming weeks, as Bill Nalley, who has been sidetracked for the last month due to an injurious crash at the Airport Speedway, will be back on the circuit this weekend with his car rebuilt. And you can bet that after being off the track for a number of weeks, Nalley will be raring to go.

On August 9, 1959, Smokey Stover won the modified feature at Winchester over Lewis Bocock in second and Earl Moran in third.

On August 2, 1960, Stover won a hard fought race over Bill Nalley and Lewis Bocock at Winchester.

On July 4, 1960, Stover won the 25-lap modified feature over Lewis Bocock in second, Earl Moran in third, Red Ninninger in fourth, and Bill Nalley in fifth in action at Winchester.

Later that day, a match race was held among the five fastest modified cars. Nalley won with Stover second and Bocock third.

On July 17, 1960, just one week before Junior Bowers' fatal accident, Stover won the modified feature at Winchester over second place Lewis Bocock.

SMOKEY PASSES AWAY

Toward the end of Stover's life, he was diagnosed with Lou Gherig's Disease; however, the story is told that he essentially died of a head injury, which he sustained after losing his balance while trying to fix a trailer he was towing, falling and hitting his head. He died August 7, 1988, at his residence in Augusta County.

When the Campbells are asked about the secret to their racing success, they are quick to credit Smokey Stover. Bobby and Tommy describe extraordinary things he could do with a racecar and say, "The man could do things with a car you'd never believe. He never tore up a car that bad and never got hurt with us."

Bobby Campbell speaks with affection when talking

about Smokey Stover. He talks about the last days of Smokey's life. "Two weeks before Stover died, he had a '34 Ford Roadster that he had restored," he says. "He was towing it and had some kind of problem. He got out to check on it and fell backwards over the tow-hitch and hit his head."

Campbell talks of his friend as he suffered from Lou Gherig's Disease, saying that he only weighed 65 to 80 pounds at his death. Campbell continues, "He'd have to put hands on his legs to push himself up a grade. He got to where he couldn't hit a golf ball 50 yards."

Campbell says, "I still miss him. We played golf every Sunday. We were like brothers."

At Stover's death, his casket was taken to an auto shop where it was painted bright red, the color of the 306 car, before he was buried. Pallbearers included Al Gore, owner of the Eastside Speedway, and Tom and Bobby Campbell. Racer Buddy Stinespring served as an honorary pallbearer and, at Stover's widow's request, brought a clean checkered flag to use in the funeral.

The Campbells have mostly stayed away from racing since they retired. Both were on hand on several occasions to present trophies at the Smokey Stover Memorial Race, which was held for some time at Eastside. But Bobby says, "When we quit, we quit. We got tired of racing three days a week, every week, 9 months a year, and working on the car every night. And I started playing golf and fishing and hunting-- doing anything to get that damn brake fluid smell out of you."

The Campbells were interviewed in their comfortable, well-decorated homes in Staunton, Virginia. Pictures and plaques of the Car 306 glory days are prominent in their living rooms. Both brothers need the assistance of oxygen due to their medical conditions, but their ill health obviously doesn't dampen their fond memories of the Car 306 and Smokey Stover.

Clyde Harris

Born and raised in Staunton, Virginia, Clyde Harris got involved in stock car racing in 1960. He opened Clyde's Auto Body Shop in 1961 in downtown Staunton and operates this business as of 2002.

Harris Gets the Racing Bug

His first involvement with racing was building a 1934 Chevrolet Coupe, racing in the modified division and driven by Earl McCrary. Clyde never raced, however, often "warmed up" the racecar prior to racing. He says, "I thought I'd make a good driver, but I had the fear of getting injured and my family would pay for it."

Work was conducted on his racecar at his body shop in Staunton; however, he parked and worked on the racecar in a bay hidden from the general public. This was done to keep away onlookers. Harris says, "I didn't want anybody to be talking about it. I didn't want 'track trash' hanging around trying to talk about racing when you've got a legitimate customer you're trying to talk to or trying to get some work done."

In addition to owning a car, Harris began scoring races at Eastside and did so there for seventeen years. He also periodically scored at Natural Bridge, Winchester, and Devil's Bowl. He is very proud of his proficiency as a scorer. He designed his own score pad, a legal pad increased to 18 inches long with wide columns. He made a checkmark for each time a car passed before him. At Eastside, a lap would take approximately 19 seconds. With 35 cars on the field, this was no small task, however, Harris was very confident in his abilities and says there were very few scoring mistakes. He was paid $70 a night to score at Eastside, good money for the day. He received $25 a night at Devil's Bowl, and at Natural Bridge $100 an event for scoring.

Harris on Al Gore

Over the years at Eastside, he formed a very close relationship with track owner and promoter Al Gore. Harris says that Al Gore was a successful track promoter "because of perseverance." Harris continues,

Clyde Harris scoring a race at Natural Bridge Speedway.

"Al Gore was a man. He was strong. He carried wooden beams by himself to build the grandstand at Eastside. One night some guy pulled a gun on him. He just backhanded the guy and put him on the hood of a car. He was a rough head, but he knew what had to be done and he did it."

He relates that there were Eastside Speedway annual awards banquets held on the second floor of the firehouse in Dooms, Virginia, within earshot of the track. These events were rather extravagant affairs, with a band, dancing, trophies, and bonus checks presented. Harris has several pictures of such events.

THE DEMISE OF DEVIL'S BOWL

Harris speaks affectionately of the Devil's Bowl Speedway, and describes its demise in 1962. Devil's Bowl initially opened as Valley Speedway in the early 50's just west of Staunton, built by Jesse Weaver and Leonard Shull. After Weaver died in 1958, the track was operated by his son, Homer Weaver, who in the later years of the track took on local TV personality partner Bill Lydell and later Bob McNeal who was a radio announcer. The name Devil's Bowl was the brainchild of Lydell. It opened under the name Devil's Bowl on April 30, 1960. The relationships with Lydell and McNeal did not salvage the operation of the track, which had to fight frequent court injunctions against closure. These legal battles were initiated by residents who lived in the area and complained about the excessive dust from the dirt road leading to the track as well as from the track itself. At least one injunction alleged that there was excessive noise.

On several occasions, Harris was the flagman at Devil's Bowl Speedway.

Harris further explains that at that time, most of the individuals in the area of the speedway had cisterns as a way of supplying water. The excessive dust would apparently accumulate on residents' roofs and then flow into their cisterns when it rained.

In an effort to curtail the dust, Weaver placed motor oil on the dirt road leading into the track, which according to residents only increased the degree of water contamination.

As far as is known, the last race at Devil's Bowl was conducted on July 6, 1962.

Harris laughs about Homer Weaver at Devil's Bowl awarding $10 for any driver who flipped his racecar. Yortha Claytor, a relative of the Claytors who at one time operated Eastside, often would have several of his crew at the bottom of the banking of the third and fourth turns so that when he rolled, his crew would roll it back on its wheels and he'd continue racing. Yortha is alleged to have said, "I made more money rolling them over than I did racing."

Harris also remembers a man by the name of Luther Painter, a regular spectator at Devil's Bowl who often was intoxicated. On one occasion, he tried to catch a wheel that had left a racecar. "He was hit in the chest and seriously injured," according to Harris.

TIRES COME TUMBLING DOWN

Harris tells the story of Lewis Bocock's wife Jean driving Lewis' tow truck to Staunton, which had a tire rack in the back. This is the vehicle Lewis towed his #500 modified racer to the tracks.

Staunton is known for steep hills. Jean Bocock drove to the top of Johnson Street in Staunton. When she stopped at the top of the hill, five racing tires came rolling down the hill behind her as the tailgate on the truck was open! Harris says, "It was something, but not one tire did damage to anything."

WENDELL SCOTT

Harris also remembers the late Wendell Scott at Devil's Bowl. He remembers several occasions when Scott would remove tires from his tow vehicle, place them on his racer, complete the race, and then return the tires to the tow vehicle and drive to his home in Danville. Scott also would often remove the radiator from his tow truck, place it on the racer, and then return it back to the tow vehicle to travel home.

THE FLYING ROLLBAR

In 1964, Harris along with McCrary built an extremely light modified racer. It was said to have been built with a great deal of stainless steel and weighed only

1200 pounds; however, it was powered by a 327 cubic inch fuel-injected Chevrolet engine. The car, #88, was known as the "Flying Rollbar" and was the result of over 300 hours of work by Harris and McCrary.

According to Harris, Al Gore had generated a great deal of hype over this vehicle in an effort to draw fans. It was widely advertised that the vehicle would be at the track and driven by Smokey Stover, who would be coming out of retirement to race the car. According to Harris, "This was supposed to be the greatest thing that ever hit a dirt track." Harris continues, "This car was so small I couldn't get in it. Smokey was a small man and could. We took the car over to Eastside to try it out. He made a half dozen laps and came in. It had so much power that it bent the traction bars."

Harris then returned to Staunton with his car and installed new, stronger traction bars. According to Harris, "It had so much power, it would do wheelies like a dragster. It had about 500 horsepower."

The next week, Harris returned to Eastside with stronger traction bars and Smokey Stover to drive in the race.

Disaster Strikes

What happened in the race is somewhat uncertain, however, there is no uncertainty that the bell housing, protecting the driver from the transmission, broke and twisted, causing the gear shifter to become a lethal weapon, and in the process severing the calf muscle from Smokey Stover's right leg.

Harris describes the scene. "At Eastside when his leg was injured, Ruby his wife was dressed in white. I remember her sitting in the red clay in the middle of the third turn with his head in her lap. She had blood on her dress. I (Harris) was holding him down on the chest. He was in great pain. I saw his leg muscle laying on the ground.
"We went with Smokey to the Waynesboro Hospital and the doctor said the leg should be amputated. They said he'd never walk again."

What ensued was a rather long recuperation; however, Stover recovered. Harris, with tears coming to his eyes, says, "But he didn't even have a limp."

Harris was close to Stover, according to him, "Smokey was great. He laughed a lot. He had a nickname he'd call people--"Bad Egg." You would hear him whistle before he walked in the door. He was a great machinist. He could do anything.

"When Smokey was sick at the end, he was going back and forth to Nevada for alternative treatments. The doctor made him believe it was all related to the Chernobyl disaster in Russia. He told him the winds had brought radiation to North America and transmitted it to humans by milk. He was desperate for a cure." The trauma of Stover's leg injury stopped Harris' involvement in racing as a car owner. He continued to score primarily at Eastside as well as at Winchester for Clem Lamaster, but in 1970 took his biggest risk by far with regard to his involvement in racing.

Craigsville Motor Speedway

In the early 1950's, just south of Craigsville, Virginia, on Route 42, a man by the name of Bobby Johns opened Johns' Speedway and operated the track for four or five years. It was originally a 3/8 of a mile track. Some fifteen years later, Harris was to lease the land on which the old Johns' Speedway sat and build his own speedway named Craigsville Motor Speedway.

Harris did all the design work himself. He designed a tri-oval dirt track just over 3/8 of a mile in length.

Once Harris received approval to build the track, he

proceeded with a vengeance, often working 17 and 18 hours a day to get the track in operation. He completed most of the work himself. First, Harris had to remove drive-in movie speakers from an abandoned drive-in movie theater that sat on the field to park cars. He then had to completely grade the track, rebuild guardrails, concession stands, toilets, bleachers, and wire the track for night racing. He's very proud of the fact that because of his experiences at Eastside, which often saw the entire lighting system go out if a car hit one pole, Harris wired the lighting system at Craigsville on three separate circuits. In addition, Harris served as both the announcer and scorer at the races. He relied upon his old friends, Smokey Stover and Buddy Stinespring (by this time retired drivers), to perform flagman chores.

Harris talks about his involvement with the Craigsville track. "I would get up in the morning, go out the road to the track, pull up to the gate, and unlock the gate just as the sun was coming over the mountain. I'd stay there all day long."

Having witnessed the unpleasant experience of the Devil's Bowl Speedway with surrounding residents, Harris made it a point to personally visit door to door within a five-mile radius of the track, having residents sign a petition in support of his endeavor.

As a way of opening the track, Harris staged a country music jamboree on June 28, 1970 at the Craigsville track. Approximately 1,500 fans attended and, ironically, Harris says that this is the only event held at the track that was profitable.

Harris offered a guaranteed purse to drivers, which meant that most, if not all, of the gate receipts went to the drivers. Concessions, according to Harris, were only marginally successful and were often times effected by rainouts and the difficulty in storing perishable food until the next week.

Notables who raced at Craigsville included Gip Gibson, Earl Moran, Dick Pappy Hansberger, Junior Beeler, Tommy Bear, Bob Dobyns, David Repass, and Ray Dovel. In one 100-lap race, Tommy Bear lapped the entire field.

Remnants of the infield concession stand at Craigsville Motor Speedway

According to Harris, "I'd work all week in my body shop and put my dollars out there at the track. I had $60,000 in it. I did all the work myself." Harris is somewhat bitter about the fact that many fans would sneak into the track without paying. The location of the track, adjacent to a major highway, coupled with the relatively rural setting, made the track vulnerable to the fans entering without paying. Harris says, "People would sneak in. I couldn't afford a fence. There were too many ways to get in. If I'd been paid by everyone who got in, I'd have realized a profit."

Harris continues, "Everybody wanted to talk to you about racing when you went somewhere, but nobody wanted to pay to get in. When I closed, I just closed it. I sold my equipment, my two water trucks, tractor with implements, and several other trucks. After I sold all that, I still had to borrow against my home to get out of debt."

After a Friday night race, Harris describes what it was like to be at the rural Craigsville Speedway. "A lot of times after the races, I'd be there by myself, 10:30 or so at night with just one or two lights on. I'd eat a still warm hamburger and a drink and sit there. Deer, bobcats, and bears would come down out of the mountains and drink from the pond inside the track. It was really neat."

Harris also describes what it was like after a Sunday race. "I would pay off the help, get rid of the drivers, lock everything up, turn everything off, and we'd go into town with the family over to the Dairy Rite and sit there and have supper. I would sit there and put the finish into a write-up to take to the newspaper so it would be in the Monday or Tuesday paper."

As Harris struggled with his track, vandalism from apparent locals as well as theft took its toll. A large freezer was removed from his concession stand and dumped in his pond. A truck, sitting for the winter in the infield of his track, was disassembled.

Rotten Meat at Craigsville

On another occasion, a very interesting mishap occurred at the concession stand at Craigsville. Harris tells the story, "My sister-in-law and my wife ran the concession stand. She had two boys. They'd always go into the freezer for ice cream or whatever.
"I had an old boy that worked for me who lived up the road from the track, and I'd ask him to stop by and check on things at the track. He came in the shop one morning and said, 'Clyde, I think somebody died up there at that concession stand. There's green flies just swarming around there.'
"I left everything at the shop and drove up to the track right away. One of those children had apparently left the door open to the freezer. There was about 300 pounds of hamburger in there and it was all rotten, loaded with maggots. It had liquefied and run all through the freezer, down on the floor of it.

"I drug the freezer through the doors into the fresh air and went to Craigsville and bought everything I could to get rid of the smell. I even put gasoline in it. I buried all the rotten hamburger. It was a year or so later and somebody would bring me a hamburger and I couldn't eat it to save my life! I had that smell on my hands and I couldn't get it off.

"I gradually got the smell out of the freezer, putting it in the sun and with the ammonia." Harris can now laugh about this incident, however, admits that it was not funny for the longest time.

Harris Reflects

Looking back on his racing career, Harris has the most respect for Buddy Stinespring and Smokey Stover. He also speaks with fondness for the late Dick Pappy Hansberger. According to Harris, "Buddy Stinespring could get more out of a 6-cylinder than anybody I've ever known."

Over time, and without profit, Harris decided to stop racing at Craigsville Motor Speedway. According to him, "It was not that hard to give up. It was something I wanted to do and I did it, but the time, money, and effort was something. But I have no regrets. If it hadn't been for the people sneaking in and if I had another $20,000, it might have worked. I didn't want to complicate things with a partner."

Harris does regret that he didn't use the parking area to stage flea markets, which could have helped his profit margin.

Clyde Harris was interviewed in the office of his body shop in downtown Staunton. He is a friendly, warm, and candid man who is an excellent historian when it comes to racing in the Shenandoah Valley.

Later that day, he accompanied the author to the grounds of the old Devil's Bowl Speedway, which is now completely covered by pine trees. Remnants of the banking can still be seen. The narrow road, the source of so much controversy because of dust, is now paved.

We then traveled 19 miles west of Staunton to the site of Craigsville Motor Speedway. Harris served as a tour guide as we walked the grounds, observing the rather severe effects of Mother Nature on man-made structures over the past 26 years. At times, a feeling of sadness emerges, seeing only the remnants of Harris' hard work and money that did not prove profitable.

Harris is sincere when he says he has no regrets. But he does say, "I come out here now and again. I lost so much money out here that anytime I want to buy a lottery ticket, I come out here to Craigsville and buy it. I figure this place owes me some money."

Clyde Harris standing near the site of the old Devil's Bowl Speedway in 2002.

CAL JOHNSON

BRUSH WITH DEATH

On the night of July 2, 1955, Cal Johnson narrowly escaped death. Driving the Car 555, affectionately known as the "Triple Nickel" and owned by Chuck Dedrick of Waynesboro, Virginia, his car exploded in flames midway through the first and second turns at the Eastside Speedway in Waynesboro, Virginia.

Car 555 before explosion.

Johnson, a man of small stature, quickly unbuckled his seatbelt and jumped through the open right window onto the track. The car continued rolling over an embankment, coming to rest near the pits, and was completely engulfed in flames. Johnson suffered burns over 17 percent of his body. The author, as a 5-year old, witnessed the accident.

Johnson describes the experience. "I was going around the turn and all of a sudden there was nothing but fire in front of me," he says. "I knew I had to get out of there quick and I did. When I got up off the ground, my shirt was burned off and I had burnt skin hanging down from my left arm. They loaded me into an old ambulance and, as it went out of the speedway turning onto the old Route 340, it went onto two wheels. I thought it was going to turn over!"

He was taken to the Waynesboro Hospital and describes what happened there. "The doctor had to be gotten out of bed," he says. "There was no doctor on duty in the ER back then. The doctor said, 'You bunch of crazy fools. A bunch of nuts trying to kill yourselves. I can't get any sleep. I've got to come patch up a bunch of crazy fools.'" Johnson continues, "He was not happy."

Later that night Johnson was transferred to St. Luke's Hospital in Richmond, Virginia, where he stayed several days. He received over one hundred get well cards. His wife and children who had accompanied him to the race followed the ambulance back to the Richmond area, which was near their home in Ashland, Virginia.

Of his brush with death, Johnson says, "I'd never made it out of 555 if they had all the safety features today."

The night before the accident, Johnson had raced in Lawrenceville, Virginia, and was planning to race a

Car 555 after explosion.

midget car he owned at Winchester Speedway the next day. Obviously, his racing the midget car in

Winchester the next day was out of the question.

A follow-up article on Johnson after his accident at Eastside from The News Virginian reads:

Cal Johnson, of Ashland, probably is one of the most experienced stock car drivers at Eastside Speedway. He is a lucky sort, and has flirted with many a mishap while driving.

It is doubtful if he will ever forget what happened here at Eastside on the night of July 2, 1955.

"It was in the feature," Cal began. "I started in 28th place. Different people told me that I had gotten up to fourth place by the 17th lap.

"When I came into the third turn, I saw two cars had spun out and were crossways on the fourth turn. When I started to pass, one of them pulled out of the pileup and hit the side of my car and spun me.

"My motor stalled, and I restarted it and continued down the front straightaway. As I went into the second turn, the whole car exploded in flames. I tried to steer toward the outside fence and managed to unhook my safety belt at the same time. When I felt the car go off the outside edge of the track, I jumped headfirst through the right-hand window. "By all rights, I should have killed my fool self," Johnson said of the accident. "I was burned pretty bad, but I didn't realize it until I had gotten halfway to the ambulance." The doctor said that 17% of the driver's body had received burns. Johnson's wife, Virginia, and the couple's three small sons were in the stand that night and saw the whole thing.

Just one week after his injuries, drivers at Eastside took up a collection for Cal Johnson by passing their racing helmets through the stands. A total of $218.30 was raised for him.

On July 23, 1955, Johnson returned to Eastside and received a tremendous ovation from nearly 1,300 fans. Johnson thanked the spectators and the speedway officials for the kindness shown him while he was in the hospital. The crowd roared its approval when he told the fans he might be back driving in August.

On August 6, 1955, the following article occurred in The News Virginian approximately five weeks after Johnson's accident:

Johnson Returns to Action This Evening at Eastside

Cal Johnson of Ashland, the driver who narrowly escaped death when his car caught fire during the July 2 trophy races, will be back in action at the Eastside Speedway tonight. The popular stock car pilot informed Eastside's officials of his planned return by phone Thursday afternoon. Johnson spent over two weeks in a Richmond hospital after his July 2 mishap. He was burned about the face, body, and hands.

The Ashland driver returned to the track on July 23 as a spectator and informed the fans that he might be back racing in August. At that time, his arm was still bandaged and in a sling.

Cal Johnson is a rather small man who is polite, friendly, and exudes a love of racing. He always has a pipe in his hand. The scars of the burns in 1955 are evident on his arm.

He was interviewed in his home outside Ashland, Virginia. He owns an active go-cart track, but is essentially a retired machinist. During his racing career he won 108 features. His son, Eddie Johnson, has been quite successful during the 1990's as a super late model driver, having won 140 features. He's also raced in several Busch series races.

Cal Gets Started

In 1949, Johnson got involved in racing. He was a spectator at the old Royal Speedway in Richmond, Virginia, on Route 301. It was a quarter-mile dirt track. Johnson describes how it happened. "These two guys were arguing who could beat who. The promoter said, 'I'll put up $25 if you guys will run a match race at intermission.' One of them backed out. I had a '39 Mercury. The promoter looked at me and said, 'You said you could beat him. How about it?' I said, 'Who me?' He said, 'Yeah, you. Get out there on that track,'"

Cal Beats the Great White Whale

Johnson says, "Well, I'd rather die than be chicken. I said, 'Okay, I'll do it.' I went out there and beat the other guy. He was a big man with a nickname of Great White Whale. I beat the Great White Whale and it was my first race.

"I then said to myself, 'Man, this is no more than I've been doing on the streets, hanging in these corners. I've found a quick way to get rich.' I made $25 and was working for about $40 a week as a machinist. That was big money. So I started racing every Sunday. I'd drive my car to the track, tape up the headlights, pump the tires up, and race it."

After he started in 1949, Johnson said, "I'd travel anywhere they paid money." He said he raced at 46 different tracks throughout his career.

Drinking and Driving

When asked about the popular perception that stock car racers of that era were hard drinking types, Johnson replied, "That's a popular misconception. I knew very few race drivers that drank before races. A lot of them did afterwards! Now did we talk about the stagger of tires? We didn't know anything about that. The only stagger we knew was what we did after drinking moonshine after the races."

Cal Johnson talks about a driver named Buddy Shuman. He says, "When he was sober, he couldn't drive. When he was drunk, Buddy couldn't drive. But Buddy half-drunk was unbeatable!"

Johnson says that Shuman owned a racing shop and had a number of 55-gallon barrels from which he sold racing alcohol. In the middle of the barrels, there was one barrel full of moonshine whiskey. "Buddy would go out and get it for you," Johnson says. "He's the only one that knew which barrel it was and you'd better hope Buddy wasn't drunk when he went out to get it for you!"

Johnson kept meticulous records of his race winnings.

Shuman apparently had a great deal of potential and had reached a deal with Ford Motor Company for sponsorship. But Shuman was destined to fail. According to Johnson, "He went to a motel, got drunk, lit a cigarette, and burned himself up."

SERIOUS TRAVEL

Johnson was serious about racing but also serious about money. He says, "I ran for the bucks. My cars always had gold on them to remind me of what I was there for."

Johnson talks of the travel involved in racing in those days. For example he says, "On Fridays I'd take my car with me to work and Friday night take it all the way to Lawrenceville. I'd come back here (Ashland), get back at 1:30 to 2:00 in the morning, get up early, go to Front Royal, Virginia, and they would check the car over. Then we'd go from Front Royal to Waynesboro Saturday night, then back to Front Royal, and then the next day run Winchester after we checked the car over Sunday morning. We ran Winchester that afternoon, come back home that night, and Tuesday I'd go to Culpepper and meet the car owners, and they'd take the car to Culpepper and then I'd bring the car back here for the next weekend." Such a schedule required traveling a minimum of 500 miles over several days with no four-lane roads, through many small towns, usually towing the racer.

"In towing the racer, you'd have to take the back axles out, change all four tires, and wire it for a brake light," Johnson says. This was before the days of transporting racecars on trailers.

Despite the grueling schedule, Johnson claims that racing was financially profitable at that time. He says, "I had a wife and three kids to support. I was only a machinist."

Johnson's favorite track was Lawrenceville, Virginia. It was high-banked and had a clay consistency which was conducive to the car staying on the track. According to Johnson, "The track was eventually turned into a figure eight and then became defunct."

CAL BECOMES A PRESIDENT

During the mid-50's, Johnson became President of the Blue Ridge Racing Association. This was a loose-knit group of racers racing at Douglas Speedway, Hilltop Speedway, and Charlottesville's Cavalier Speedway. According to Johnson, "We tried to form a club to keep the promoter from cheating us too bad and make a few rules."

In the early 50's, a young man from Charlottesville named Reasel "Gip" Gibson started racing at Hilltop Speedway at Zion's Crossroads, Virginia. Johnson says, "He was wild. He was taking all sorts of guys out. Other drivers raised a petition to ban him from the track."

Another win for Cal.

Johnson, who was President of the club, said, "No, he's trying to learn." Johnson continues, "He turned out to be a really good driver, but he had everybody hating him for a while 'til he settled down a little bit. He was a real nice fellow." Gibson became a successful and respected driver.

Johnson also speaks of a controversy at the old Hilltop Speedway. The promoter had a brother who was a driver. Johnson says, "He used to try to drive. I said try. He took about three guys off the track, so everybody came to me as President and said, 'We ought to ban him for one or two weeks.' He runs to the promoter and so the promoter comes to us and says, 'You can't suspend him.' I said, 'Yes we can. The club says so.' He said, 'No you can't do that. Well, he's going to run if nobody else does.' I said, 'Okay.' The next week we went up there, the following Sunday, and there he was on the track. I said, 'He can't run. He's suspended.' The promoter said, "No he isn't. He's going to run if nobody else does.' I said, 'All right. If that's the way you want it.' I called the guys together. We voted. We all loaded up and went to Unionville and left him there by himself.

"We then put an ad in the Charlottesville paper explaining why we did. We said, 'We're very sorry about you fans who showed up last week and didn't get to see a race,' and we explained why. And you'd be surprised how many fans said, 'You did exactly right!'"

DEATH AT SALUDA

Later, on July 14, 1974, both Johnson and Gibson entered a race at Saluda, Virginia. They pitted next to one another. As it turns out, Johnson was the last person to see Gibson alive because Gibson was involved in an accident that severed an artery. According to Johnson, Gibson's shoulder harness cut his neck. Gibson bled to death at the scene. To this day, Johnson refuses to wear a shoulder harness.

JOHNSON AND NALLEY

Cal Johnson has always had a great deal of respect for Bill Nalley. He also got along well with Smokey Stover saying, "He was a good old boy. I spent a weekend at his house one time. I drove his go-cart at Winchester." Later, when Stover was suffering from Lou Gherig's disease in a veteran's hospital in Richmond, Johnson had his last contact with him. Johnson remembers, "He was in real bad shape."

Both Johnson and Nalley laugh about an incident that occurred at Fort Ashby, West Virginia. Johnson remembers it this way. "We were rained out at Winchester so a bunch of us, including Bill Nalley, decided to go up there to Fort Ashby," he says. We called it Fort Apache. Somebody had dug a track out in the field with a scraper. There were weeds and all still in the track. It was so rough that we busted three brake rotors. Nalley won and everyone went down to the judge's stand for payoff after the race. They called us up one at a time and called Bill first. It was on an old announcer's booth. The promoter told Nalley, 'I got about $200 here for the payoff. How much would you usually get for winning?' Nalley quickly replied, 'About $150.' He took the $150, came down the steps grinning, and walked off. The rest of us went up there and didn't get but $5 or $10 a piece. We cussed Bill all the way home! A lot of things are funny now that weren't funny then."

OLD TRACKS

Johnson talks of the many tracks that he raced that were ill designed or built with a limited budget. As his reputation grew, Johnson was sometimes offered "appearance money." He remembers driving at a racetrack outside Roanoke, Virginia, named Starkey in 1950. He'd been offered $100 over and above winning money to go to Roanoke. He remembers little of the race, however.

In the early days, there were very few safety rules and no yellow flags. The red flag only flew if the track was completely blocked.

At one time Lynchburg, Virginia had two tracks.

Johnson says, "There was a half-mile dirt track. They had 100-watt bulbs about every 100 yards. When you looked at cars running down the backstretch at night, it looked like cars running in and out of tunnels." At one time, there was also a fourth-mile asphalt track called Shafer's Field in Lynchburg.

Petersburg, Virginia had a track in which turns one and two ran over a dam. According to Johnson, the late Wendell Scott was a winner there on one occasion. There was also a track outside Brookneal, Virginia and in Unionville, Virginia. He describes the Douglas Track at Ruckersville, Virginia, which according to him was dug out of a side of a hill.

Johnson took racing very seriously. He says, "The harder you worked, the more money you made. If you're out in the garage at 2:00 in the morning, that's one thing. But if you're sitting in a beer joint telling all your friends what you're going to do the next race, it doesn't always work out too good. Then they'd say, 'Well, I had the worst luck. My car broke.' But we won because of hard work."

During most of his racing career, Johnson's wife and children accompanied him to the races. He says, "Ninety-five percent of the other drivers were friends. You knew their wives, their families. We'd run for 40 percent of the gate. There were no computers, calculators--it was all on pencil and paper. They'd figure how much they'd cheat you out of. The payoff took a long time to figure, so the drivers, owners, and families would go out to some trees after the race and have a picnic; break out a couple of six-packs and there might be a fight, but that would be over soon. Mostly we'd just sit around, re-run the race, and have a lot of laughs. We just had fun. Then we'd all go home."

INTERRUPTED LUNCH

Johnson recounts with humor a Sunday afternoon at Winchester when a wheel came off the car of Doug Bailey, hit the track fence, went 20 feet in the air, crossed a field, and hit a house, knocking down the screen door and coming to rest against a refrigerator while the family ate their Sunday lunch. A wayward car also destroyed the outdoor men's restroom at Winchester.

CAVALIER CAL

At the old Cavalier Speedway in Charlottesville, Johnson won 11 features in a row. According to him, "You'd get $111.50 if you won the feature and a free steak dinner if you won the heat and the feature." The track was owned by a man named George Durham, who also owned the Tip-Top Restaurant in Charlottesville. Johnson continues, "After I won a few races, the steaks started getting small. I ended up going back in the freezer and picking out my own. I'd wait till I'd won three or four, then go up there and feed the whole family!"

Cavalier Speedway was near the old stockyards and the river in Charlottesville. At one time races were held there on Friday nights and Sunday afternoons. Johnson won so much there that a bounty was placed on him.

JOHNSON GOES TO LYNCHBURG

On one occasion, Johnson visited the asphalt track in Lynchburg, Virginia. He did not do well. Johnson was fairly well known and he was being lapped by the regular racers there. One apparently said, "He's the one who's been winning all those races at Hilltop (Zion's Crossroads)." Johnson continues, "They thought they could beat me and win all that money. So the next day they all came to Hilltop. I lapped all of them. They never came back. I did not go back to Lynchburg!"

Cal Snookers Nalley and Irwin

In the mid-50's, Johnson entered a 300-lap race at Winchester Airport Speedway. He was competitive with the chief competitors at that time, Bill Nalley and Tommy Irwin. Johnson continues, "We were all good friends. They were my two toughest competitors. We were talking and we said we'd run 250 laps, stay out of trouble, and then race it down amongst us. We all agreed and I meant it. On the pace lap, however, we had to start in the back and a crazy thought struck me. Instead of taking it easy, I started out like a maniac. Tommy and Bill watched me and they couldn't take it. I was too far ahead and they took out after me. I ran like that 10 or 15 laps in second gear and then I shifted into high gear, which cut down power but enhanced my gas mileage. Well, here comes Tommy and Bill by me. After a while, there's Tommy in the pits; then there's Bill getting oil, tires, and gas.

"After 100 laps my right-hand fender broke off. All I could hear was a roaring noise. I stopped for a quart of oil and I see Tommy and Bill back in the pits again. At the white flag I put it in second gear and off the fourth turn for the checkered flag I was flying. I wanted to show them. Tommy and Bill cussed me after that but it turned out to be a pretty good strategy."

Cal and Al

Johnson speaks of an early altercation with Al Grinnan. Grinnan now lives and works near Johnson and the two are the best of friends. On this particular night at Cavalier Speedway, however, they nearly became enemies. "Grinnan kept hitting me every time I passed him," Johnson says. I got tired of him banging on me. I won that feature and just as I came across the finish line, he was right ahead of me. Payback time! Wham! I hit him and saw his trunk lid go up.

"It was just my dad and I there down in the pits after the race. Here comes Al. My dad said, 'Here comes trouble.' I picked up a jack handle," says Johnson, knowing that he was very small in stature compared to the tall, lanky, well-built Grinnan. Johnson continues, "Grinnan said, 'Cal, you totaled my car.' I replied, 'Looks like that to me, too, Al.' Grinnan replied, 'You really tore me up.' I said, 'I did, Al. You had it coming.' Grinnan said, 'You know, you're right. Are we even now?'" Johnson continues, "We shook hands. Ever since, we've been good friends. I tell you, I thought we were in for a big fight!"

Close Calls

Johnson speaks of several other close calls in addition to his exploding car at Waynesboro. He says, "At Winchester, my car was broken and a man asked me to drive his car, number 713. I said, 'Sure. I'm here to make a buck.' I'd never been in that car in my life. On the second turn, first lap, something broke in the front end and I hit the fence, went into the air, and Bill Nalley ran underneath me. I hit the ground hard.

"In Rocksboro, North Carolina, another driver hit the dirt bank on the backstretch, went up in the air, and I went under him. I didn't enjoy that one either."

Johnson says that he was in cars that flipped on seven different occasions. He says, "At South Boston, a guy in front of me broke his spindle and dropped the wheel, tire, and axle right in front. There was no where I could go but just straddle it. It took out the steering gear and the brakes, and I just sat there and watched that white wall come to me. The next thing I knew I woke up in the ambulance going to the South Boston Hospital. I had a hell of a time trying to get them to turn around and take me back. They wouldn't do it, but I was okay."

In March 1957 at Valley Speedway in Staunton on

the first lap, Johnson was flying down the front stretch when his car seemed to jump out of gear. "I looked and there wasn't a gear-shift lever," Johnson says. "It was gone. I pulled off to the side. I looked and here comes Lewis Bocock. Lewis said, 'Your transmission came out and hit me.' He was the second car behind me, so it went under the first car, bounced up in the air, and hit Lewis. My drive shaft was in the infield and looked like a pretzel. It hit the top of Lewis' car. If that had been a foot lower, Lewis would have been killed!"

FIGHTS

Johnson says there were fights. Johnson's philosophy is that, "It's better to fight and get it out of their system. After the fight, it was over and they'd be drinking out of the same bottle of beer. Now they can't fight, so what happens? They go home, stew about it, get madder, and then you'd have a year-long feud and bust up a lot of pricey equipment hitting each other."

One night at the Royal Speedway, a driver by the name of Runt Harris and Johnson were going to fight. "After the race I went over there, took my glasses off, and threw my helmet in the seat of the car," says Johnson. "Here came Runt with all of his pit guys behind him. I was mad, too, and I was ready to fight. He was hot also.

"Runt had been bumping me around and Ray Hendricks was driving my car. I was driving another car. I saw him knock the hell out of Ray. That did it. I went back on the track and tried to run him through the fence.

"Runt said something and I said something, and about that time one of his pit crew hit one of my pit crew and knocked him on his ass. Everybody went to fighting except Runt and me. We were leaning up against a racecar and watched the whole fight, and then there was a fight in the grandstand. Runt and I ended up laughing about it."

On another occasion, a driver by the name of Buck Mason and Johnson were in a heat race. Johnson says, "Both of our cars were running lousy. I had a spark plug wire off. We got to playing, bumping each other and laughing about it. We came in the pits after the race and a fight started up in the grandstand fighting over us."

Johnson continues, "I always had respect for the other drivers. I never started anything, but I finished some."

JOHNSON'S BUMPER

Johnson was noted for an innovative rear bumper that featured coiled springs between the bumper and the body of this car.

CAL AND PATSY CLINE

Johnson tells a story about the late Patsy Cline, the famous country singer. At Winchester she came to present the trophy after a feature race. One of the drivers (or spectators) said, "Hey Patsy, what are you doing tonight? Hey Patsy, want to go out for a beer tonight?" According to Johnson, "Patsy Cline said, 'I wouldn't be caught dead with any of you rotten greasy son-of-a-bitches.' Everybody just walked off and turned away from her."

COLORADO CAL

Johnson once raced in Colorado. He went to visit his wife's in-laws and there was a racetrack nearby. He had gotten a letter from a NASCAR representative to get him in the pits, which described Johnson as, "One of the top drivers on the East Coast." Johnson continues, "That got me in the pits. They rolled out the red carpet and introduced me to all the drivers. Then they asked me if I wanted to do a match race against the track champion. I said, 'Sure.'"

Johnson got his choice of two cars with stock engines. He noticed at this particular track that everyone ran on the inside in the curves. According to Johnson, "They would almost stop in the middle of the turn to make the turn." Johnson said he was used to running on the outside, keeping his RPM's up, and getting momentum.

Johnson continues, "The track promoter said to me, 'You want to flip for the inside?' I said, 'Naw, I'll take the outside.' Well, they looked at me like I was crazy. We ran five laps and I beat him by a backstretch. They couldn't believe it. 'How do you drive like that?' they asked. I was taking it down in the corner with the throttle flat out, kicking a big rooster tail, and they were just doing the opposite on the inside. It was a blast."

In the feature, however, Johnson got "boxed in" behind a wreck and didn't finish well. He still cherishes the experience, however.

CLOSE CALL AT LANGHORN

One of Johnson's accomplishments was being invited to the 1952 National Invitational Race at Langhorn, Pennsylvania. According to Johnson, "That's one thing I'm proud of, but I've seen the tape. I can't believe I was stupid enough to get out there! All the top drivers from the local tracks were invited. There were 102 cars circling a one-mile track. I started in the 75th position. Can you imagine 102 old pieces of junk out there on a one-mile track?"

Johnson says, "They'd already run midgets, sprints, and sport cars on the track and the track was torn to pieces by the time we got out there. I was trucking along. You could run flat out. You didn't have to back off. But then my hood flew up and I got the black flag. When I went to go into the pits, I had no brakes. Finally I stopped the car and looked down and the floorboard was a half-inch deep in gas! The track was so rough that it tore the brake lines loose. It shook the pickup out of the gas tank. That ended my race but it certainly was a close call."

PRIDE

Johnson is proud of the Car 34 that he owned. He won 48 feature races with this car and a state championship. "Car 34 was a dirt car," he says, "but it was a stinker on asphalt. It was a 1934 Ford Coupe, Flathead Ford, 205 cubic inches motor. It ran on 70 percent methanol and 30 percent nitromethane." He also ran the car number 41, a 1934 Ford Coupe with a DeSoto engine.

SELECTED EVENTS

On May 11, 1957, Cal Johnson out-dueled Bill Nalley, Lewis Bocock, and Robert Peer to win a 25-lap sportsman feature at Eastside. This apparently was one of Johnson's first races using alcohol as fuel.

On May 25, 1957, approximately 900 racing fans at Eastside watched Johnson defeat Al Grinnan, Tommy Irwin, and Bill Nalley in a 25-lap feature race.

Cal Johnson in 2001.

Johnson ceased racing in the late 1970's saying he was "burnt out. We'd reached the point of diminishing returns."

Johnson continues, "I was a lucky guy to come along when I did and have a lot of good fortune. I ran with a great bunch of guys, the nicest bunch of guys in the world. I really enjoyed it. Now many of them are dead and I can tell all the lies I want to!"

Tommy Irwin

Originally from Mt. Jackson, Virginia, Tommy Irwin moved to Purcellville, Virginia, in Loudon County in 1945 and opened a garage. He describes how he got involved in racing: "The Winchester Speedway had been closed for a number of years because of World War II. In the winter of 1953, Kermit Batt, the owner of Winchester Airport Speedway, traveled to northern Virginia to garages with a list of rules to come and race at Winchester. He started races with stock cars in 1953 and began to draw a crowd. Prior to World War II and directly after World War II, Batt had run so-called jalopies or roadsters, which were essentially cut-down Model A Fords; however, they failed to draw a crowd."

Tommy Irwin

Batt visited Irwin and talked him into entering the world of dirt stock car racing. According to Irwin, "I had never given much thought to racing before that, although all the police knew me. I was what you might call a highway hotrod man."

Irwin built his racecar, a 1933 Plymouth Coup, and raced in the sportsman class at Winchester. It was a turquoise and white racer and bore the number P-12.

Irwin's First Race

Irwin continues, "I won the first heat I ever run in there at Winchester. But during the feature, I lost a right front wheel. I remember there were a lot of accidents. As long as you could get through, you raced, unless the track was blocked. There were no yellow flags."

After 1953, Irwin began to race regularly to the point that in 1956 he supported himself solely on monies won from racing. He raced at tracks at Waynesboro, Virginia, Staunton, Virginia, Hagerstown, Maryland, Keezletown, Virginia, and Winchester. He took championship honors at Winchester and Waynesboro.

Irwin Not Liked in Waynesboro

Irwin says that in 1957 at Eastside he won so many races that local fans lost interest. He said, "God, they hated me up there! They'd boo. It sounded like a thunderstorm! My wife quit going because women couldn't go in the pits and she didn't like to sit in the stands where I was booed all the time."

He says on one Saturday he was about to leave for Waynesboro and said to his wife, "Let's go." Her reply was, "I'm not going to go. You don't know how they talk about you in the grandstand. What if people found out who I really am!"

STAUNTON-WINCHESTER RIVALRIES

Irwin substantiates the story told by many that there was a great deal of rivalry during the '50s between Winchester-based and Staunton-based drivers. To make this point, Irwin says, "At Waynesboro-Staunton you had to take a couple of big guys along. This was for protection. At Staunton they'd throw sockets at you. When you got out of the car, you'd better leave your helmet on. You'd hear them in the air whizzing by. They'd hit your car and make a dent in it. You never knew where they were coming from because it was so dark."

IRWIN GOES TO NASCAR

After winning the first three races of Winchester's 1958 season, Irwin sold his Ford Coupe and graduated to NASCAR. He bought a 1957 Ford factory car formerly driven by Eddie Pagan with the Holmond-Moody Organization.

In late 1958 he read in the Winchester paper that a Thunderbird convertible had been stolen from a physician, set on fire, and later found.

According to Irwin, "I got to thinking that would still make a good racecar, so I called the doctor's wife who then referred me to an insurance company. I called the insurance company and they told me about a salvage outfit in Washington, DC, they had sold it to. I called them and they had sold it to a junkyard in North Carolina. I went to North Carolina and bought it."

He refurbished the car and bought a regular Thunderbird hardtop and bolted it on the body. That way he could race the car either as a sedan or as a convertible, since they raced convertibles in the late '50s in NASCAR.

He raced this car until 1961, driving for such notables as Bud Moore and Buck Baker. He points out

A young Tommy Irwin (left) receives a trophy from Winchester Airport Speedway owner Kermit Batt.

that in those days, NASCAR, known as Grand National and not Winston Cup as it is known now, drove numerous half-mile dirt tracks in the south. The only long tracks he remembers were at Darlington, South Carolina, and Daytona.

When Irwin was racing at Daytona, the NASCAR circuit at that time averaged approximately 150 miles per hour around the two and a half-mile track. According to Irwin, "We didn't think we were traveling that fast. NASCAR told us that but we didn't believe it. We went to a mathematician. He measured the tire diameters, gear ratio, and RPMs and figured that the cars were racing approximately six miles per hour faster than what they were being clocked at. Wheel slippage was not figured, so it was accurate that we were indeed traveling around 150 miles per hour."

In terms of driving at 150 miles per hour, Irwin says, "It's like riding a roller coaster. After you ride it three or four times, there ain't nothing to it. After ten laps, you're used to speed. After 100, it's just like driving the interstate."

During his NASCAR career, Irwin registered a third place at Daytona, a fifth place at Darlington, and a third place at Martinsville. He was oftentimes close to the top of the leader board in terms of points.

IRWIN ALMOST DROWNS

Tommy Irwin has the distinction of being the first racer to plow into the infield lake at Daytona. It was 1959 and Irwin was racing in the 125-mile qualifying race. According to him, "Everybody was running the low and middle lines and nobody was running the high line. There was a whole pack of cars bunched up that couldn't get away from each other. The top groove was wide open. Every time I'd come through the turn behind that pack, I'd almost have to put my brakes on to keep from getting sucked up into them.

"I said, 'I wonder how that high groove is up there?' So I backed off a little bit and slid up right next to the wall. I knew there was some loose stuff up there but I was all right. It stuck so good coming through the turn, I just put it up close to the wall, floored the accelerator, and just went by everybody.

"Coming off turn two, Johnny Bauchamp slid under me, caught me on the corner, and turned me sideways. Another car hit me in the door on the left side. The only window that would open was the driver's window. I went out across the grass, sliding. I pumped the brake again and again. I twisted the wheel. I pumped the gas. I just kept sliding and sliding and sliding. I guess I went sliding on the grass and sand a quarter of a mile. There were puddles of water and I thought that would catch me and flip. I anticipated flipping, but the car just slid over them like nothing." He eventually plowed into the lake.

Irwin continues, "I hit the water hard enough that it pushed the grill back into the radiator and I went into the water 50 or 60 feet from the shore. The water was right at the window. I thought I was on the bottom, but then water rolled over the hood. The car sat there an instant, so I unhooked my harness thinking I was on the bottom. At that time, the front went straight down sinking in the water. I felt it go down and down and hit. It put me under the dashboard. It was standing on its nose completely under water!

"By the time I got out from under the dash, the car was full of water. I went to crack the window down on the left side driver's side, but it wouldn't open from the impact of the previous crash on that side. I had to go to the ceiling and put my face up against it to get about a half-inch of air.

"I struggled frantically with the window, getting it down so I could get my helmet out, but then I really needed air and there wasn't much left. I told myself, 'That's all there's going to be. There ain't going to be no more air. I've got to get out of here.' If I had panicked, I'd been dead right there."

Irwin continues, "I weighed about 120. I knew if I could get my helmet through the window I could get through, so I got out, scratched my back a little bit, and rose to the surface of the water. By the time I got to the surface, I was just busting for air and I didn't know how far up I had to go. I found out later that I was in eighteen feet of water!

"When I popped up and got some air, I just laid back, floated, and rested. I said to myself, 'It's going to take a whole lot more to worry me from now on after going through all that.' I looked to the shore and the rescue squad had run up to the shore but they were doing nothing. They were standing on the bank watching me! I kept saying when I was in the car, 'If I can hold on, they'll be here to rescue me.' However, little did I know they weren't doing a thing. When I swam over to the shore, one of them held out a hand. I splashed some water on him and he stepped back. I should have just pulled him in the water with me!

"They took me to the infield care center at Daytona. As we were getting there, I saw Cotton Owens' wife holding my wife up. She was white as a ghost and I saw her legs buckling. When I saw that, I jumped out of the ambulance and grabbed her and propped her up. I then went to the Holmond-Moody Building with her. They gave me some dry clothes. She sat there a half-hour not saying anything, being in shock. I was smacking her in the face and talking to her. I got a wet rag and finally brought her around. Thirty minutes later they got the car out of the water, drained all the fluids, and I ran it at Daytona the next week."

In recollecting his NASCAR experiences, Irwin says that he ran well but never won. "To keep up with those guys," he says, "I had to run the car too darn hard and I'd break it, or a tire would go before the end of the race."

Myrtle Beach

At Myrtle Beach Raceway, Irwin had lapped Buck Baker with Lee Petty running in second place. With two laps to go, Irwin's tire blew. He went over the bank in the second turn and slid across some one hundred feet into mud.

Shortly after, he heard a singing sound. At first he thought it was his radiator. However, someone tapped him on the shoulder. Irwin said, "It scared me to death. It was a tow truck driver. He says, 'I got here as soon as I could.'"

The tow truck driver had pulled on the track while the race was still going to get to Irwin. Since Irwin was the only Ford in the field which was competitive, and the tow truck was owned by a local Ford dealership, the driver felt a sense of obligation to get him back on the track as soon as possible. The tow truck driver was severely admonished by NASCAR.

Irwin Injured

In 1963, Irwin was hospitalized for one month after severe injuries sustained in an accident at the Spartansburg, South Carolina raceway. Irwin tells the story:

"When you came into the infield at Spartansburg at the number one corner, they had a board fence around it and a gate to get off the track. The track was very banked. I had a brand new car and we had just practiced, and when they threw a red flag for us to quit, the cars in front of me stopped pretty quick. I had laid my arms up on the steering wheel just resting, and I went down on the brake hard to keep from running into them. At that time the left front brake grabbed, and I just lost it. I flipped end over end four times and then rolled sideways several times."

Irwin continues, "I had a stock bucket seat in a 1963 Ford. The top and bottom of the seat were fastened to the roll cage, but the seat came apart and there I was with my harness on bouncing inside the car. It knocked my left eye out of the socket and laid it down on my cheek. I suffered a broken back, injured hip, and cut on my hand. My arm had gotten out the window. We didn't have window nets then. The next day my arm was completely black. I remember I had mud all over my helmet."

Irwin was hospitalized three weeks in a Spartansburg, South Carolina, hospital. Ironically, Irwin was leading in NASCAR's points race going into the Spartansburg race. According to him, he had suffered severe flu-like symptoms before the race and thinks it contributed to a mental lapse, which led to the accident.

Irwin Goes Cold Turkey

While he was hospitalized, Irwin relates, "They gave me a shot of morphine every hour on the hour for the first week. The second week they gave it every three hours. Then the third week I'd get one at bedtime and two or three in the morning and then they turned me loose."

Irwin continues, "I came home with a big brace on my back and shoulders. I had no idea what I was in for 'til bedtime that night. God, it was hot summertime, but I was cold and shivering! We had an old floor furnace. I got me a plastic kitchen chair and sat on the furnace with a big, heavy wool blanket and sat there and just shivered and sweated. You could hear my sweat dripping down on the furnace. I thought I was going to die."

Irwin was experiencing severe withdrawal from narcotics, without medical supervision or monitoring.

Irwin continues, "People talk about getting diseases from dirty needles. At that point I would have put dope in me with a rusted nail if I had it. About daylight, I passed out and got in bed and slept until dinnertime. I got up and felt wonderful. The next night the same thing. Right on that furnace, just a'dying. Well, the third night I didn't need the blanket. The fourth night I got in bed and my wife piled a bunch of covers on me and I finally made it. It got less and less after that. I was all right after a week.

"When I went to see the doctor in a week, he walked in the room and started laughing. He said, 'How was it?' I said, 'It wasn't nothing but hell.' He said, 'If I had told you about it, you'd have wanted me to give you something to take with you and you would have become addicted.'"

Irwin recovered and raced three races in Asheville, Bristol, and Langhorn, Pennsylvania, during the 1963 season.

Irwin continues, "I was hearing through the grapevine that Ford was dropping everyone except the Wood brothers and Holmond-Moody, so I decided to quit for good."

Irwin on Petty and Jarrett

The top racers in NASCAR during Irwin's heyday were Junior Johnson, Lee Petty, Fireball Roberts, Ned Jarrett, David Pearson, Fred Lorenson, and Richard Petty. For all the drivers he knew, Irwin said his favorite is Richard Petty. "He's the same guy whether he wins or loses. I got to know him pretty well and I've always respected him," says Irwin.

Irwin also had a great deal of respect for Ned Jarrett. He felt that Jarrett was a gentleman and refers to him as "one of the best fellows that ever walked on two feet."

Irwin tells a very poignant story told to him by Ned Jarrett regarding Fireball Roberts' fatal accident at Charlotte in 1964. Roberts' car had overturned and was aflame. Jarrett stopped to rescue him and ran to Roberts' car. Roberts told Jarrett, "Ned, this has got me." Jarrett reassured him, to which Roberts said, "No. I won't make it this time, Ned." Jarrett later related that the entire top of Roberts' overturned car was full of burning gas. Irwin says Ned Jarrett was deeply affected by Fireball Roberts' death.

Irwin also says that Junior Johnson quit racing soon after Roberts' death because of the accident.

Irwin Races in the Valley

Before Irwin went to NASCAR, he raced throughout the Shenandoah Valley of Virginia. He was quite dominant at Winchester and Eastside, in particular. He relates the following event from Waynesboro:

"In the first heat I was lapping a car and got spun out, went into the mud, and came out in fifth place, which put me on the pole for the feature. The other racers obviously felt they didn't have a chance if I started on the pole. When they called for us to go out there, I went out and no one else came out. The race didn't happen and the promoter at Waynesboro paid me the winning money for the race and told everyone else in the stands that their rain checks would be honored the next week. Ironically," Irwin notes, "the fans blamed me!"

Kuda Bux

Irwin speaks with amusement of the "man with x-ray vision" called Kuda Bux, who appeared at both Eastside and Winchester. This man was noted for driving cars around racetracks and obstacle courses blindfolded with two dough balls on both eyes wrapped in a towel around his head. He also would often take a .22 rifle and shoot balloons blindfolded. To this day, Irwin and other racers who saw Kuda Bux's act marvel at how he did it. Interestingly, women would often run from Kuda Bux because they truly thought he had x-ray vision and could see through their clothes.

Irwin Scares His Passengers

Irwin was known as a daredevil and hell-raiser. In 1956, the Joey Chitwood Thrill Show was preparing to perform in Waynesboro at Eastside Speedway. Irwin with four other people in his car drove unauthorized onto the track. After a couple of laps, Irwin made the ramp-to-ramp jump Joey Chitwood had planned to make as part of his show, scaring the daylights out of his companions and drawing the ire of track and Joey Chitwood personnel.

Selected Events

On July 14, 1956, in the Class A feature at Eastside, Tommy Irwin took the lead and the win on the last lap from Bill Nalley by a car length. Third place went to Junior Bowers.

On June 1, 1957, The News Virginian had this account of a race at Eastside won by Irwin:

A crowd of 1,512 paying customers watched the 28-year old Purcellville, Virginia driver, Tommy Irwin, jitterbug his way to victory as he started in 14th place in a 15-car field.

Irwin, driving his red and white number 5, appeared to be on the verge of being denied his chance to take home the big trophy and the $187 in prize money that went with it.

Lewis Bocock of Greenville, piloting Car 500, had a comfortable margin and seemed like a shoe-in to capture first place in a 20-mile feature. But Bocock hit a wet spot in the track at the west turn and spun out on the 36th lap.

"I wanted to take you," Irwin told Bocock in the pits after the race, "but not this way."

On June 15, 1957, at Eastside, Tommy Irwin won the 25-lap feature over Lewis Bocock and Junior Bowers. Al Grinnan was fourth and Smokey Stover in Car 306 was fifth.

On June 22, 1957, Irwin narrowly edged Junior Bowers in a 25-lap feature at Eastside.

On August 6, 1957, Irwin dominated the field at Eastside, winning the feature over Junior Bowers, Al Grinnan, Lewis Bocock, and Bill Nalley in that order.

On August 24, 1957, Irwin continued his domination of the Eastside track, easily outdistancing Junior Bowers and Lewis Bocock.

After dominating Eastside during the 1957 season, Irwin won his first feature of the 1958 season at Eastside on May 6, 1958. He won over Junior Bowers, Bill Nalley, and Ray Dovel in that order.

On May 24, 1958, Bill Nalley won the 25-lap feature at Eastside but only because of a bumping incident. The News Virginian has this account:

Nalley, Irwin, and Lewis Bocock of Greenville in Car 500, battled for the first spot for four laps. Nalley in S-3 was on top with Irwin and Bocock riding his tailpipe and battling wheel to wheel for second. The two cars tangled coming out of the number two turn, dropping Irwin back to seventh and Bocock even further back yet.

Irwin lead footed his way back into the thick of the race with an outstanding display of daring and driving. The "Purcellville Flyer" finished second.

On July 14, 1958, Irwin won the 25-lap sportsman feature at Eastside, out-dueling Smokey Stover. Bill Nalley, who was usually a contender, was out with a broken axle.

In this race, Irwin chased Stover most of the way and overtook Stover on the inside in turn number two on the 25th and final lap. He beat Stover to the checkered flag by a car length.

On August 11, 1957, Irwin won the 25-lap sportsman race at Eastside over notables such as Bill Nalley, Al Grinnan, Wendell Scott, Bob Crosen, Lewis Bocock, Cal Johnson, Red Ninninger, and others. Second place was taken by Ray Dovel, followed by Bill Nalley, Wendell Scott in fourth, and Grinnan in fifth.

On June 15, 1958, Irwin won the 25-lap sportsman feature at Eastside by some 45 feet over a hard-charging Bill Nalley.

On June 8, 1958, Irwin won the Class A sportsman feature over Nalley and Ray Dovel at Eastside.

On April 19, 1958, at Eastside, Irwin won the Class A sportsman feature over Junior Bowers who finished second.

Tommy Irwin was interviewed in his spacious and pleasant home in Winchester, Virginia. He is gracious, friendly, and enjoys speaking of racing. He laments the fact that he didn't keep better records and can't recount exactly how many heats or features he won. He does have many of the trophies and awards he received; however, he isn't a man who seeks the limelight. His scrapbook, though it could be bulging, is relatively thin. According to him, "That part of racing just wasn't that important to me." In the year 2001, Irwin is still involved in racing, offering advice and mechanical expertise to his son who drives regularly at Winchester, Virginia and Hagerstown, Maryland in the super-modified late model division.

Tommy Irwin in 2001

Buddy Stinespring

Buddy Stinespring operated a service station with his father in Staunton. In 1955, he and his father bought a racecar from Claude Baldwin and Johnny Scott for $300. At the time the Stinespring's service station was the sponsor of the car.

Stinespring and his father began working on the car. His father was steadfast that Smokey Stover would drive it. After a great deal of thought, Buddy said, "Daddy, why can't I drive it?" When his father said, "You ain't never drove a racecar before." Buddy replied, "I know, but I can learn." Stinespring was persistent and eventually his father relented.

Buddy's First Race

In Stinespring's first lap in his first heat at Eastside, he overturned the car in the number three curve. Stinespring said, "I got out, checked it over, everything looked good." He went on to win the heat, win the feature, and win a trophy at his first attempt at racing. His racing career would last another thirteen years.

According to Stinespring, "Junior Bowers, Lewis Bocock, and Earl Moran gave me a fit. They said, 'First time you ever drove a racecar in your life and here you won a trophy.'"

Baldwin's number was 703, the initials of the first three men who owned the car. The Stinesprings eventually changed the car number to 501.

In the early days of racing at Eastside, there was the "three in a row win". The rule was that if you won three races in a row you had to sell your car for $250. After winning his third race, Stinespring refused, simply coming back again with a different car number.

The Bow Tie Racer

In the 50's, service station attendants wore bow ties. Stinespring was no exception. He often drove the racecar in his service station uniform with a bow tie during his early days of racing.

Getting Nervous

Describing himself before a race, Stinespring says, "I'd get nervous and I'd have to go by the house to go to the bathroom and then go again and maybe again. After I got my helmet on and got in the car, it was all over."

Stinespring and Junior Bowers

Stinespring speaks with deep affection of the late Junior Bowers. He says, "When we first moved to Staunton from Waynesboro, he was the first person who came by to visit. When my daughter was born, he was the first person who came to visit at the hospital."

He says, "Junior was a nice guy. When I had a station, Junior would bring his bankbook, checks, car payment book, and utilities by, and when I went to the bank, I'd take care of it for him. Often he would come to hang out at the station, bringing both of his daughters, having one on each knee."

A Unique Car

Stinespring and his father were mechanical wizards.

The primary engine they used in their car was a 6-cylinder GMC 302 cubic inch truck engine. They bored it out to 330 cubic inches. Their first race engine had been built for them, but the Stinesprings built their own engines thereafter.

The original car was a '36 Chevrolet Coupe; however, the finished product was eclectic. The front end was out of a '34 Ford and was attached to a '35 Chevrolet body. They chopped it in four ways and made it a small car, leaving just enough space for the driver to sit. The fact that the car was chopped and lightened often was a source of controversy, as Stinespring drove almost exclusively in the sportsman division, won consistently, and was competitive with the higher modified division.

BUDDY BECOMES DOMINATE

Stinespring quickly became a regular at Eastside and Valley Speedway. He was, however, so dominant in the sportsman division that he was often protested and was the center of a great deal of controversy because of his car's unorthodox body and frame. This eventually led him to leave Eastside in the mid-60's and start racing at Pilot, Virginia. Pilot is a small town 15 miles east of Christiansburg, Virginia. Buddy recounts his first visit there:

RACING AT PILOT

"For some reason we'd heard about Pilot and we decided to go there. It was raining but we decided to go anyway. As we got closer, it quit raining. We were meeting racecars coming out. When some of the drivers saw us, they turned around and followed us back. I remember there was a garage and you had to drive through a junkyard to get to the track.

"When we got there, the owner, Mr. Gearhart, said, 'We called off the races but go on down there.'"

Stinespring continues, "We went there and cars were down there in the mud, old jalopies. There were a number of people sitting in cars on the hill. There were no grandstands. Most of them were drinking and some of them were drunk."

The Pilot track was quite unusual to Stinespring. He continues, "The front straight was downhill and then went uphill on the backstretch. I think it was a quarter-mile track. I've never seen anything like it. "They really had a good announcer. He said, 'Folks, if you want to see a racecar, you ought to come on down here,' referring to Stinespring's car. The announcer continued, 'We got a racecar down here.' "Mr. Gearhart and the announcer came to see us and said, 'Are you going to run this thing?'" Stinespring replied, "I don't guess so, the races are called off."

Gearhart said, "Let me ask you, would you take that thing out there on the track?" Stinespring replied, "If you're not going to have any races, it's no use unhooking." Gearhart said, "No, but we might get the track in shape. We'll just take up a collection and have a race."

Stinespring continues, "Dad and I talked about it and we decided to give it a try. We put the axles back in, took the cord off of the brake lights, and got it ready. We never had a starter in the car and Dad would always push me off in a truck. Two drunks took up a collection, went around twice through the crowd and collected $65. The idea was winner takes all after a short meeting with all the drivers who were still there."

Stinespring started in the rear. He was unsure of the unusual configuration of the track. He continues, "Well, shoot, all I had to do was goose that thing once in a while and I'd go by them. It wasn't nothing to it. They didn't have anything to hold a light to me. I got the $65 and I went back every Saturday night after that."

For the next three and a half years, Stinespring and his father raced at Pilot, never losing a race unless they experienced mechanical difficulties. Stinespring says, "I think that happened three times."

What ensued was a great deal of controversy with many people concerned about the legality of Stinespring's car, and repeated unsuccessful efforts to find the secret to his success, despite the fact that he was "torn down" on many protests.

Despite the controversy, Stinespring and his father often forfeited all or some of their winnings to an unfortunate driver who may have had an accident or other mechanical breakdown at Pilot.

Stinespring continues, "On one occasion at Pilot, my radiator came loose and it punctured the fan belt. We had no means to fix the radiator and we were about to pack up and go back to Staunton. At that time a spectator came up to us and said, 'I've got a soldering gun. Here's the key to my car, but don't let anybody know where you got it. I just wanted to see you run.' We got the iron, fixed it, and won the feature."

Eventually Stinespring's chopped down car was outlawed at Pilot and he was forced to race a full-body car. Despite this change in the configuration of the car's body, he continued to dominate races.

STINESPRING BLACKBALLED

As Stinespring's notoriety grew, the owner of the Pulaski Speedway invited him to race. This was a half-mile dirt track, which is now the paved 3/8-mile New River Valley Speedway outside Radford, Virginia.

Stinespring continues, "The owner--I forget his name--said, 'I'll advertise that you'll be there.' The following Sunday we went there."

Stinespring's appearance immediately caused controversy. The flagman came to Stinespring and said, "501, do you want to qualify?"

Stinespring was flabbergasted. He had never before had to qualify his car for a sportsman race and replied, "Do sportsmen have to qualify?" The flagman replied, "No, but they want you to qualify." Stinespring continues, "I said what the heck. So I went out to qualify. I went down the backstretch and asked the flagman for a couple of laps to warm up. He said no. He said, 'When you come around you're going to get the flag.'"

Stinespring continues, "I knew that the cards were stacked against us, but I went into the curve and sat there waiting for the engine to warm up. Then I called on it."

Despite never having raced or qualified on the track, Stinespring's speed was only .03 of a second off the track record set by the more powerful modifieds.

Stinespring relates what happened after his first lap. "Here come about six guys down to the car," he says. "One guy said, 'Where do you think you're going to drive that car?' I said, 'Well, we came to run it here.' Another driver said, 'I don't think so.' I said, 'The track owner invited us to come.' One of the drivers said, 'We'll just have to have a meeting to see if you can run.' I said, 'Okay.'"

Stinespring continues, "They came back and said, 'We decided that we'd let you run in the modifieds if you start in the rear and give them one lap.'"

Stinespring felt this was outrageous. He'd been invited to race at the racetrack, had a car for the sportsman division, and here he was being asked to begin a race one lap down in the modified division.

Stinespring said, "No, I don't think so. You're crazy, not me." He told his dad to put the tow hitch on the racecar and he'd pull the axles. He put the jack under the car and was pulling the axles when some spectators came down the hillside asking what happened to the car.

Stinespring says, "I said nothing. They said, 'What are you doing?' I said, 'We're going home.' I told them what the situation was."
Spectators, unhappy with the situation, said, "Wait a minute. They advertised you were going to run and that's what we're here for, to see you run. We'll tear this place down."

Stinespring was so disillusioned that he continued to prepare his car for towing and started to leave the track. There were four couples who had traveled to the races with the Stinesprings. Stinespring says, "Two of the couples came with us and the other two stayed, reporting later to the Stinesprings that a fight occurred in the infield because of the controversy."

It should be noted that Stinespring did return to Pulaski twice, winning two sportsman races there.

Stinespring Meets More Controversy

Stinespring also raced at Callaway, Virginia, Ferrystone Park, Virginia, near Martinsville, and Stuart, Virginia, home of the legendary Wood Brothers. He raced against 8-cylinder cars in a sportsman division for the first time in Stuart.

In his first race at Stuart, the starting order was determined by a drawing. Before the drawing, someone came to Stinespring and said, "This is your first time here, isn't it?" Stinespring replied in the affirmative. The other person continued, "There are two brothers here. You've got to watch them. If one of them starts up front or is in the lead, the other one is going to hold you off."

At Stuart during the warm ups, because he felt the track was too long, he set the timing back on the car to "kill some of the power and go further down the straightaway." After three laps he had the lead and eventually won the heat race. Stinespring says, "That son of a gun was sailing."

Stinespring notes that at Stuart in the backstretch there was a dip, and if a driver were going fast, he would actually go airborne when he hit the dip. Stinespring finished second in the feature but knew something was wrong with his car. After racing, he inspected his motor and says, "The whole left side of the block was black from hot oil. A bearing was going out of it. If I would have pushed it, I would have blown it."

Stinespring is proud of the fact that he never blew an engine. He changed his bearings each year and rings every two years.

At Callaway, Virginia, there was a bounty on him. One day the track owner said to him, "Buddy, if you win today, you're going to run in the modified division after this. If I were you, I'd back off." Stinespring says, "I told him I'd think about it," and asked his father, "Daddy, what do you want to do? Back off or win it?"

Stinespring's father replied, "We didn't come down here all this distance just to back off."

Stinespring won the heat and the feature, got their money, and left. Stinespring says, "The next

Sunday we went down there to Callaway and saw this old guy in a ticket booth. He said, 'Damn, I'm glad to see you here. They were saying you weren't coming back.'"

Stinespring says, "Other drivers were glad to see us because they didn't think we would come back because we had to run with the modifieds." During the warm ups, Stinespring experienced a problem with his flywheel. With the help of another mechanic, he repaired the loose flywheel, entered the modified feature with street tires, and lapped the field except for one car.

Stinespring also ran at Hillsville, Virginia. He describes the track as "beautiful" and says, "Man, you could fly there."

At Ferrystone Park, other sportsman drivers went on strike because of Stinespring's appearance. The owner told the flagman to call the sportsmen out and whoever went on the track would race. Eventually the other drivers came out, but Stinespring won handedly.

Valley Rivals

Stinespring staged epic battles in the sportsman division in the Shenandoah Valley against Jackie Clore and later Charlie Beeler. At Eastside, Stinespring describes a run-in with Jackie Clore. "I was trying to get by him," he says. "He kept coming over and beating on me, and finally put me up in the fence in the number three curve. I went up on the fence, but it didn't hurt the car. I came back, turned it on, and put him over the bank. I came around and took the checkered flag.

"In the pits, here he came, whole Cox's Army following him. He wanted to fight so bad. I told him, 'Jackie, you beat on me long enough that I got tired of it. If you want me, you just come on.' He stood there and run his mouth and they left. I didn't have any more trouble with him."

Stinespring was very close to Junior Bowers and Smokey Stover. Stinespring says, "When Smokey died, it was like losing a brother. He was a good friend of mine. The last time I saw him he was on oxygen and just a shadow of his former self."

Driving Smokey's Car

On one occasion Stinespring was asked to drive Stover's Car 306 at Winchester. Because Stover was not able to drive in the race, the Campbell brothers and Stover came by Buddy's service station to ask him to drive. Smokey told Stinespring, "Don't get on the gas till you get out of the corners."

When they got to Winchester, Stinespring says, "When I got in it, that son of a gun didn't fit me. I was too big. We got there late and I didn't get to warm it up. I started in the rear and brought her on. I finished fourth in the heat."

In the feature Stinespring was leading after passing Bill Nalley and Al Grinnan. He continues, "Darn it if I didn't lose it going into turn one and backed it up in the fence. It just got away from me and I had to wait there until everybody came by. I finished third to Grinnan and Nalley, finishing on seven cylinders."

Stinespring speaks with respect of Car 306 owner Tommy Campbell, saying, "Tommy was sharp. He got his horsepower from valve adjustments."

Sabotage

On one occasion at Pilot, Stinespring's car was sabotaged. He described what happened, "I was adjusting the valves on another boy's car who was running against me and Daddy had gone to the john. Somebody dumped rocks, dirt, and sand in the oil intake. I was leading the race and the motor just let go. Before this, my father heard somebody say, 'Well, he won't win this race.'"

After the motor malfunctioned, they returned to Staunton, tore the car down, and found evidence of the sabotage.

BUDDY'S NICE CAR

Stinespring and his father were meticulous in working on their car. The car, with its unusual closed hood, was shiny, bright, and clean. They got their tires off of ambulances and hearses and often ran whitewalls. The right side door was chopped down so there could be an easy exit in case of a fire. They ran one set of Ford stock brake shoes for three and half years. They made their own manifolds and linkage from soda machines. At one time they ran the car with a tractor implement tire on the left front, with a 16-inch tire on the right front, to improve handling.

HOLDING BACK

At Devil's Bowl, he once won $125 for winning a race, with a $15 under-the-table bonus if he agreed to let the second place car finish close to him. His father didn't like it and said, "All you have to do is slip and you've done lost it." The track promoters were concerned about one car dominating and wanted to create the illusion of close races. One night at Devil's Bowl, Stinespring was running second to Lewis Bocock. Stinespring says, "I thought I'd make this thing look good. I'd get beside him in the straightaway and I'd get behind him on the curve on purpose. With two laps to go, I won after pulling up beside him. I got a tongue-lashing from Dad after that."

"DURTY"

Because of controversy with Jackie Clore, Clore's wife Marie nicknamed him "Durty." People in the Staunton area still comically refer to him by this nickname. He says, "Jackie Clore's wife would cuss me after the race was over. She said, 'You're the dirtiest driver.'"

INJURED AS A FLAGMAN

After Stinespring retired, he was the flagman at Eastside for a number of years. He is proud of the fact that he cleaned the flags, made by his mother, before every race.

Stinespring was injured when his old nemesis, Jackie Clore, rode the guardrail coming off the fourth turn and hit the flagstand where Stinespring was flagging, injuring Stinespring's back and ribs. The injuries turned out to be not serious, but he was carried from the flagstand and taken to the Waynesboro hospital.

SELECTED EVENTS

On July 23, 1960, Stinespring won the Thunder in Carolina Trophy Race at Devil's Bowl Speedway in Staunton. The race consisted of three 20-lap races and the best average finish between the three denoted the final order of finish. Stinespring was second behind Jackie Clore of Madison in the first 20-lap section and won the two remaining 20-lappers before a crowd of over 2,000 fans. Clore finished second and Bill Nalley was third.

On July 14, 1957, Buddy Stinespring won the 20-lap amateur feature at Eastside over Earl Moran and Roy Neff.

On August 9, 1958, Buddy Stinespring won the 20-lap amateur feature at Eastside over Herb Breeden of Orange, Virginia, Bill Rodeffer of Penn Laird, Virginia, Dick Pappy Hansbarger of Mount Jackson, Virginia, and Earl Moran of Staunton.

The News Virginian had this account of the August 16, 1958, races at Eastside:

Stinespring, Nalley Get Double Victories at Eastside Speedway

For the first time in three weeks a racing program was run off at Eastside Speedway without the lights going off. There was nothing wrong with the power plan at the track, but the drivers seem to have a strange liking for ramming light poles.

Maybe it was the white paint applied to the bottom of the poles, or maybe the drivers just decided it was time to run with the lights on. Whatever the reason, it was to the liking of amateur driver Buddy Stinespring of Staunton and the sportsman ace Bullet Bill Nalley of Winchester.

With the lights on for a full evening, Buddy Stinespring showed that he is the hottest thing around in the amateur division. His feature win makes two in a row for the ace from Staunton. Finishing second to Stinespring were Jackie Clore followed by Al Grinnan and Earl Moran in that order.

On May 16, 1959, Stinespring won both his 10-lap heat and 20-lap amateur feature at Eastside in the inaugural Eastside event of 1959.

On July 22, 1961, Buddy Stinespring won the sportsman-modified feature driving a sportsman vehicle. The News Virginian had this account:

Buddy Stinespring, the Waynesboro native who now operates a service station in Staunton, drove Car 501 at a high-speed rate throughout the feature to gain the win. Finishing second place in the feature was Lewis Bocock of Greenville in a modified Car 500.

Stinespring's win was surprising to many fans as the modifieds are supposed to run the sportsman cars in the ground. But Stinespring was not of this school of thought Saturday night as he turned the four-tenths mile oval at top speed. Stinespring and Bocock staged a real dual for about 3/4 of the 20-lap feature.

On April 21, 1962, at Eastside, Stinespring took the lead on the third lap of the 20-lap feature, and at the end of the race was lapping most of the field.

On April 28, 1962, Buddy Stinespring won the 20-lap sportsman feature at Eastside, gaining the lead on the fifth lap and driving on to victory. He began lapping other cars in the field on the eighth lap.

On May 19, 1962, Buddy Stinespring won the 20-lap sportsman feature at Eastside with ease. Later he drove Lewis Bocock's number 50 car to third place in the modified feature.

On June 9, 1962, Stinespring dominated in the evening racing at Eastside. The News Virginian had the following account:

Stinespring Takes Three Flags in Two Classes at Eastside

A first was established for the 1962 season at Eastside Speedway Saturday night when one driver picked up three checkered flags during the evening stock car racing program.

Buddy Stinespring, a native of Waynesboro who

now lives and works in Staunton, entered the winner's circle three times during the evening. The first checkered flag was picked up by Stinespring in a sportsman heat when he drove his Car 501 to a win. Then he changed cars, driving Lewis Bocock's Car 50 to a win in the modified heat. Finally, Stinespring gained the third win for the evening with a victory in a sportsman feature driving his own car.

On August 6, 1962, Buddy Stinespring won the 20-lap sportsman feature at Eastside edging Charlie Beeler.

On July 6, 1963, Stinespring won the 25-lap sportsman feature at Eastside after a spirited battle between himself and Charlie Beeler. Second place went to Bob Cabe of Broadway, Virginia, with third place going to Charlie Beeler.

On May 2, 1964, Stinespring captured the checkered flag in an abbreviated sportsman feature at Eastside, which was called after 18 laps because of a spectacular accident off the fourth turn. Robert Gordon of Staunton spun out and into the rail, coming to rest straddling the fence as his car caught fire. Gordon was unhurt. The fire was extinguished by the Dooms Fire Department. Charlie Beeler finished second.

On June 13, 1964, running in a sportsman consolation at Eastside, Stinespring nearly demolished his 501 car when he tangled with Bobby Hite. Stinespring collided with Hite on the first turn and rolled over twice.

Pop Becomes Ill

Soon after he had quit racing, Stinespring's father became ill. By chance late one night, Stinespring encountered Mr. Gearhart, the former owner of the Pilot Speedway, who was driving a tow truck to pick up a car in Staunton.

As they talked, Stinespring told Gearhart that his father would love to see him and that he was seriously ill. Gearhart wanted to visit, but felt uncomfortable and self-conscious because of his appearance, saying that he was dirty from working on cars. What happened next is described in the chapter dedicated to W. W. Gearhart.

Stinespring's father, Cecil Ward Stinespring, died on June 22, 1974, at the age of 73. Buddy also had a brother, Tommy, who also drove racecars in the early 50's.

Stinespring was interviewed in his modest, well decorated home in Staunton along with his wife of 47 years, Virginia. Buddy looks in great shape and younger than his age. He is talkative, friendly, outgoing, and relishes the opportunity to talk about his racing days about which he is justifiably proud.

Buddy Stinespring in 2001

Lewis Bocock

One of racing's all-time nice guys is Lewis Bocock. He drove his own cars from 1953 to 1963. He was interviewed along with his wife, Jean, in his spacious, well-decorated ranch home outside Staunton, Virginia. He has suffered horribly from arthritis and the effects of medication over the years. The sense of loss related to his disability has been psychologically devastating. Nonetheless, he retains his friendly smile and warm personality. In interviewing Lewis and his wife, the author felt most at home.

The Bococks were proud to show the author Lewis' second hobby after racing, which was restoring cars. A 1937 Chevy Coupe sits in his garage. Sadly, after having it restored, Lewis and his wife were involved in an accident, not his own fault, returning from a car show. The car has yet to be repaired, but Lewis hopes to do so in the near future.

Lewis and his wife Jean have been married 51 years. He went to his first roadster race in the late 40's at Winchester Airport Speedway, won by Shorty Bowers. He was then hooked on racing.

Lewis and his wife were married in 1950 and went on their honeymoon to the Indy 500. The race, which was won by Johnny Parsons, was stopped because of rain after 230 laps. According to Lewis, "We were glad, because we were hot and tired."

He was known as an expert tile setter.

Bocock and the Grease Pit

Bocock had gotten the racing bug in 1953, and he and a friend, Charlie Propst, had prepared his racer. Lewis admits that he was quite nervous as they towed the car to a filling station to check grease in the rear end before going to race at Valley Speedway in Staunton, Virginia. Bocock continues, "I took it there. About six to eight guys gathered around looking at the car. I got in the car and I had been working most of the night to get the car ready. I was nervous and tired. Nobody was watching to see if I was okay. All of a sudden I felt the whole right front drop down in the grease pit!

"I ran out to see if we'd torn up anything. I put it in reverse and it wouldn't move. This old big guy said, 'We can push it out of there.' Sure enough they did.

"Charlie and I, along with his wife, left to go to the track at Valley Speedway. Before we got out of the busy part of town I said, 'Charlie, you're going to have to drive this thing. I'm too nervous. I couldn't get around the track with it.' Charlie said, 'I can't drive it.' I said, 'You're going to have to. I just ran it into the grease pit up at Moomaw's Filling Station.'

"Finally we got on the road that leads out to the track and I said, 'You're going to have to drive it.' He said, 'I can't drive it. I'm too nervous.' I said, 'I might as well turn around and go back.'

"Kitty, his wife, said, 'Charles, you can drive it.' He

didn't say anything, so I just kept going. We got to the track and Charlie got in the car.

"At Valley Speedway those days there was a driver by the name of Ace Denkins. He was real crazy and he and Charlie got together on turn two. I saw Charlie coming back on the track sideways and he bumped Ace. The announcer said, 'Number 4 has had a little problem with Ace Denkins up there on number two.' Charlie didn't do too bad, but Charlie said when he got back in the pits, 'You better take that thing out there. I'm not going to drive it in the future. I've had enough trouble with Ace Denkins today.' I said, 'I don't know if I can.' Charlie said, 'Go on. Get used to it.' So I got in it and I went around a few times. It had a half windshield and the wind was coming through there and I thought, 'Wow. This thing will fly.' And so I made three or four laps and went back in. I said, 'It runs pretty good, doesn't it?' Charlie said, 'Yeah, but you're going to have to take it out there and run it really fast.' I thought, 'That's as fast as I could go!'"

What Bocock is referring to is the fact that few people appreciate the real speed racers achieve and how it is experienced inside the car. The author of this book found out firsthand when on September 7, 2001, my wife and children gave me as a gift 25 laps in a late model modified car at New River Valley Speedway in Dublin, Virginia. It took a number of laps to realize how slow I was actually going compared to the racing speed of the cars who drive there. Not only does it give one an appreciation for the actual speed and concentration required to achieve the speed, but also being surrounded by 30 or 40 other cars.

Bocock continues his description of his first race. "I drove it in the feature and there were two guys from West Virginia," he says. "One of them was lined up right behind me. When we got the flag, it reminded me of a bee. He was on my bumper and I could just feel him hitting me again and again. When we got to the curve, he was gone. I began to realize that I really wasn't driving fast at all as I tried to keep up with the others. I got used to the speed. I really didn't realize how fast they went. Later, I took a couple of people out and had them ride in my car at race speed. They couldn't really believe how fast it seems."

Rough Driving at Lawrenceville

From this first experience, however, Bocock was hooked and began a ten-year all-consuming commitment to stock car racing. Bocock talks about racing at Lawrenceville, Virginia. He started the first heat in fifth place. After the first lap, he came out leading. In eight laps he had lapped most of the field. In the next race, a local driver, resentful of Bocock's speed, hit Bocock on purpose from the rear, sending Bocock into the fence. Bocock says now, "I can't remember his name but I'd sure like to talk to him. I didn't have anyone with me that night. I wasn't about to make an issue of it in a fight. Only one I knew was Cal Johnson and he was a nice guy and pretty small at that. We fixed it before the feature and then the same guy did the same thing to me again. I never went back.

"I had raced on a Friday night at Lawrenceville and this was Saturday morning. I got back to Staunton at Standard Tile where I worked at 7:00 in the morning and the guys were there waiting to go to work. Then I had to come home, put the car together, go to Waynesboro that night, and then go to Winchester the next day. I was ready to go to work on Monday and get some rest!"

Bocock worked on his car in a garage he built.

Bocock's Crosly

One of his most prized racecars was a Crosly body, which was attached to a 1936 Chevy chassis, shortened to accommodate the Crosly body. The idea was to build a lighter car with a strong motor. To this day, Bocock cannot remember where he found the Crosly body.

The first race with the Crosly was at Valley Speedway. Bocock says, "It was quicker than I was used to so I had the lead in the first race and I thought I'd see what it could really do. I went into the number three and four curve. You went down in as you come out of it. I went off the track. I just went straight up in the air off the track and landed on the road on all four wheels. It wouldn't restart. The force had put the distributor back in the firewall. That was some ride just flying through the air but in ten years I had never had one upside down."

This Crosly racer was unusual and interested most of the drivers and fans. Bocock says the car especially ran well at Winchester.

RUNNING THE HIGH LINE

Bocock said that when he went to another track he had in his mind that he needed to drive like the other drivers at the track. He says, however, that he had his best luck running on the outside high line. In fact, he says, "I wish I would have done that more."

BOCOCK WITHOUT A HELMET!

When Bocock started driving, he used leather football helmets for protection and then eventually went to the Cromwell helmet. His wife would polish the helmet with white shoe polish before every race. She went to most every race, although she never drove in a powder-puff race. His wife continues, "When he was on the track I had my eye on his car only. I always had a paper cup in my hand and when the race was over it was like a mouse had torn it up.

"One night they were lining up and I said, 'He doesn't have a helmet on!' I was getting ready to go down and stop that race, and I motioned to one of the guys."

Bocock continues the story. "Smokey Stover and I were in the back," he says. "I remember coming down the front stretch on the warm-up lap. He gestured I didn't have a helmet on. It was lying on the floorboard, so I reached down and got it on in time for the race to start."

His wife says, "I was going to stop that race. I had two small children at the time!"

A FAMILY AFFAIR

According to Jean Bocock, "Our kids never knew anything on Saturday nights except the racetrack. We'd start early, get baths, pack meals, and then go."

BOCOCK'S FAVORITE TRACK

Bocock feels that Winchester was his best track. He says, "When that track was dry and slick, about the third lap I would take the lead. I did it all in the curves. But with a wet track I'd finish third or so to Nalley or Stover."

KUDOS FROM SHORTY

Bocock always looked up to Shorty Bowers. Bocock continues, "One Sunday after a 10-lap heat race at Winchester, Shorty Bowers was just there looking. Smokey Stover was there with a couple of other fellows, and I noticed that smoke was coming off his rear tire. Bowers was looking at my car and put his hand on my rear tire and said, 'Feel that.' It was just a moderate temperature in it. It was recapped and it still had the little tags on it. He said, 'Man, that guy's really getting good traction.'"

Bocock believes that handling was the key to his success. He noticed that Al Grinnan had a very powerful car at Waynesboro, about the most powerful car he had seen, but he had difficulty getting the power to the rear tires, preventing good handling.

Bocock says that the most he ever made in a race was $120 at Eastside. He says, "I probably finished second more than any other driver, mostly to Stover."

BOCOCK FINDS AN ENGINE

Bocock restored some of his racing engines but on occasion bought the original cam and pistons from a racing shop in California. He took one block to Norfolk to be balanced and bored. This particular motor, according to Bocock, was his most powerful motor, but it never had adequate power. Bocock has this account. "In Waynesboro on a Saturday night, coming out of turn two, all of a sudden it just cut off dead," he says. "I just pulled to the infield and sat on the track away from the racing, and my buddy was in the pits. He came running across the track. He had a flashlight. I said, 'Check the wires. I think there's a wire come loose because it just quit all of a sudden.' He looked around and said, 'You might as well get out.' He said, 'There's a hole in the pan about the size of a fist.' It didn't smoke or anything. It ruined everything in the engine except one head in the intake.

"I went to Winchester the next day. I didn't have any parts. Those guys down there at Winchester weren't too interested in helping me since I was from Staunton. I was running third at points both at Winchester and Waynesboro, so few wanted to help. I asked everybody around there but I didn't have any luck. I ended up not racing.

"I was just lucky that I came back through Harrisonburg and at a Dairy Queen, while I was eating ice-cream, this little short fellow came up and said, 'Racing at Winchester today?' I said, 'I blew an engine last night.' He says, 'I've got parts for an old engine. I'll let you have it.' I said, 'What have you got?' He replied, 'I got the block, cam, two sleeves. It's an engine out of an old truck they pull trailers with.' I said, 'What do you want for it?' He said, 'I owe those people $40. If you pay the bill, you can have it.' I got everything I needed! The next week I went to the Chevy place and got a new set of rods and fuel injector pistons. This was 1958 and I put it together, having a total of $142 in it.

"This motor had double the horsepower than any other engine I'd had. Before that I hadn't won. After that I won seven straight races at Winchester. I ran it three more seasons before I had the heads off of it. I did put new bearings in the motor twice a year."

BOCOCK AND STOVER

Bocock has a great deal of respect for Smokey Stover and Bill Nalley. Bocock continues, "Smokey was cocky. He was kind of wild with everything. He had a '56 Ford and he had it painted every year. He was in North Carolina one day and had a loud exhaust on it. He got a ticket in North Carolina and coming home in Rocky Mount, Virginia, another cop pulled him over and told him his exhaust was too loud. Smokey said, 'You're not going to give me a ticket are you? I just got one in North Carolina.'"

Bocock says that on a personal level he and Stover never had conflict. Bocock acknowledges, "I never could beat him unless he had problems. When he wrecked, hardly before the car would stop, Smokey would unbuckle and jump out. One night in Lawrenceville he jumped out of a moving car and his crew had to run to get it."

On July 15, 1961, at Eastside, a car had blown an engine through the fourth turn, putting a great deal of oil and water on the track. Bocock says, "I was behind the car that blew up and went to the right and got around him. A bunch of cars wrecked and Smokey went into the pileup." As was his custom, he got out of the car quickly. At that time another car hit the Stover car and broke several of Stover's ribs. Bocock continues, "They took him to the hospital and I thought, 'I've got it made tonight because Smokey's hurt.'"

BOCOCK'S DUEL WITH DOVEL

After the track was cleaned and Stover taken to the hospital, the race continued. Bocock continues his account of the race. "Ray Dovel was running behind me," he says. "Everybody got out shovels to cover up the oil in that curve. We still had ten laps to go." Bocock continues, "I started in front. I went to the inside to get away from the oil. Dovel followed me. On the second lap I did the same thing. All of a sudden I heard this engine roaring and looked and he was coming around the outside. I was in second and I thought, 'Man, I've lost this again.' So I took after him and ran the high line. Dovel was the type who wouldn't give you anything. So I would catch him but I couldn't get around him. He wouldn't give a bit. I watched him and he would slide up through the curves. I could get along side but I'd have to lift.

"With two laps to go, I pulled up beside of him on the outside. We went into the curve. I slammed on my brakes as hard as I could. As he slid up, I poured it on and went under him. He tried to catch me but he couldn't. I won the trophy. Smokey had given it to me by getting hurt, but I had to take it from Ray Dovel that night."

BOCOCK AND NALLEY

Bocock describes one of the few times he was able to beat Bill Nalley. He says, "At that time Nalley was running at Hagerstown and wasn't running Eastside that much. One night going into turn one, about halfway through the race, Nalley was pretty good at putting you out of the way if he wanted to. On the straightaway he was easing up on me and on the curve he rubbed up against me. I could see the sparks coming off the car. It hit me. I'm always giving into him and I don't believe I have to do that anymore. So I got back on it and drove away from him."

Bocock says Nalley told him after the race, "These guys run a little rougher than they used to when I drove here before!"

BOCOCK AND DOVEL

Bocock had a number of duels with Ray Dovel. He describes Dovel as "a real nice guy but at Eastside, if the lights blinked, Ray Dovel had hit a light pole. One time we had to take a half an hour to fix it after he had done it. Ray raced for Ray. In Winchester one day he flat out would not let me pass and I had the fastest car."

WIVES

Bocock's wife Jean says, "Racers' wives got along well. After the race was over, we'd go to somebody's house or to Buddy Steinspring's gas station, especially after a race at Devil's Bowl." She describes the late Helen Bowers, widow of Junior Bowers, as happy-go-lucky, just full of fun.

BOCOCK AND JUNIOR BOWERS

Bocock becomes visibly sad when speaking of the late Junior Bowers. He considered Junior and his family good friends, but Bocock had protested one of Bowers' wins at Eastside and the protest was upheld. Bocock continues, "The Sunday after I protested I wished I had told them to forget about it because a year there, there was a great deal of bitterness. But finally we were good friends again, and that's when he got killed. We'd run together a lot and started going to Manassas some."

Bocock was present the day Bowers was killed at Winchester. Bocock continues, "It was the strangest thing. I very seldom had problems at Winchester but I spun out at the start of the race. I was in the rear and the next lap was when he wrecked. Most of us stopped the cars and went to see Junior. I saw where his helmet was cracked. I looked at him in the ambulance and he was unconscious."

Bocock would go on to win this race. Jean and Lewis Bocock went to the Winchester hospital the night of the accident. With Bowers in a coma, Bocock was responsible for bringing the wrecked Junior Bowers' car back to Staunton and putting it in Junior's basement where he worked on his cars. Jean Bocock says, "It really tore everyone up and Lewis couldn't sleep over it. I had grown up with Junior." Bowers and Jean both had brothers killed in World War II.

The Bococks referred to Bowers as "June." Jean continued, "June was so full of life. I don't think June met a person who didn't like him. He just was such a likable person. He had so much fun about him and was eager to help everybody."

One week after Bowers' death, Bocock entered the Junior Bowers Memorial Race at Winchester. Before the race, Smokey Stover and Bocock had agreed that if either won the trophy, they would present it to Bowers' widow, Helen.

During the race, Bocock spun and saw Smokey Stover spin out, saying to himself, "Doggone, we're not going to get the trophy."

"We were determined to bring Helen back that trophy. I don't think I've ever run any harder in a race. I worked my way back to the lead with three laps to go. As I got the white flag, my whole drive shaft and rear end went apart, and everything came out. Charlie Almond, the flagman, had to run to keep from getting hit by the drive shaft. Smokey passed Bob Dobyns on the last lap and won the race." He gave the trophy to Bowers' widow.

In this race, Dobyns finished second with Jackie Clore, driving a sportsman car, third. As Clore was the highest finishing sportsman car, he also won a trophy.

CLOSE CALL FOR BOCOCK

Bocock was never seriously injured; however, narrowly escaped serious injury or death in March 1957 at Valley Speedway. In a heat race, Cal Johnson's transmission tore loose from beneath his car, hit the track, went into the air, narrowly missed Bob Dobyns' car, and hit the top of Bocock's car, just a few inches from the windshield. Had the transmission hit a few inches lower, it most certainly would have killed Bocock. Bocock suffered a few cut fingers from the broken glass but sustained no serious injuries.

Bocock describes the event. "It hit so hard the car hesitated and shuttered. It happened so quick I didn't know what it was." Bocock says, "I never thought more about it." But his wife says, "I realized how dangerous it was and maybe that was a warning at that time."

BOCOCK'S SECOND CAR

At one time Bocock had a second modified car, number 50. He was especially fond of Buddy Stinespring and felt that he was one of the better drivers. For one year Stinespring drove Bocock's second car, which was a 1958 Pontiac. Bocock says, "During that time, Stinespring finished third 14 weeks in a row. I'd be second and Smokey would win.

"Buddy's Pontiac had a direct drive. It had a high gear and no other gears. That way we had more horsepower. I told Buddy, 'Don't kill the engine.' We had to push it off. It was hard on brakes. "After finishing third fourteen weeks in a row, the fifteenth night Stinespring got his bumper locked with another driver and sat on the turn the whole race." Bocock emphasizes that there were no cautions at that time, only red flags when the track was blocked.

SELECTED EVENTS

On August 25, 1956, Bocock won the feature at Eastside over Jimmy Aleshire in Car J-5.

On September 8, 1956, Bocock won the feature in the Class B sportsman division over Claude Baldwin of Staunton, Gip Gibson of Charlottesville, Smokey Stover, and Charlie Sipe of McGaheysville.

On August 17, 1957, Tommy Irwin, who was dominating the track at that time, had mechanical difficulty. The News Virginian has this account of a Bocock win:

Long overdue Lewis Bocock of Greenville, driving Car 500, took advantage of Irwin's mishap to capture the first event of the 1957 season.

The 25-lapper started off as a battle between the two. Bocock led for the first eight laps, but the hard-driving Irwin overtook him on the ninth. They fought fender to fender and wheel to wheel for several laps and finally it appeared that Irwin would easily outdistance Bocock. It was then that Irwin was forced to retire, leaving the field to eat Bocock's dust the rest of the trip.

On May 16, 1959, it is said that Lewis Bocock provided the big thrill of the evening in Car 500 as he came off the track on the number four turn and did a ten-yard broad slide in front of the fans at Eastside.

On August 6, 1961, promoter Al Gore at Eastside pitted four modified cars against four hobby cars in a special four-lap feature. The idea was for the modifieds to catch the hobbies, although the hobbies had been given a half-lap lead at the start. Bocock caught two of the hobbies before the green flag was dropped. He eventually went on to win.

On August 19, 1961, Bocock won two of three modified features at Devil's Bowl, winning one 25-lap feature and finishing second and third in the other two. Finishing second for the evening to Bocock were Jackie Clore, Bill Nalley, Ray Stinespring, and Smokey Stover in that order.

During August and September 1959, Lewis Bocock won eight straight modified features at Winchester Speedway. The string was broken in a special match race on September 30, 1959, as Ray Dovel defeated him by a car length, holding off repeated attempts by Bocock to win the race. This is the race recalled earlier by Bocock where he felt he had the fastest car but was blocked by Dovel.

On May 25, 1960, at Devil's Bowl, Bocock lost a close duel with Smokey Stover when his car caught fire. He was not injured.

On October 7, 1961, Bocock won the final race of the 1961 season at Eastside Speedway before a shivering crowd of approximately 500 people. Bocock won over Smokey Stover with Bill Nalley finishing third and Buddy Stinespring fourth.

BOCOCK RETIRES

Bowers' death started eating at Bocock. His wife Jean says, "I think he got to thinking more seriously. We had small children and it made you think what could happen. I thought about it a lot but I knew it was so much in his blood to race. While we were going together, he was always heavy-footed. He was always ready to race on the road and he knew I didn't like it. But I knew he had to make that decision to quit on his own."

When Bocock told his wife he was quitting she said, "Are you sure? The only way I think you can do this is to advertise and sell your car. If that car sits here, it will always be a temptation."

Bocock admits that he didn't have the spirit to race after Bowers' death. Bocock continues, "The year was 1963 and I didn't even win a heat race that year. I thought, 'Well, I'm losing it and I'm not enjoying it like I did before.' Our lives centered around racing. I worked all week for the weekend, but I just wore myself out." Continues Bocock, "Racing was the best part of my life."

Jean and Lewis Bocock in 2001.

Dick "Pappy" Hansberger

Dick "Pappy" Hansberger was a regular racer throughout the Shenandoah Valley during the 50's, 60's, and 70's. Known affectionately as Pappy because he was somewhat older than other racers at the time, he won over 50 features in his career, mostly racing in the amateur, later to be called sportsman, division. His racing career began in 1952 and ended in 1979 when he retired from racing at the age of 63. He died on January 25, 2002, at the age of 87 from congestive heart failure. The interview about Pappy's career was conducted with Delores Hansberger Kagey and P. C. Hansberger, two of Hansberger's five children, approximately two weeks after his death. P. C. spent much of his youth as a mechanic for his father, and later went on to produce his own car and drive during the 1970's.

Pappy Hansberger

Pappy Hansberger raced throughout the valley, including Winchester, Eastside, Devil's Bowl, Keezletown, and Red Banks. He raced on one occasion at Pilot Speedway and for some time was a regular at Fort Ashby, West Virginia Speedway. His favorite track, however, was Winchester.

Miss Airport Speedway

Delores was third runner-up in the 1955 Miss Winchester Airport Speedway Beauty Contest. The winner, Carol Hamrick, never returned to the speedway after her win. Allegedly, she had entered the contest under protest, being forced to do so by her parents. When second place Barbara Ballinger was not regularly in attendance at the raceway, Delores

Miss Airport Speedway, 1955. (Left to right) Delores Hansberger; Barbara Ballinger; Carol Hamrick (winner); Track owner Kermit Batt; and unknown woman.

Hansberger, as third runner-up, inherited track duties, which often involved presenting trophies and checkered flags to race winners and having pictures taken. Since Delores always accompanied her father to the races, she was a natural to function in this role. Delores went on to win several other beauty contests during her youth.

Pappy and Wendell Scott

P. C. Hansberger remembers his first contact with the late Wendell Scott at Winchester as he and his father drove into the track. Hansberger says, "When we got to Winchester in the afternoon, Wendell Scott was already there up on a hill under some oak trees outside the track. Wendell was up there with his boys and had the car jacked up. They had pulled it behind an old panel truck. He carried all of his parts in his panel truck.

"As we pulled in, Daddy said, 'Who is that?' We'd

never met him before. We stopped and asked him if he needed any help to find out really who he was. Scott said, 'I'm trying to find a gear to run here. I've already walked over the track to measure the distance, and measured as much as I could stepping it off.'"

Hansberger continues, "Scott changed his rear end and came in on the track. During warm-ups he had to change his rear end again. He ended up winning the feature that day and stayed at Winchester that night, and the next day went to Hagerstown. Daddy won the amateur feature that night at Winchester. The next day we went to Hagerstown. Scott again won the feature and Daddy won, winning about $100. Scott was allegedly given less than $10 for his feature win and told not to come back." Hansberger says this slight was obviously racially motivated.

Hansberger continues regarding Scott, "Scott was a nice man. At Winchester he'd take his boys up to the grandstand. He'd say, 'You stay right here,' and they would, and then he'd go and race. Those were about the only blacks you'd see at the track in those days."

Hansberger continues, "Scott's car ran well, but it didn't look like much, never fully painted. It was just an old black car with a number smeared on it." Hansberger also relates that Scott was accepted by all the racing community. He readily borrowed gas and oil from the other drivers and it was given to him freely.

Racing at Fort Ashby

Hansberger describes how his father began racing at Fort Ashby, West Virginia, Speedway. He says, "The way we got to Fort Ashby was this guy who owned an Amoco station close to that track came to Winchester one day and said, 'Why don't you come to Fort Ashby? I know you could win. Them guys back there don't run like you guys. You come and stop at my station and I'll fill all your vehicles up with gas, including hi-test.' We went there and he did."

Hansberger says that at Fort Ashby, "If you won, you not only won money but also a free meal at a local restaurant, a wristwatch, or a bushel of apples. I don't know how many watches Daddy did win."

Pappy Hansberger, according to his son, was very successful at Fort Ashby. P.C. says, "We outclassed those guys. We had gears and supped up our cars. All they had was a stock body and the biggest motor they could find. We just ran over top of them."

Because of Hansberger's domination at Fort Ashby, he was often protested but always found to be legal.

Hansberger describes the Fort Ashby track. "They didn't have any running water except for a big pond where you got water for your radiator," he says. "It was old river bottom dirt, and they tried to run on Sunday afternoon but it got so dusty. That river bottom dirt would dry out quick, but at night they'd water it all day long and get it all muddier than heck and it would get good at night, but you'd tear holes in it and it would get rough."

Racing at Devil's Bowl

Hansberger describes his father racing at Devil's Bowl. "At Devil's Bowl, if you went over the third or fourth turn, you could just call it quits for the night. It was like a 75-foot drop."

Hansberger remembers Lewis Bocock going airborne off that turn in his Crosly. There was no guardrail.

Hansberger continues, "Devil's Bowl had no grandstand to speak of. Everyone just parked on the hillside.

"One night at Devil's Bowl, we had a brand new car, #2X4. It was black. We didn't have any time to put any paint on it. We never did anything to the brakes because we thought they were okay. We went there and as the race went on, it just looked like Pappy's car kept slowing down slower and slower. Pappy was up with the leaders but started dropping back. He pulled into pits and said, 'This thing just won't go. It acts like the brakes are locking up on it.' Sure enough, the brakes were locked. We tried to push it and you couldn't move it a bit!"

Pappy and Roy Neff

Hansberger remembers the outspoken Roy Neff and says that on one Sunday afternoon at Winchester a driver by the name of Tiny Slader and Neff got into an argument. Roy's wife Hilda apparently chimed in and Hansberger recalls this exchange. He says, "Tiny walked over and told Roy's wife, 'Old woman, you ain't got nothing in this. Keep your trap shut. You probably ain't washed your breakfast dishes yet!'"

Being Wrecked at Eastside

Hansberger also remembers one night at Eastside when his father was leading the race and an unidentified driver intentionally hit him in the number three turn. According to Hansberger, "It drove him clear off the track, he just pounded him. Daddy went off the track through a board fence and hit a car on the outside and tore it all to pieces."

Favorite Drivers

Delores Kagey and P. C. Hansberger's favorite drivers were Buddy Stinespring, Bill Nalley, Tommy Irwin, and Junior Beeler. Adds Delores, "We were all like a family. You'd have your differences, but after a few weeks you'd be over it." Delores adds that her entire family would go to the races, usually packing picnic lunches.

Working All Night

P. C. Hansberger remembers a race in the early 1970's at Winchester in which both he and his father were involved in a spectacular crash. He continues, "We were at Winchester and the track was muddy. We had a heck of a wreck. Red Ninninger flipped over Daddy. About six cars rolled over in the first heat coming off the fourth turn. It tore up about four or five cars."

He continues, "I'd bought a 14-inch tire and wheel and spent about $165 and put it on the car. After the wreck, three of my tires were flat and this new one was the only one that wasn't. It had driven the door into the transmission. Before the race, there was a guy from Craigsville signing up cars to race there. (This was probably Clyde Harris.) And the contract Daddy signed was something he just didn't read. He just wanted to race at this new track. In the fine print it said, 'If you don't show, you owe them $50. If you showed, you got $50.' So here the car is all tore up from this wreck and we're supposed to go to Craigsville the next day. So we came home right after that heat, loaded on the truck, and came straight home. We worked all night till 3:00 in the morning. We thought we were finished. We had to replace three A-frames, line up the wheels, put a spring on the rear, hammer the door out, and in the process woke up a lot of neighbors.

"Then we realized that the contract called for a full windshield, so we went back in the junkyard and got a windshield out of a '62 Ford and put it in with straps."

Wrecking at Craigsville

"We headed out without sleep to Craigsville. We got up there and Charlie Beeler was supposed to drive for us and didn't show up. So Daddy got in it and adjusted the seatbelts for himself; got out and then walked out saying, 'He'd drive it in a little while.' My brother-in-law, Paul Baker, said, 'Why don't you take it out there?' I said, 'All right,' and got in it. I put Daddy's helmet on and didn't fasten any seatbelts. Bob Dobyns was there and he was dominating races at that track. So I'm out there running around and here comes Dobyns and he's really going good. I tried to follow him and picked up my speed.

"The flagman was on a platform and could look down at the cars. He sees I don't have any safety belts on. He comes in off the platform and across the track and motions for me to pull in. I pull in and he said, 'Get some damn belts on.' I said, 'I forgot.' I put the belts on but they didn't fit too good because Daddy had adjusted them for him and he's bigger than me.

"I'm out there trying to follow Dobyns at full throttle. I was going around pretty keen. I went into the number one turn and the steering broke. Out over the fence I go, down the back and upset.

"Dobyns pulls up and gets out of his car and asks, 'Are you okay?' I said, 'Yeah,' but when I got out of the racecar it was a funny feeling. When I stepped out, I was in a ditch and I couldn't stand up straight. I had some cuts from the windshield and burn marks on my neck from the shoulder harness.

"Daddy ran over and said, 'My God, get the ketchup bottle. He's white!'"

A Long Night Home

On another night at Craigsville, P. C. Hansberger, Dick Pappy Hansberger, and a man by the name of Dick Foley piled in the front of a flatbed truck and transported Dick Pappy Hansberger's car to Craigsville Motor Speedway. P. C. Hansberger explains what happened. "I thought I'd never get home that night," he says. "We had the car on the truck and it was the three of us in the cab of the truck. Coming down the road from Craigsville after the races, the headlights went out on the truck. The generator quit working on the truck. The battery was dead.

"We pulled over to the side and Dick Foley says to Dad, 'I believe we need a drink.' Daddy said, 'We need more than a drink. We need a generator.' "Back then, when you went to the races, you had some form of a trouble light. So we had one that worked off the battery. This was about 2:00 or 3:00 in the morning. Dick Foley said, 'We're not going to be able to get to Winchester.' Pappy said, 'Oh, yes we are, Dick Foley.'

"We hooked the trouble light to the racecar battery and we were going down the road pretty good and a cop pulls us over. He said, 'You need more lights on that truck than just one headlight.'

"Daddy said, 'Well we'll just have to wait till daylight.'

"Dick said, 'Well, why don't we just wire both headlights into the racecar's battery?' So they did, but then the battery on the racecar started to go down. There was a small generator on the racecar to keep the battery up, something that Lee Stultz had invented. It didn't take much power to pull it.

"So then we had the idea to go back and start the motor on the racecar so that the generator would keep the battery up and provide lights to the truck. So, here we are going down the road in the wee hours of the morning with a racecar on top of a truck with the motor running to keep the lights going on the truck." They made it home and raced the next day.

Selected Events

On September 21, 1957, at Winchester Airport Speedway, Hansberger won the amateur feature trophy over Robert Peer, just as he could barely keep his engine from overheating.

On June 28, 1959, Hansberger finished second to Earl Moran in a long-distance race, which required two pit stops with a complete wheel change on each stop. Moran finished just a few yards ahead of Hansberger.

On August 2, 1959, Hansberger won a 10-lap sportsman heat at Winchester with his windshield obstructed by the hood of his car, which came loose on the very first lap. The Winchester Evening Star has this account:

Because Hansberger started fast, he didn't have to worry about passing any cars, but he had to be a contortionist to see through the small gap left between the hood and the windshield.

In September 1962, Hansberger won two consecutive sportsman features at Winchester, both over Charlie Beeler, who finished second.

On September 7, 1958, Hansberger received the nickname "Hard Luck" when he skidded through an oil patch and lost the Class B feature. In this race, Hansberger was making a move to pass leader Sonny Kisner on the 39th lap of the 50-lap trophy feature race when both cars sailed in opposite directions. Hansberger's car came to rest on the edge of the infield and was out of contention.

HANSBERGER HURT

In 1958, Hansberger suffered his only injury, albeit a serious one. A car driven by Fudgie Fauble went airborne in the fourth turn at Winchester. As Hansberger drove under the airborne car of Fauble, Fauble's car brushed the left side of Hansberger's car. The contact severely cut Hansberger's left arm.

Hansberger, holding his arm with his right hand to curtail the bleeding, drove slowly to the front stretch where an alert Bill Nalley, who was standing in the pits, ran to Hansberger's car and helped steer and stop the car.

Hansberger was hospitalized for several days after the accident.

CLOSE CALL AT WINCHESTER

Quick thinking and alert driving by Hansberger avoided tragedy at a race in Winchester in the late 50's. The Winchester Evening Star has this account:

Fast thinking by Mount Jackson's Dick Hansberger saved Bob Crosen of Winchester from serious or fatal injuries in Sunday's Class B feature at the Airport Speedway.

With every one of the 1,500 fans keenly watching the start of the 25-lap race, Crosen's car went out of control on the east turn and rolled over crazily five times, dumping the local driver out on the track about half-way through the turn.

Running in second place at that time, Crosen was followed closely by Hansberger, a veteran driver.

As Crosen's car went up in the air, the Mount Jackson ace let off the gas and hit the brakes.

Either the rolling car of Crosen or Hansberger's racer could have killed Crosen as he laid in a semi-conscious state on the track. He was treated

Car in which Hansberger was injured in 1958.

for a cracked shoulder at Winchester Memorial Hospital and released.

The only person at the speedway that didn't see the crack-up was Crosen's wife, but there wasn't a person in the place who would have given a plugged nickel for Crosen's chances in this spectacular accident; but he rose half-way to his knees before the ambulance arrived, even though he had no later recollection of it.

LOSING AN ENGINE

P. C. Hansberger last owned a car in 1979. "Charlie Beeler was driving for me and blew up my car at Eastside." He continues, "He was out there running and I was motioning for him with a flashlight, trying to get him to come to the pits. The car was putting off more and more smoke. He had burnt a piston and when he was finished it was gone. It burnt the whole motor. He came into the pits and said, 'Something went wrong.'"

Hansberger continues, "I put an open Coke can under the exhaust pipe and I had about a half a cup of oil in no time at all. Man, that car was looking good up to that point." Hansberger never owned a car again.

Both Delores Kagey and P. C. Hansberger speak with deep respect for their father. They admire his tenacity and his commitment to racing. Pappy Hansberger was a truck driver who was also employed by the Virginia Game Commission and Forestry Service. In addition, he cut pulpwood to augment his income. He also liked to trap game.

Hansberger was buried in a racing decorated casket. He is buried at Trinity United Church of Christ in Bayse, Virginia. A picture of him in Car 2X4 is on his headstone.

In terms of racing, Hansberger made the most out of limited resources. In addition to being a solid and steady driver, Hansberger was an accomplished mechanic. P. C. Hansberger sums up his family's commitment to racing. "Racing was a heck of a commitment," he says. "It was about all we did. Daddy drove a truck and we cut pulpwood through the week. When Friday came, we were done. It was time to focus on racing, someplace, somewhere, somehow. We were going to the races if we had a car capable of racing, or we would be going to watch others. The whole family went. This was an every week occurrence."

Charlie "Junior" Beeler

Charlie "Junior" Beeler is a native of Winchester, Virginia. As of 2002, he is the Truck Service Foreman at Winchester Ford. Beeler started racing in 1956 when he first presented himself at Winchester Airport Speedway. Kermit Batt, owner of the Airport Speedway, said, "Boy, you don't look eighteen years old. Well, I'll let you go, I guess. You sign your name and I want to be able to read it, too."

Winchester track champion Charlie Beeler in the Lee Stultz #3 car.

Beeler started racing with a 1935 Ford sedan owned by Mitchell Pappas of Strasburg, Virginia. Beeler was a mechanic throughout his racing career. Before Beeler retired, he won more features in the history of the Winchester track than anyone else, including notables such as Tommy Irwin and Bill Nalley. Beeler always raced in the sportsman division after getting his experience in the jalopy division.

Beeler was later to drive the #3 car for Lee Stultz, owner of a legendary S-3 piloted by Bill Nalley. Nalley ran the modified division and Beeler the sportsman division.

Beeler is a humorous, fun-loving guy who often took adversity in stride. He laughs now over the fights and controversies. He laughs that on one occasion his wife got into a fight with another driver's wife because of adverse comments made by the other wife.

Protests

According to Beeler, both Nalley and he were protested on multiple occasions. In those days, a driver who protested another car as being illegal would need to post a certain amount of money, anywhere from $25 to $150, to have a car "torn down" and examined. If the car was illegal, the driver was usually stripped of his prize money, which went to the protesting driver. A certain amount of the money posted initially went to the mechanic who tore down the car. If the car was legal, the driver of the car under protest was able to keep that money less the mechanic's fee.

In 1963 and 1964, Beeler dominated the sportsman division at Eastside and became the focus of controversy.

Beeler continues, "The last time I was protested at Waynesboro, the other drivers were taking up a collection to do it. We had to wait till the motor cooled before he tore the motor down. The mechanic came by and said, 'Who's here protesting this car?' Nobody said anything. I said, 'There ain't none of them here. They took up a collection to do it and then they all go home.' The mechanic said, 'Well, if the guy's not here who's protesting, then you're legal.' He gave me the money, picked up his toolbox, and went home. The owner of the track, Al Gore, proclaimed, 'This won't happen anymore.'"

Beeler says that he was oftentimes protested by Buddy Stinespring. He says that Stinespring told him, "We know you're legal, but you might put it back together wrong." Beeler is proud of the fact that his motors were never disqualified. Beeler fondly remembers "Pop" Stinespring waving a flashlight at Buddy, exhorting him to the lead, as he raced Beeler.

Beeler talks also of the rivalry between Winchester and Staunton area racers. According to him, "Whenever those guys from Waynesboro asked me questions, what I told them was sure to be a lie."

SELECTED EVENTS

On July 22, 1961, at Eastside, Charlie Beeler, driving in the hobby division, caught fire coming off the fourth turn. According to newspaper accounts, "Members of the Waynesboro First Aid crew responded quickly to douse the flames as Beeler escaped unharmed."

In the inaugural race of the 1963 season at Eastside Speedway which was held on May 6, 1963, Beeler, who was driving Nalley's old S-3 vehicle, won the old hobby-sportsman feature, maneuvering through a two-car smash up involving Buddy Stinespring and Buck Shipp with ten laps remaining. At the time, Stinespring and Shipp were battling for the lead. Beeler won by a wide margin.

On June 22, 1963, Charlie Beeler won the 50-lap sportsman trophy race at Eastside. The race started with Buddy Stinespring going from the rear of the 20-car field to the first position by lap five. He held the leader's position until he ran into heavy traffic on the fourth corner at the end of the 37th lap. Attempting to jockey around the slower moving traffic, Stinespring spun out in the backfield. It was there that Beeler made his bid. Beeler had caught up to Stinespring in the 33rd lap on the same fourth turn when the Staunton ace had run into some more difficulty. Beeler led thereafter and won the race.

On June 29, 1963, Beeler won his second race in a row over Buddy Stinespring in a 25-lap sportsman feature. Stinespring, who had led the first 10 laps of the 25-lap sportsman feature in the 17-car field, developed engine trouble on lap 22.

On August 10, 1963, Beeler won the 25-lap sportsman feature at Eastside; however, a week later, Beeler saw misfortune at Eastside, much to the delight of the Eastside crowd who favored Beeler's nemesis, Buddy Stinespring, in a very exciting race. On the fourth start of the 50-lap feature, Beeler jumped to the head of the 17-car field and was moving out for what seemed like another sure win. At that time Car 0, driven by Glendon Good of Stanley, bumped the rear of Beeler's #3 car, hanging his front wheel over the rear of Beeler's car. Hooked together, the two cars continued through the third and fourth turns to the front stretch where they managed to unhook after coming to a complete stop. Because of this mishap, Stinespring then had approximately three-quarters of a lap lead over Beeler. The lead must have seemed insurmountable; however, Beeler worked his way back through the field and passed Stinespring in the 49th lap. The News Virginian continues the account:

Setting a terrific pace, Beeler and Stinespring flew around the track just inches apart. Then on the third turn of the last lap, a near spinout by Beeler returned the lead to Stinespring.

Stinespring finished the race with Beeler breathing right down his tailpipe in the closest Eastside race of the season.

On May 9, 1964, Beeler won the 20-lap sportsman feature despite a determined come-from-behind run by Buddy Stinespring. Stinespring attempted to pass Beeler on the fourth turn of lap 19 of the 20-lap feature, but swerved off the turn and across the infield for a second place finish. Earlier, Stinespring had led the race but had lost control on the first turn, yielding the number one spot to Beeler.

Regaining control, Stinespring battled Beeler almost bumper to bumper until the 19th lap.

On May 23, 1964, in a 20-lap sportsman race at Eastside, Buddy Stinespring took an early lead and moved out well ahead of the pack. Beeler reeled in Stinespring at the midway point and thereafter was never challenged, winning by a large margin. Following the race, Beeler's engine was checked by track officials to see that it was within regulations. The Chevrolet engine was figured at 276 cubic inches, well within the 290 cubic inch maximum.

On June 15, 1958, Beeler, driving a Bayliss Garage Studebaker, won the Destruction Derby at Winchester Speedway over five other entries.

On September 27, 1959, Beeler won the jalopy feature at Winchester.

On August 22, 1963, at Eastside, both Beeler and Buddy Stinespring, who finished first and second in the feature, were protested by Bob Hite of Waynesboro who posted the $25 bond to have Beeler's motor checked. Track management posted an equal amount to have Stinespring checked. Just the week before, Stinespring had protested Hite and it was found that his racer carried far more than the maximum limit of 290 cubic inches. On this night, however, both Beeler and Stinespring were determined to be legal.

On May 16, 1964, Charlie Beeler won the 20-lap sportsman feature at Eastside over Lewis Newland of Woodstock, Virginia, and Buddy Stinespring.

Beeler left Lee Stultz in 1964 after both he and Nalley won the track championships for sportsman and modified divisions at Hagerstown Raceway and Winchester. All in all, he had driven three years for Lee Stultz. He came back in later years to race sporadically. He says that he won enough money to make a down payment on his first house through racing.

Beeler was interviewed at the home of Tommy Irwin in Winchester. He laughs frequently about the good old days of racing and still closely follows NASCAR.

Charlie Beeler in 2001.

Al Grinnan

In the late '40s, Al Grinnan was in the Army stationed in Fort McClellan, Alabama. Nearby, there was a dirt track named Hefflin Speedway where he would often attend the races. According to Grinnan, "I was there one night and this car didn't have a driver. Somebody said, 'Who's going to drive it?' I said, 'I can drive!'" He had never raced before.

Grinnan continues, "About halfway through the race, two or three of us got together and I turned that bird over! I'll never forget it [laughs]. After that I drove every Saturday night there for the next two months. I wasn't anything great, but then I got discharged and went back to my hometown of Fredricksburg, Virginia."

According to him, "We and a bunch of guys bought a car. I ran it at a speedway in Alexandria, Virginia. Man, that track had more rocks in it. You'd throw rocks and break windshields!"

Grinnan then became a regular at the Fredricksburg Speedway, a now defunct speedway at the fairgrounds in Fredricksburg, Virginia. Notables who raced there include Wendell Scott, Richard Petty, and Curtis Turner.

Al Grinnan poses with his original coupe in 2001.

Grinnan's Career Grows

Grinnan soon branched out, driving just about anywhere there was a track. He ran often in Wilson, North Carolina, Elizabeth City, North Carolina, Trenton, New Jersey, Pulaski, Virginia, Charlottesville Speedway (Cavalier Speedway), Winchester (Airport) Speedway, Waynesboro (Eastside) Speedway, Lonesome Pine Speedway in Coeburn, Virginia, Devil's Bowl Speedway, Natural Bridge Speedway, Lawrenceville Speedway, South Boston Speedway, Unionville Speedway, and Pilot, Virginia, among others. He won over 400 features and drove briefly in the Grand National Division of NASCAR.

Grinnan is notable in that, unlike most racers described in this book, he continued racing well into the 1970's. His last race was in Elizabeth City, North Carolina for old-timers. He started tenth, and on the first lap after a big wreck, passed most of the other cars and got to the front. He led the whole race, although according to him, "The second place car was faster but I wouldn't let him by. We really put on a show. I won and the whole place went wild! I really had some fun--my last race."

He recalls driving at Pilot Speedway and says, "That thing had a big bulge in the middle of the straightaway, and you had to drive around it. Man, was that something. The announcer was sitting up there with a quart of corn liquor.

All Night Driving

"After winning one night in Fayetteville, North Carolina, the announcer summoned me to the announcer stand saying that I had a phone call. It was Ashton Lewis, owner of Lewis Chevrolet in Norfolk. He said, 'Can you be in Dover, Delaware, in the morning at 9:00 to qualify the car?' It was 11 p.m. then." (As of 2002, Ashton Lewis' son is a driver in the Busch Grand National Series.)

Grinnan said, "'Yeah, I think we can.' I came down and told my wife, 'We've got to be in Dover, Delaware, in the morning.'

"We lit out from there. My wife was driving. I went to sleep. We had to come back to Richmond, go to Norfolk, and go up the Chesapeake Bay Bridge Tunnel. You're talking about a trip! But we made it. I ran third, drove all night to get there."

Grinnan and Patsy Cline

While a regular at Winchester, Grinnan developed a relationship with country singer Patsy Cline, of whom he speaks fondly. He was driving a car that was housed close to her home. According to him, "I used to go up there to race and sit out there on the swing with her. I got to know her real well. Patsy was real nice."

Bounty on Grinnan

Grinnan was such a contender at Wilson, North Carolina, Speedway and won so many races that the promoter put a bounty on him. Veteran driver Sam Ard was also there. The bounty was $350 for anyone who could defeat Grinnan.

According to Grinnan, "Ard approached me before the race and said, 'Let me win tonight and I'll give you the bounty,' which is more money than if I'd won. I said, 'Okay.' Everybody agreed including the owners."

Grinnan continues, "I'm leading the race and Sam's running second. About five laps to go, I dropped a valve and kept on going, slowing down as we went. Sam ran by me. I was missing real bad. Sam won the race. We hadn't said anything about dropping a valve. He gave us the bounty and we didn't tell him 'til two races later. He was hot when he heard that!"

Grinnan and Dale Earnhardt

Grinnan tells a story of racing against the late Dale Earnhardt. He recounts the story at Russell, North Carolina, Speedway where he qualified eighth and Dale Earnhart, at that time a youngster attempting to make his name in NASCAR, qualified sixth. Earnhart won the race with Grinnan finishing second.

Woman Throws Shoes

At Unionville Speedway, outside Orange, Virginia, Grinnan speaks of the sister of Cotton Shiflett, a fellow driver. He says, "She's quite a buzz saw. She used to get on the flagman. One Sunday she became so mad at the flagman she threw her shoes at him."

Grinnan says, "Everywhere we went we had fun." In terms of other drivers, "We were all friends."

Grinnan and Rick Mast

While racing at Natural Bridge Speedway, Grinnan met a young Winston Cup racer, Rick Mast, who was the son of the track owners. Grinnan gave Mast his first driving suit.

Top Dollar for Grinnan

Grinnan's top prize money was $5,000, won at a racetrack in Maine the same weekend in 1974 that fellow driver and friend Gip Gibson of Charlottesville was killed at a track in Saluda, Virginia.

Grinnan Loses His Steering

When asked what was the wildest race of his career, Grinnan speaks of running a track in Maryland for Sonny Hutchins. He says, "I went out to qualify. On the first lap I did well with the best time. The next lap, the steering wheel came off in my hand when I was getting ready to go into turn one. I got on the brakes. I went all the way across the infield and stopped on the backstretch. Didn't hit a thing. Everybody came out and asked me what happened. I just handed them the steering wheel out the window. Somebody forgot to put the nut on the steering wheel."

Selected Events

On July 28, 1956, at Eastside, Grinnan started at the rear of a 12-car field, winning over Tommy Irwin.

On July 20, 1957, at Eastside Grinnan won the 25-lap feature over Tommy Irwin and Lewis Bocock. He also won his heat race.

On July 21, 1957, an extremely hot day in Winchester, only three cars showed up to race in the sportsman class. Al Grinnan was the apparent winner in the 25-lap feature; however, his win was protested. Grinnan then refused to have his car torn down, saying it was, "Just too hot to fool with an overhaul." He was then disqualified.

On August 17, 1958, Al Grinnan won the 25-lap Class B feature at Winchester.

Grinnan was interviewed along with his wife Carolyn in his cozy and well-decorated home outside Mechanicsville, Virginia. His walls are covered with pictures and memories of his long racing career. He's a friendly, fun-loving man who enjoys talking about racing. He currently owns Al's Auto Parts outside of Richmond and is quite active in the business. He often interacts with fellow driver and friend Cal Johnson who lives in nearby Ashland, Virginia.

Al Grinnan poses in front of his wall decorated with racing memorabilia in 2001.

Earl Moran

Earl's Big Lincoln

Another colorful and sometimes controversial figure was service station owner and "pint-sized" driver Earl Moran. Originally from the Verona, Virginia, area, Moran began his racing career at Valley Speedway in Staunton after his discharge from the Marine Corps in 1953. He says, "I didn't have no money so I took a 12-cylinder Lincoln out there. It was a 1941 model. The rollbar I used was a head-

Earl Moran with the checkered flag.

board of a bed and I drove it to the track. It was so big nobody could pass it. I ended up taking second place in my first race."

At Johns Speedway at Craigsville, Virginia, he blocked the track with his large car. Moran was a regular driver at Valley Speedway, Eastside Speedway, Airport (Winchester) Speedway, and Hagerstown, Maryland. He drove frequently in Manassas on an asphalt track. Like Smokey Stover, he was unable to unseat Jimmy Mears, who was often the winner at Manassas.

Moran liked to party. He says, "Whenever we made trips, we'd drink. I guess that's what got me out of racing because I'd rather party than race." His career started in 1953 at Valley Speedway with the Car 35A. Moran says, "I bought a Car #85 and they already had an 85 on the track so I changed it to 35. They had a 35 on the track. Wendell Scott used to always have an A on the end of his number, so I just put an A on the 35."

Moran Burns Alcohol

Moran burned alcohol in his early cars and had a coffee can in the back for an exhaust. Car 306 owner Tommy Campbell says, "The whole rear would light up at night when he let off of it."

Moran says further, "When you back off the gas going into the corners, a little old ball of flame would come out of it."

Earl Learns About Mechanics

Moran eventually put a Plymouth engine in a Crosly body. According to him, "It took me a year to get the handling right, but when I did I won a bunch of races with it." Asked where he obtained his motors, Moran replies, "Anywhere I could."

Moran continues, "I didn't know much about mechanics at the time. If Tommy Campbell would have helped me, I might have won some more. He's told me how many mistakes I've made over the years. I could drive a car but I just couldn't build it exactly right."

Tommy Campbell continues, "Smokey Stover used to get so mad at me. I'd go over and work on Earl's car. He'd say, 'What the hell are you doing? You work more on his damn car than mine.'"

Earl Moran won two championships at Winchester and one at Hagerstown, even though in that particular year he only won one race, consistently finishing high.

Winchester Fans

Moran remembers that the fans at Winchester Speedway were hostile to the Staunton racers. He felt that Eastside fans welcomed the Winchester drivers. This is refuted by Winchester drivers.

Moran and Wendell Scott

Moran speaks with respect of the late Wendell Scott. "Scott in those days never had much of a car, but he carried a bucket under his radiator," he says. "I asked him about it. He told me it was because he didn't want to drop water on the track." Later Moran learned that the can was for the overflow. "When you'd run down the straightaway, it would pick up the water. When you let off, it would flush it back out."

Moran remembers an instance with Scott. "It was a muggy night at Eastside and Scott wore white pants and a white T-shirt. He laid down on the ground and was working. At least they were white sometime or another. He got his boys to get towels that were just as dirty as his shirt, and hollered, 'Fan me, boys. Fan me. Your daddy's hot.'"

Moran continues, "Scott was a good driver. He was a comical person. We were at Devil's Bowl one time and he spun a car around and around while a clown walked in the middle. I couldn't believe it."

Asthma and Shoulder Harnesses

Moran was known as one of the first drivers who wore a handkerchief across his face to protect himself from the dust and dirt. Bobby Campbell says, "I think they threatened him with ugly pollution and that's why he did it."

Moran says that he suffered from asthma and that was the reason for the handkerchief.

Moran detested shoulder harnesses and after these became mandated, he had shoulder harnesses sewn to his shirt, which gave the illusion of his being secured in the vehicle; however, he did not attach the harness. Moran continues, "I couldn't stand being cramped up. I think about that now since Earnhardt was killed. I had a handle built in every car on the floorboard, and when I lost it and felt I was going to flip, I'd just duck down as far as I could and get a hold of that handle and not let it go."

Moran Injured

Moran tells the story of a harrowing accident at Hagerstown. "I got a concussion one time," he begins. "My safety belt broke at Hagerstown in 1968. I was driving two cars that day and I'd fired the sportsman driver because he wouldn't get off the damn pinball machine at my station and help me load it. So I told him to stay there and just run the damn station. I took both cars up there to Hagerstown.

"I passed a couple of cars going into the corner and all of a sudden the track was blocked. And when I caught him I flipped over the top and landed on the wheels. The safety belt broke. It wasn't hooked up right.

"I was knocked woozy. They took me to the hospital. I tried to talk the attendants into taking me back to the track. Eventually, this mechanic brought me back to the track. I sat in a pickup truck and went to sleep. I didn't know that was a bad sign with regard to a head injury. So when it was time for the race to start and they couldn't get me awake, they took me back to the hospital where I woke up the next day with nobody around, not knowing where I was."

Moran Visits Stover

Moran speaks of visiting his friend Smokey Stover in the hospital after his injuries at Hagerstown in 1968.

"I went to visit Smokey in the hospital and noticed that his mouth seemed to be burnt shut. He was so swollen I couldn't see his ears. I did see that one ear was almost completely burned off. He did come back in pretty good shape as far as looks were concerned, although."

Moran at Zion's Crossroads

Moran was especially fond of the track known as Hilltop at Zion's Crossroads, Virginia, which according to him was less than a quarter of a mile long. Moran continues, "When you stuck your foot in the gas, you just held it there till the race ended. You kept the car sideways the whole damn race."

Both Moran and Tommy Campbell remember with humor Cal Johnson's rear bumper on #40, which was secured with coiled springs to absorb any blows.

Moran and Tommy Campbell also say that some drivers welded steel on the side of their cars for the sole purpose of puncturing other drivers' tires.

Moran on Junior Bowers

Moran speaks with sadness of the late Junior Bowers, saying he was "a nice guy." Moran says that he helped build Bowers' first car.

Bowers had two cars. One was #1/2 and the other #1/3. The #1/3 had a 348 cubic Chevrolet engine, and Moran felt it was too much of a motor for Bowers to drive. He later changed the number 1/3 to 1/2 and was killed in that car.

Moran was in the race the day of Bowers' accident and describes what happened. "I rode the straightaway behind Junior," he says. "He went over another driver's tire and he just flipped and flipped and flipped, maybe five or six times."

Moran jumped out of his car and ran to Bowers' aid. "He rolled his eyes at me and didn't say anything." According to Moran, Bowers died of pneumonia ten days later; he goes onto say that for a while Bowers' insurance company didn't want to pay the Bowers' family.

Moran says that Bowers' car was flipping in the air while other cars went beneath and continues, "Stuff was flying off his car. He was in first and I was in second. I was thinking about letting him win because I was winning all the races right then. I had just gotten through the pack. Junior wrecked trying to pass some lapped cars."

Selected Events

On Monday, September 18, 1961, the Waynesboro newspaper, The News Virginian, had this account of Earl Moran winning race:

Earl Moran, the pint-sized stock car racer from Staunton, proved that his size is nothing to sneeze at Saturday night when he piloted the small modified racer bearing the number 35A to a win at the main feature at Eastside Speedway.

The end of the main 75-lap feature had more than 900 fans on their feet cheering. Moran took the lead in the feature in the 35th lap from crowd-favorite Smokey Stover, also of Staunton. At the end of the feature, Stover was in third place, the second slot being held by Greenville's Lewis Bocock.

The gold cup went to Moran for his winning efforts. The cup was just icing on the cake for the driver and provided a proper finish to a well-driven race.

On September 1, 1957, Earl Moran won the 20-lap amateur feature at Eastside over Charlie Sipe and Buddy Stinespring.

On June 27, 1959, Earl Moran won the 20-lap amateur feature at Eastside, winning over Jackie Dennison and Buddy Stinespring.

In the inaugural race of the 1962 season at Eastside on April 21, 1962, Earl Moran beat Bill Nalley to win the 25-lap modified feature.

On April 28, 1962, Moran won the 25-lap modified feature at Eastside, finishing only inches ahead of Bill Nalley. Nalley had led for most of the race, but was overtaken by Moran with only a few laps remaining.

In May 1962, Devil's Bowl Speedway ran three 20-lap sections of a Memorial Day Sweepstakes feature. The winner would be the driver who consistently finished highest in the three races. Although Smokey Stover won two of the three 20-lap sections, it was Earl Moran's consistency in all three sections that made him the overall winner.

On August 25, 1962, Moran won the 25-lap modified feature at Eastside over Smokey Stover and Buddy Stinespring who was driving Lewis Bocock's #50 car.

On June 6, 1964, Moran won the 35-lap modified feature race at Eastside, winning over Winchester's Chuck Brannon, who had battled Moran throughout the race.

On June 29, 1959, Earl Moran won the sportsman feature at Winchester, which required the cars to make two pit stops with a four-tire change on each stop. It took the crews an average of two laps to change all four tires. As the track was 1/3 of a mile in length, and lap speed was approximately 20 seconds, that meant changing four wheels in 40 seconds. At that time, such a task was relatively Herculean. In addition, the crews had to work in 95-degree temperatures that day.

On August 3, 1962, Earl Moran won the first night race ever at Winchester in the modified feature.

On May 25, 1960, Moran won his third straight feature in the sportsman division at Devil's Bowl.

Rough Driving

Moran last raced in 1970 at Natural Bridge in a late model car. Moran was known as a very aggressive driver and says, "Back in those days, there was no protected groove. I used to call it blocking. If I could catch a car, we were going by him or we were going out the fence." He goes on to say, "Smokey Stover would put you in a situation where you were going to hit the wall or hit him."

Moran on Nalley

Moran speaks of Bill Nalley. "Nalley was the best cowboy of all of us. Between Lee Stultz and Bill Nalley, they always came back to win races."

Earl is still a very colorful, humorous, and animated man. He is not one to mince words. He was interviewed in the home of Tommy Campbell. He currently manages the Moose Lodge at Verona, Virginia, and retains much of his fun-loving and maverick demeanor.

Earl Moran in 2001.

Red Ninninger

Red Ninninger began racing full time in 1951, although he had dabbled in racing starting in 1948, not long after he had been discharged from the Navy. Originally from the Fincastle, Virginia, area near Roanoke, he raced at Starkey Speedway outside of Roanoke, Virginia, and at the Fincastle and Covington, Virginia Fairgrounds, where only a few races were held. He also remembers racing in the early days at Victory Stadium in Roanoke.

Red enlisted in the Navy at the age of seventeen and served during World War II in anti-submarine warfare. Upon his discharge from the Navy, he was an automobile mechanic at a Hudson dealership in the Roanoke area. He received an offer he couldn't refuse and moved to Brunswick, Maryland, where he continued to work on cars. It was at this point that he began serious involvement in racing.

Ninninger remembers racing at St. Thomas, Pennsylvania, and Fort Ashby, West Virginia, Langhorn, Pennsylvania, Lincoln, Pennsylvania, Winchester, Eastside, Mountain Top, and Unionville raceways. He never raced at Devil's Bowl; however, he did accompany Bill Nalley there to see Nalley race.

For seven years during the 50's, Red drove a '34 Ford Coupe with a 312 Mercury engine. The car was owned by Richard Bonebrake.

The "Flying Redhead"

Red was often referred to as the "Flying Redhead."

Red Ninninger wins one in the early days at Winchester.

He considered his home track to be Winchester. He cannot recall how many features he won. According to him, "We didn't keep records back then. I didn't even put the dates on the old pictures."

Red won the 1969 Point Championship for late model cars at Winchester.

September 22, 1968

An infamous day was September 22, 1968. This was the day that Smokey Stover was severely burned in a sprint car accident at Hagerstown. Red also was injured that day and spent the night in the hospital. He recounts what happened. "Smokey Stover, Johnny Crum, and me ended up in the hospital at Hagerstown," he says. "I had a head injury. Gerald Chamberlain's axle broke in front of me and I went over the fence. I can still see that fence and guardrail. It barrel-rolled and came back on its top. I didn't know what was going on. I had my eyes closed. The next day at the hospital I was discharged. When I was leaving the hospital, I saw Smokey Stover's wife (Ruby). At the time I didn't know about Smokey's wreck. His wife said, 'He's burned bad.' I felt like it was time to quit racing."

Red Flies in the Trees

In 1969, this author saw Ninninger catapult off the third turn guardrail at Hagerstown and vault through the tops of trees. Ninninger remembers this happening. "I remember seeing the tops of the trees. I landed in them. That's what saved me. It cushioned my car. We pulled leaves and limbs out of that thing for the next three weeks!"

Tragedy

Ninninger had a friend by the name of Red Matthews who raced at Winchester but mostly at Maryland tracks. Ninninger relates the tragic events that led to Matthews' death in 1963 at Condon Speedway near Fredrick, Maryland. "He had come to the track late. He started at the end of the field in a heat. On the second lap, he hit something and flipped and flipped and flipped. Red came out of the driver's window as if he was diving off a diving board. He went as high as the light pole with his hands held straight up, and came down and landed on his belly. He laid in the hospital for a month and died of pneumonia."

Just a week or so before, Ninninger had seen Matthews in a rather severe accident at Winchester. Ninninger continues, "He was leading the feature and slipped coming off the fourth turn. The steering gear broke loose from the frame. He went out of the fence and he really tore it up."

Mom Asks Him to Quit

Ninninger's mother never liked his racing. After Red Matthews was killed, that tragedy stuck in her mind. Ninninger continues, "I came home. My mother was in bed sick. She asked me to make her a promise to stop racing until she died. What are you going to do? I told her okay. So I did. I didn't race for a year or so, and then she passed away. I started racing again and raced until 1987, but my last full season of racing was 1985."

Red on Racing

Red was often referred to by other drivers as a "courteous driver." He also was described as "cautious." Red continues, "Being cautious pays off; chargers win races, but overall they lose more than they win."

Ninninger felt the relationship in the pits among the crews and drivers was like a "family affair." He says, "Ninety percent of these men regret seeing a fellow driver wreck his car. They realize the money and the expense involved," said Red.

Red and Patsy Cline

Red talks of the early days at Winchester and notes the day that Patsy Cline, the famous country singer, came to the racetrack. Red continues, "I knew this guy who was an official at the racetrack. Patsy was there to sing a song and she had to go up this ladder to get to the judge's stand to sing. Patsy's going up the ladder and this guy's behind her. He said, 'Go on, Patsy, I'll be right behind you.' She said, 'Yeah, and I'll piss on you, too.'"

Red said, "I never will forget that! It startled me. I wasn't used to hearing a woman talk like that. She didn't care what she said, but that's the very words she said."

Red and the Flagman

Red also remembers with some consternation the fact that he almost hit flagman Charlie Armel at Winchester on several occasions. Back then, the flagmen were on the track with the racecars. There was no flag stand. Armel was known as a risk-taker and was somewhat dramatic and unpredictable. According to Ninninger, "You never knew where to look for him."

Al Gore Hypes Red

On August 17, 1962, The Waynesboro News Virginian had this article:

Promoter Says Ninninger, Nalley Will Enter Races

What a race the modified feature of the Eastside Speedway on Saturday night is shaping up to be!

One of Maryland's top stock car drivers has informed promoter Al Gore he will be present to give local stock car racing fans a top-notch driving exhibition.

The Maryland driver who will be here is Red Ninninger. The fast driving Ninninger hails from Brunswick, Maryland.

The appearance of Ninninger and Bill Nalley will make the modified feature a rip-roaring affair. They take the backseat to no one and will give Smokey Stover, Earl Moran, Lewis Bocock, Buddy Stinespring, and other regular modified drivers a run for their money.

In the race that night, Red nosed out Buddy Stinespring in the modified heat; however, in the feature, his car developed a miss and was out of contention early.

RED AND ROY CLASH

Red laughs when he speaks of an incident at Winchester that occurred during the late 50's. "I'd won quite a few races and everyone had it in for me," he says. "Roy Neff put a huge bumper on his Car P38, and I'd heard through the grapevine he was going to get me. That is, put me out of the race. His driver in the P38 was Robert Peer. In the race, I decided to pass Peer but he wouldn't let me, so every time I went into the corner I'd hit that bumper and hit it again. About the fifth time I hit it, I bent it into his tire and busted the tire. I wasn't trying to do that, but it happened. The next time I came around, Neff had a huge rock and threw it at me! Later we became good friends."

RED ON FIRE AND GREEN

Red says he always had a fear of fire while racing and feels lucky that he was never involved in a fiery crash. He also was somewhat superstitious regarding the color green, following an old Southern racing superstition that green around a racetrack signifies "bad luck."

SELECTED EVENTS

On May 13, 1956, 1,800 fans at Winchester saw Red Ninninger win the amateur feature over Jackie Denison.

On July 29, 1956, Ninninger won the mid-season trophy feature at Winchester Speedway over Jimmy Aleshire and Robert Peer.

On September 3, 1956, Red Ninninger earned an extra $100 by winning the amateur feature at Winchester.

On August 12, 1956, Ninninger won the sportsman feature at Winchester over Shorty Bowers.

On September 9, 1956, at Winchester, Ninninger intentionally rammed the wall rather than take a chance on hitting several cars that had wrecked and the flagman who was trying to stop traffic.

On July 29, 1962, Ninninger, driving Chuck Brannon's car, won the sportsman feature race at Winchester after his own car had blown an engine during a heat. Bill Nalley was second, followed by Jackie Clore in third place. Ninninger had won the heat with a steaming engine, which blew before the feature, and thus drove Brannon's car.

In June 1958, Red Ninninger was involved in an end-over-end crash at Winchester. At the time he thought he wasn't injured; however, he later learned that he had suffered a fractured leg just below the knee joint. He had walked around for a few days with a broken leg and did not know it. After it was diagnosed, he missed several weeks of racing.

On June 10, 1971, Red started at the rear of the track at the 50-Lap Coca-Cola Trophy Race at Winchester. By the 35th lap he was in second place, and on the 44th lap he took over, winning the race.

Red is still involved in racing. He does mechanical work on his son's and grandson's cars. Recently at Winchester, he took his grandson's car for some hot laps at Winchester. He was told he was turning laps in some 18 seconds, which amounted to a 95 mph average, much to the surprise of track personnel and Red.

Red and his wife Shirley have three children and numerous grandchildren. He acknowledges that this ongoing commitment to racing can be consuming, but continues to this day, supporting his son and grandson who are actively involved in racing as of 2002.

Red was interviewed in his camping trailer parked next to his sister's home near Fincastle, Virginia, where he was visiting relatives. He is a friendly, gracious, and gentlemanly individual who seems justifiably proud of his accomplishments and racing career.

Red Ninninger in 2001.

Ray Dovel

Ray Dovel raced for approximately thirty years throughout the Shenandoah Valley and beyond. He began in the sportsman division in the early 50's, graduated to sprint cars in the mid-60's, and finished his career in 1980 driving late model cars.

Dovel's First Race

Dovel's first race was in 1950 at Keezletown, also known as Massanutten Speedway. He was 16 years old at the time, driving a car for Charlie May who owned a garage outside of Shenandoah, Virginia. Dovel won his first race driving a 1949 Mercury.

Later he drove the Car J5 owned by Granville Batten of Luray. In 1965 he took over the Lee Stultz S3 ride from Bill Nalley and raced until the late 1970's with Stultz.

Dovel on Lee Stultz

About Lee Stultz, Dovel says, "Stultz was a great man to drive for. You couldn't ask for a better guy. He never got excited, no matter what happened. One night I totaled the car at Winchester and won with the same car the next night at Hagerstown.

"I wiped it out. They had to cut the whole front off. They worked all night till the next evening, just got to Hagerstown in time for the show, and won the race. The car had even caught fire and they had to rewire the car."

A Full-Time Commitment

Dovel talks of his nearly full-time commitment to racing throughout the 50's, 60's, and 70's. He often raced on Wednesday, Friday, and Saturday nights and Sunday afternoons. During the week, there was often an additional trip to Winchester to consult with Lee Stultz regarding repairs to the car. During the winter, he often went on Sundays to the garage in Winchester.

Dovel's favorite tracks were Hagerstown, Winchester, and Eastside; however, he speaks fondly of the Lawrenceville, Virginia, track, the favorite track of several other racers at the time because of the high banking and soft clay. According to Dovel, "Man, that was a real track."

Near Riot at Winchester

On June 21, 1959, Dovel was involved in a spectacular crash at Winchester which many felt was caused by Bill Nalley. The Winchester Star has this account:

Speedway Feud Flares

The stock car fans at Winchester Airport Speedway yesterday had ringside seats to what almost developed into the fight of the year.

It became so rugged that the modified feature was halted at the end of seven laps and the money added onto next week's purse for the same event.

Already in a temper over earlier incidents, the crew of Ray Dovel's car flew out of control when it rammed onto the top of the fence in front of the grandstand and tore out 30-feet of post and boards. When it couldn't ride the fence anymore, Dovel's car started a spectacular flip down the track but didn't injure the driver.

It did start something worse, though, as the Dovel crew blamed the wreck on Brunswick Bill Nalley and began hurling rocks and 2x4's at his S3 when it came around for the next lap.

Flagman Charlie Armel stopped Nalley at the finish line, but it nearly took the National Guard to halt Dovel's crew and friends from tearing up the Marylander as well as his car. It's just as well the mob didn't reach S3 because Nalley's friends had piled onto the track by that time and were waiting for them.

After that display of violent temper, the track management decided to call it off and wait a week for tempers to cool down.

Most of the spectators wanted to see the finish of the race, but it would have been too dangerous to let Nalley run any further. What may happen next Sunday is anybody's guess.

It was one of those accidents when even the closest fan would have a hard time telling if Nalley's car actually hit the other, but the black flag was out indicating that the collision was Nalley's fault.

When interviewed, Dovel was asked about this controversial day. He replied, "I don't remember much about it. I remember the crowd got caught up in it more than the drivers. The people with the J5 car I was driving for got caught up in it more than I did. It was just a racing accident. There was no bad blood between Bill Nalley and me. It was a heck of a wreck, though, I end-over-ended down the track and busted the roll cage."

Ray is Injured

When asked about injuries, Dovel says that he was driving a sprint car at Hagerstown, got airborne, left the track, and when he landed, broke his left leg in two places. While he couldn't drive, Jackie Denison and Ray Tilley drove the S3 car.

On June 28, 1958, at Eastside, Dovel flipped his car in the first turn, spun in the air, and crashed into a fence. He was relatively uninjured, requiring only five stitches; however, track personnel deemed it one of the worst flips in the history of the track.

Just one month later, Dovel overshot the number one turn at Eastside again when his steering mechanism snapped. The car he was driving was almost completely demolished when it dropped off the side of the track and rolled over, slamming viciously into a light pole. The track was without lights for twenty minutes. With five stitches above his eye barely healed from his last crack up a month earlier, he required additional facial stitches and treatment for a broken nose. He returned the following week to race at Eastside.

Driving a Racecar

Ray was asked to describe how best to drive a modified or sprint car around a track like Eastside. He replied, "If the track's in good shape, you can almost run the car flat out with its good clay at Eastside.

"You drive the car deep in the corner in the lower part of the track 'til you feel the car settle in, and you get out of it for just a minute. And as the car comes around, you gas it and go through the turn to the straightaway wide open. When you set it in to start sliding, you may tap on the brake. I'd often use the power of the car to bring the car back around.

"Depending on the moisture and where it was on the track would often dictate what line you took. At Hagerstown in the evening, the moisture would be at the top. I ran the high line near the fence.

"Driving late models was very different. It was all together different. The car had a different feel. It was a heavier car with a wider wheelbase. You couldn't sling it around like a sprint car. With a sprint car, you could just run off of power. You point it and it would go there."

THE TRIPLE NICKEL

Dovel also drove the Car 555 for Chuck Dedrick of Waynesboro. He says, "The car was spotless. He hated us to take it on the track because it was so clean."

MOST EXCITING WIN

When asked to describe his most exciting win, he recalls a sprint car race at Hagerstown, a Johnny Roberts Memorial Race. He ran the last 12 laps door-to-door with Johnny Crum and won by a half car length. When he came around to take the checkered flag, his right tire was flat.

AIR WINGS

Dovel continues, "When I took over the S3 in 1965, that was the only car without an air scoop on top. From then on, everyone had an air scoop. You couldn't drive those things without having it. It was a whole different feel if you didn't. You couldn't imagine it. The down force of the car changed it completely. You couldn't drive it deep in the corner and you couldn't set it in.

"The air wing had to be differently set up for different tracks. One time we went to Hagerstown with the Winchester wing set up. I started going down the front stretch and both front wheels came off the ground!"

CONTROVERSY

Dovel was asked about the frequent controversies that occurred at the track. He replied, "I tried not to get caught up in the controversy. I just concentrated on driving. When people got involved in fighting and such, I just got out of there."

When asked if he was protested a great deal, he replied, "Not a lot. They'd already torn down Nalley so much they didn't think it would do any good."

DOVEL ON FELLOW DRIVERS

Dovel remembers fondly many members of the racing fraternity. He was asked to give his reactions to the following drivers:

Lewis Bocock - "Nice guy, nice to talk to, good racer."

Buddy Stinespring - "One of a kind, never got excited, and always had good equipment."

The Campbell brothers, owners of Car 306 - "They always had really good equipment. They were nice guys, never had any trouble with them."

Dick Pappy Hansberger - "I raced with him a long time. He'd show up with his big family at the racetrack. I remember Pappy. He was always nice to me."

Jackie Clore - "Real good person. I really liked him. He was smooth. One of the first alcohol burners."

Al Grinnan - "He's a real card. A good racer."

Clem Lamaster - "A good driver. The wreck that hurt him didn't seem like it would hurt him. They gave him a tracheotomy at the track that night. We didn't think he was going to live."

When asked to remember his stiffest competition, he replied, "With sprint cars it was Mitch Smith. He'd run up against the fence all night. You'd think he'd tear the fence down, but he kept his rpm's up and would win a lot of races." He also mentions Donny Campbell, Bill Nalley, Sam Nalley, Tommy Bear, and Denny Bonebrake as good drivers.

Turning Down NASCAR

Ray had the opportunity to drive in what was then called the NASCAR Sportsman Division and is now called the Busch Grand National Division. He had been contacted by Tom Pistone, an ex-driver who owned a car. Ray declined the opportunity, saying, "I was doing good and enjoying what I was doing so I didn't go." He says he has no regrets.

Too Hot and Dry

On August 18, 1957, Dovel won the sportsman feature at Winchester; however, only four cars were entered in the feature race. It was an extremely hot day and only 750 spectators braved the heat. The Winchester Star had this account:

Track owner Kermit Batt said, "It's too hot and too dry." The prolonged drought had made it impossible to control the dust on the 1/3-mile oval.

Most $

The most Dovel claims he won in a race was $2,000 in a sprint car race at Hagerstown in the late 70's.

During his career, Dovel won three Winchester 200 races. He doesn't know how many features he won, but guesses it was well over 100. He also won track championships but cannot remember how many.

Dovel's Last Race

Dovel's last race was in October 1980, when he drove a late model car in the Winchester 200. In this race, Dovel ran second to Denny Bonebrake for much of the race and has this account about what happened next. "It was the latter part of the second 100 laps that I passed him," he says. "I'd followed him the first 100 laps or so, and he never made a mistake. It was late in the race with about 25 laps to go and he got in traffic. He went down low under some lapped cars, and that left the outside open. I knew the cars were so equal and I knew the line he ran. So I went high and ran his line the rest of the race and won. He followed me and I was sure not to make a mistake. I think we lapped about every other car there."

Dovel's Garage

Ray Dovel in 2002.

Throughout his racing career, Dovel owned a garage, which he still operates outside Shenandoah, Virginia. He's been in this business 37 years. At one time he sold cars and had a gas station as well as a grocery store on the property. Later, in the late 70's when he owned his own racer, he serviced the car at his garage.

Ray Retires

When asked why he retired from racing, Dovel replied, "I'd gotten married for the second time and I had a new baby girl, plus I was getting some age on me. I'd raced 30 years and it was time to quit." He has two children by his first marriage.

Dovel no longer attends races at the local tracks. "I went to Eastside on only one occasion," he says. "I knew that if I went back that I'd get involved. Oh, I still miss it," he says with lament.

Ray Dovel was interviewed in the lounge of his garage outside Shenandoah, Virginia. He is a somewhat low-key and friendly man who was introspective throughout the interview. What was striking to the author is the affection and respect he shows for his fellow drivers.

Clem Lamaster

Clem Lamaster started racing in 1952 at a three-eighths mile sand track in Georgetown, Delaware. In 1953 and 1954, he began racing in earnest. In 1954 and 1955, he was the promoter at Hagerstown Raceway in addition to having his own racecar.

Lamaster says his favorite tracks were Hagerstown and Eastside. He doesn't know how many features he won; however, he does know he won 27 features in one year.

In 1954, racing with teammate Shorty Bowers, he won a 300-lap race at Winchester. When talking about Shorty he says, "I got along well with him, but he was a cocky little devil."

The drivers he respected the most were Bill Nalley, Tommy Irwin, Red Ninninger, and Smokey Stover.

In the early 60's, Lamaster was voted "Most Popular Driver" at Hagerstown. While he is unsure of the exact year, he says, "I'm more proud of that trophy than all the rest."

He says that during his racing career, he rolled over "three or four times." He describes what it's like to roll over in a race by saying, "When you're up in the air, you just pray."

Lamaster Injured

On the night of April 16, 1965, Lamaster, driving in the modified division, was injured in a race at Winchester. The injuries resulted in his being in a coma for four weeks in a hospital in Fairfax, Virginia. This accident ended his racing career. Lamaster still has speech and equilibrium problems, and has since been superstitious of the 16th day of each month.

Lamaster describes what happened. "Bobby Burns drove into the side of my car. My back wheel walked over his front wheel, and I flew up in the air and landed on all four wheels at the same time. My head hit the top of the car and bruised my brain-

Clem Lamaster poses with his modified racer in April 1965 at Hagerstown Raceway. One week later, he was to suffer near-fatal injuries in a crash at Winchester.

stem. The seat had no springs. It was just bolted to the frame. The impact sent all the energy up my spine."

Lamaster's wife and four children were at the track. His wife, Ollie "Doll," describes her experience. "I didn't see it happen. We'd gotten our seats and some fans for another driver came in and sat down behind us. I knew that would upset my son, so I took them all the way to the top of the grandstand. When the accident happened, everybody stood up. I had a child in my lap and I didn't see it. When it happened, I went straight to the hospital with Clem and friends."

Lamaster was taken to the Winchester Hospital and then transferred to Fairfax. Lamaster describes further his recuperation. "I came home in six weeks. I couldn't speak, just whisper. I thought we were going to Hagerstown where we used to live instead of Winchester where we lived at that time. I've never been 100 percent back."

LAMASTER OPERATES WINCHESTER SPEEDWAY

Three years later, Lamaster was promoting races at Winchester Speedway and continued to do so until 1982. He says when he started promoting, approximately 300 to 400 fans were in attendance at any given event. Under his leadership, one race attracted 3,400 fans. He says the track was averaging 1,500 fans per night when he retired.

He reports that the job of being a track promoter is a tough one. He says, "There were a lot of headaches. I sometimes dreaded to see Saturdays or Sundays come. You'd have to walk the line between the fans and the drivers. No matter how nice you are to both sides, there is always someone who is unhappy."

At Hagerstown in the mid-50's, Lamaster, who was the promoter, says the gate was split 50/50 with the drivers. With an average crowd of approximately 400 people at the time, it wasn't much money. He admits that money was made from concessions, which was directed by his wife. He says that oftentimes, the gate receipts would not meet expenses and, if there were a guaranteed purse, they sometimes could not meet it. Lamaster then had to pay drivers out of his own pocket.

At Winchester, he says, new red clay was brought in every year from a location near Stephens City, Virginia. Lamaster says this was "the best clay." He also got red clay from Perry's Quarry in Berryville, Virginia. The cost of this per year? Approximately $1,500. Lamaster guesses that it would cost approximately $5,000 per year now to put clay on a track.

He says the best clay at a racetrack he ever experienced was at Eastside, and referred to it as "swamp clay." According to him, "You just stick on it."

Lamaster owned a mobile home sales business outside Winchester. He leased Winchester Speedway from the two owners known as Dixon and Snyder. The owners got a percentage of the gate.

In the early 70's, Lamaster tore down the old grandstand on the front stretch at Winchester, changed the front stretch to the backstretch, and built a new concrete grandstand on the new front stretch. This configuration continues to this day.

While, according to Lamaster, "The old grandstand was rickety," (an opinion shared by the personal experience of this author), "the thing was well built by Kermit Batt and we had a hard time tearing it down."

Lamaster describes the work that was involved in preparing for a Saturday night race at Winchester. He said that work started Friday night with watering the track until 1:00 or 2:00 Saturday morning. There was a local pond and well from which Lamaster obtained the water to fill his 2,000-gallon tanks mounted on flatbed trucks. He estimates that approximately 78,000 gallons of water was applied to his one-third mile track for one race. He goes on to say, "You didn't want any dust."

Clem was a strict taskmaster at the track. He knew that fans would get antsy if there were a great deal of time between races. Therefore, he says, "We didn't fool around getting wrecked cars off the track. We gave them five minutes to get it cleared up. If they didn't, you'd hear somebody say, 'Here comes Clem. You'd better move it.'" Lamaster motored around the track on a four-wheeler.

Clem also set a curfew of 12:00 a.m. for the races to conclude. This curfew was never broken.

Lamaster provided security at Winchester by hiring

a private company because he could not convince the local sheriff's department to provide deputies on a regular basis. He often hired off-duty game wardens.

At the track, Lamaster was all business and did not tolerate violence. He was known to bar drivers from racing at Winchester because of fighting. He notes that he barred Buddy Armel for the bulk of a season because of fighting. According to him, "We're friends now."

In talking further about being a promoter, Lamaster says, "When you're a promoter, you pray for rain sometimes and you pray for it not to rain sometimes."

When asked to explain, he says, "When you're paying a $3,000 purse and have about 1,500 people in the stands and it's raining all around the speedway, which has kept the crowd down, but not raining there, you're at the mercy of the weather and you're going to have to pay that $3,000 regardless."

Lamaster remembers rather fondly how during the era of the 50's and 60's, fans would bake cakes with their favorite drivers' car on them and present them at the track.

Lamaster on Stultz

Lamaster speaks affectionately of Lee Stultz, owner of the Bill Nalley and Charlie Beeler cars, noting that Stultz was nicknamed "Noodle." Lamaster continues, "He was my buddy. A lot of people didn't like him because he won all the time, but he was one of the best mechanics ever and made a lot of money. His secret? He had to have everything perfect." Lamaster was an honorary pallbearer at Stultz's funeral.

Protests

During his racing career, Lamaster says that he was protested often and was found to be legal on every occasion. He says this happened quite often when he raced at Chambersburg, Pennsylvania. He notes he won track championships at Winchester, Hagerstown, and Chambersburg.

Batt Distributes His Purse

In the early days at Winchester Speedway, Lamaster describes how then-owner Kermit Batt would distribute the winnings for the day. Lamaster continues, "There used to be a tree next to the judge's stand in the infield near the front stretch. Kermit had built seats around the tree. When it came time to payoff, the drivers would sit around the seats. Batt would get in the middle and point at drivers saying, 'What did you do?' One would say, 'Ran second.' Batt would reply, 'Five bucks. What did you do?' Another said, 'I won.' 'Here's ten bucks. What did you do?' 'Sixth place.' 'Four dollars.' That's how he did it. Us drivers would sit around and wait for money, and he'd arbitrarily decide."

The most money ever won by Lamaster was $450, which he split with Shorty Bowers, when they won the 300-Lap Pair Race in 1954 at Winchester.

Lamaster, Patsy Cline, and Kuda Bux

Lamaster remembers Patsy Cline, who would sing at the speedway and also appeared at his mobile home sales lot in promotions.

While his memory is somewhat vague in this regard, Lamaster remembers paying Kuda Bux $100 to appear at Winchester Speedway. He admits that he never understood how Kuda Bux was able to drive the track blindfolded.

Going to Eastside

Lamaster's wife notes that Clem hated to be late. He would often depart Winchester at 3:30 p.m. to arrive at Waynesboro for the races that started at 8:00 p.m. One must remember, however, that there were no interstates at that time and towing the vehicle from Winchester to Waynesboro would take some two and a half to three hours. The fact that Clem wanted to have his pick of the pit areas is one of the reasons he wanted to leave early.

His wife, however, suspects that. "I think they did more racing on the highway going to the races than they did on the tracks!"

The Flying Rebel

Lamaster was oftentimes known as the "Flying Rebel" during his racing career. In August 1964, he won a modified feature at Winchester, setting the record for the 25-lap feature at 8 minutes, 14.2 seconds.

Lamaster made quite a stir during the 1963 season at Eastside. He'd often duel with Smokey Stover and whether or not he would appear at Eastside was often a topic of discussion and anticipation among local fans. Newspaper articles often speculated whether or not Lamaster would show, and the battles between him and Stover were embellished, obviously to draw a crowd.

On June 10, 1963, The News Virginian had the following account of a feature race that had taken place two days earlier:

Lamaster Proves Speed in Whipping Staunton Stover in Feature Race

The reign of Staunton's Smokey Stover came to a jolting halt Saturday night at Eastside Speedway when his modified Car 306 failed to match the speed of his top threat this year.

That threat (the man who has whipped him in consecutive weeks at Winchester's Airport Speedway) is Clem Lamaster of the Apple Capital (Winchester).

Although Stover's experience kept him within short yardage of the Winchester speedster in the turns, 306 couldn't make up for the distance lost on the straight stretches. The other big threat, Bill Nalley of Winchester, blew the motor in his S3 in the first heat.

In Saturday's top race, Lamaster won simply by getting the jump on Stover and making his lead stick. He was almost caught time after time by the Staunton driver, but averted any lost ground when reaching the stretches. Stover came close to passing on the 30th lap, but was in too tight and spun sideways long enough to lose all the ground he gained. Running behind Stover when the checkerboard silk dropped was Lewis Bocock of Greenville in Car 500. Earl Moran in Car 35A was 4th to give the Staunton area crowd another thrill.

This win was especially meaningful for Lamaster considering just the night before at a feature race in Winchester, he was involved in a fairly serious accident. All day Saturday--the day of the Eastside race--Lamaster and his crew installed a new axle, motor mounts, and rear end.

Selected Events

On July 27, 1963, Lamaster ran second to Stover for slightly more than half of the 50-lap modified trophy race and then slipped past him to win handedly at Eastside.

On August 24, 1963, Lamaster won his third straight trophy race at Eastside, plus an extra $100 purse for driving a Ford-powered car to victory in the 50-lap modified feature.

Excerpts from this victory are found in The News Virginian:

More than 2,000 race fans were on hand for Saturday night's Baugher Chevrolet Trophy Races - the top crowd of the season.

Driving a flawless race, Lamaster put his newly rebuilt number 12 car in front of the pack in the fifth lap of the 50-lap feature race. And for the next 45 laps there was little doubt as to who would carry home the trophy and top honors of the evening.

Lamaster attributes Saturday's win to a new body - still unpainted which he installed on his car prior to the race. The new body puts the major portion of its weight on the rear end of the car and according to Lamaster, "halts its spinning in the dirt."
In this race, Bill Nalley finished second, followed by Smokey Stover in third, Earl Moran in fourth, and Lewis Bocock in fifth.

As the 1964 season opened at Eastside, once again there was speculation regarding Lamaster and his racing there. The following article occurred in the Saturday, April 25, 1964, edition of The News Virginian the day of the second race of the '64 season:

Lamaster's Return Is Uncertain

Heading into the second Saturday night of the season at Eastside's stock car oval, the top question among area fans is, "Will Clem Lamaster run?"

Sporting a $4,000 motor in his specially constructed modified racer, the Winchester ace was in an accident last Saturday night which caused $400 damage to his car. The damage wasn't as important to Lamaster as the problem of whether he could make enough money on this track to risk such an expensive motor and the necessary repairs which come with the normal knocks of a hard race.

Lamaster's problem is the same as many drivers. This year for the first time, modified cars are right up in the sprint car class, except for a hood over the driver.

Lamaster is a chief threat to Bill Nalley's reign here because of the retirement of Smokey Stover. Lamaster feels he could make more money at Pennsylvania tracks, thus he may not be returning to Winchester. However, the fans aren't taking Lamaster's threat of moving to Pennsylvania tracks too seriously because the Winchester driver has picked up a pile of money racing on Friday at the Winchester Speedway, on Saturday at Eastside, and on Sunday at Hagerstown. That's a lot of traveling around, but Clem and his crew can make more money working the three tracks than they will make by selecting a high-priced event in Pennsylvania and running down in the money.

Clem Lamaster poses in front of his many racing trophies in 2001.

Clem Lamaster was interviewed in his spacious country home in rural Fredrick County, Virginia, along with his wife, "Doll". Clem is friendly, warm, and hospitable. He still shows impaired speech as a result of his 1965 accident. His mantle is filled with racing trophies, and pictures of his racing days adorn the walls.

Roy Neff

One of the most colorful and entertaining owner/drivers during the 1950's in the Shenandoah Valley was Roy Neff. A World War II veteran who had earlier raced motorcycles, Neff was a heavy equipment operator for the Virginia Department of Transportation.

He built a garage and practice track on his land in downtown Toms Brook, Virginia. He is famous for two cars, P-38 and Z01. He often drove the P-38; however, his primary driver in the Z01 was Robert Peer from Star Tannery, Virginia.

Racing Hucksters

Roy Neff (right) with driver Robert Peer after a win in the early days at Winchester.

Neff tells the story of how he got involved in racing. He says, "Peer and two other hucksters from the Valley would race their trucks back to the Valley from Washington where they sold groceries. They'd drink beer and race all the way home. Peer, Louis Newland (who later raced for Neff and others), and John McCoy raced their trucks home. On Fisher's Hill outside Strasburg, [Virginia], they were all half drunk and on the last turn Peer didn't make it. He rolled that thing until it looked like a gumball."

Neff Builds His First Car

Neff continues, "He called me and said, 'By God, we'll just have to make a racer out of it.' Peer was a smart-ass and said, 'Let's build a racecar.' It was a new GMC truck. We cut that thing down and put rollbars in it and took it to the track. Had a straight six-cylinder Ford motor in it, and that son-of-a-bitch would fly. That was P-38."

Neff says that he worked long hours on his cars in the garage near his house. He says, "I spent all my spare time in the garage. Sometimes all night long."

On days or evenings of racing, a caravan of cars with Neff's extended family and friends would follow Roy and his cars to the races.

Mr. Krunk

Neff speaks affectionately of his father-in-law, Mr. Krunk, who was always there to help. He was also willing to fight if necessary.

Neff continues, "Shorty Bowers hit Peer coming off the first turn, knocked him off the track and we had to stop the race. When they came around, Mr. Krunk met Shorty out there on the track. He was just a little fella, but he grabbed Shorty and was shaking the shit out of him. We had to take him off him."

Krunk was always there to help Roy, often working on the car during the day while Roy worked in his regular job, or ran errands. It was on one such errand to Woodstock, Virginia, to buy a part for Roy's racecar that he died of a heart attack. According to Neff, "He never missed a race. He loved sports."

Neff says about Krunk, "Ain't nobody said anything about Roy Neff. If he did, he got hit in the jaw. He really had a temper."

Roy's Garage Burns

On one occasion, Neff was testing the engine in his racecar in his garage. It backfired near a gallon of gas sitting near the exhaust. The garage quickly became engulfed in flames and was a total loss. According to Neff, "I had a hell of a fire. It didn't do much to the car. It was really burned, but we were able to run it again."

Neff Changes Engines

On one occasion at Winchester Speedway, John Miller, a local owner's car blew an engine. Robert Peer had wrecked Neff's Z01, so Miller and Neff swapped engines between races. It took 35 minutes to change the engine, and Miller's car later won the race with Neff's motor.

Neff primarily saw himself as a mechanic. He drove on a limited basis and won some heats; however, he says, "I didn't like to drive. It was all I could do to keep them cars running." Neff often painted the cars and Mr. Krunk worked on the cars during the day.

Neff Experiments

Neff was quite innovative. On one occasion he arrived at Winchester with snow chains on his rear wheels in an effort to gain traction. On another occasion he arrived with dual truck tires on the back.

Neff says that Robert Peer was testing one of Neff's cars on the small track built by Neff on his land. The track left a lot to be desired. It was rough and uneven. On one occasion, Robert Peer rolled one of his cars. Neff and others ran up to him as he was sitting upside down in the car. Neff said, "Get the hell out of there." Peer said, "Eh?" Neff continues, "You know, he'd had a few beers. He'd drink right much. He rolled it end for end. He tore the car all to hell."

Powder Puff

On one occasion, Roy's wife Hilda raced in a powder puff race at Winchester. Coming off the second turn, she inadvertently hit the accelerator instead of the brake. The car hit the guardrail, went over the bank and flipped. Roy's wife sustained three broken ribs and never drove racecars again. Roy's reaction was a good hardy laugh.

Car in which Hilda Neff suffered injuries in a powder puff race at Winchester.

Neff and Wendell Scott

Neff remembers the late Wendell Scott. On one occasion at Waynesboro, Scott, for some reason, had brought a goat to the racetrack. According to Neff, "Some of those crooks took the goat with feed and water and put it inside Scott's truck. So when Scott called for the goat, it didn't answer. Scott was so mad he turned white! Scott said, 'Well, I'm not going to do any racing 'til I find that goat.' About that time, somebody made a goat sound and the goat answered. Scott said, 'Where in the hell do they have that thing?' I said, 'Probably in between the seat of your truck!' Scott was a good clean driver. I had a lot of respect for him. I'll tell you that."

In 1956, Roy won a demolition derby at Winchester.

PEER WRECKS

In 1958, Neff's driver, Robert Peer, was involved in two serious accidents.

On May 31, 1958, The Winchester Star had this account of Peer's accident:

Robert Peer of Tom's Brook came within inches of killing himself and flagman Jim Ellmore at Sunday's stock car races at the Winchester Airport Speedway.

It was so close that Peer, the driver of Z01, ripped out 40 cinder blocks in front of the judges' stand as Ellmore dove to safety behind the building.

Left in the wake of Z01 were blocks of the building which were thrown completely through it and out the other side as well as all of Ellmore's flags and various parts of the racer. Peer's controls locked in the straightaway and he headed on a direct course for the all-block building.

The instant before Peer's 70-mile an hour racer ripped into the building, Ellmore made it behind the scenes.

A few seconds later, while officials were trying to determine any injuries to Peer, Denzil Dillman of Baltimore crashed head-on into the cement-filled water pump and demolished his front end.

On July 27, 1958, in the Class A feature at Winchester, Peer hit the guardrail of the number three turn and sailed over the fence into a field as his tire blew. He suffered an injury to his right hip and seatbelt bruises.

This accident helped end Roy Neff's involvement with racing and is noted in The Winchester Star:

Robert Peer of Star Tannery left the track so suddenly in the second lap of the second heat that his Z01 cleared the fence without damaging it at all. His car hit hard enough at the bottom of the 20-foot incline to bounce back into view of the horrified spectators.

Swift work by the Friendship Ambulance crew got Peer to Memorial Hospital in time for emergency work on an injured chest and badly cut face, but he was in considerable pain late Sunday night.

Peer's wife, in her anxiety to reach the injured driver, cut a leg severely on the wire barricade between the track and the demolished car. She rode in the ambulance to Winchester with her husband.

ANOTHER CONFRONTATION WITH SHORTY

The driver Shorty Bowers was a controversial driver indeed. And he had more than his share of confrontations with Roy Neff. Roy's enmity for Bowers reached a crescendo on September 9, 1956.

With Neff's driver Robert Peer, Tommy Irwin, and Junior Bowers fighting for the lead, Bowers was bumped from behind and spun onto the infield with a blown tire. The Winchester Star had this account:

For some reason known only to Bowers and his crewmen, Bowers pushed his racer directly to the middle of the track and into the path of on-rushing cars.

What happened then would have done justice to a horror movie, but did little good for the other cars. In their anxiety to miss the white and yellow number 5 car Bowers, the cars blasted into each other with fenders and parts flying. If anyone had hit Shorty Bowers' car, it would have killed him since he was standing right behind it. He then added to the trouble by soberly walking across the track in the face of the rest of the cars.

That halted the affair fast and brought crewmen and fans from the grandstand hot on the trail of Bowers. Before a few cool heads could break it up, Shorty had taken a couple of stiff jolts from Roy Neff of Toms Brook, owner of Peer's car, and was in danger of being mauled by an angry crowd of about 250 men.

As it was, fights broke out on the fringes and the arguments were still hot and heavy three hours later as darkness fell across the track.

HEART ATTACK AT THE TRACK

One year later in June 1957, Shorty Bowers, who is now deceased, suffered a heart attack at Winchester Speedway after finishing a strong fifth in the sportsman feature. At that time, physicians gave him a 50-50 chance of survival. Bowers, from Hagerstown, Maryland, collapsed beside his racer at the end of the sportsman feature and was rushed to Winchester Memorial Hospital. He had first complained to track officials that he had swallowed a rock thrown by another car; however, it was soon determined that indeed he was suffering a heart attack.

NEFF RETIRES FROM STOCK CARS

The constant work and commitment to racing, along with an injury to his driver Robert Peer, prompted Neff to give up racing. Peer was hospitalized for a week with broken ribs and other injuries after he went over the turn two guardrail at Winchester. Because Peer had two small daughters, Neff felt responsible for Peer and eventually quit racing.

NEFF STARTS PONY RACING

After retiring from stock car racing, Neff got involved in pony racing. His best horse ever was Little Lady Lee, a horse for which he had paid $40. Neff broke, trained, and put the horse on the track and became very successful.

Neff says that a psychiatrist in Pennsylvania wanted to buy the horse. He continues, "A damn head shrinker from Pennsylvania kept on calling me and wanted to buy her. He and his wife came down here on a Sunday and looked at Little Lady Lee. I said, 'She's not for sale.' He said, 'Well everything has a price.' Well, that pissed me off and I said, 'I'll take $4,500 for her.' He swelled up like a balloon and said, 'You don't want to sell her.' I said, 'You're exactly right!' He walked around his station wagon and said something to his wife, came back and said, 'Mr. Neff, we're going to have to go home and think this thing over.' I said, 'All right.'

"The psychiatrist called that night and said he'd be there the next morning at 10 a.m. to pick the horse up for the agreed upon price of $4,500. After the transaction, Neff says, 'Peer and I went out after that to celebrate and got so damn drunk we didn't know which way was up.'"

According to Neff, the psychiatrist only raced Little Lady Lee twice, won both times, and put her to pasture.

Roy Neff in 2001.

Neff was interviewed in his pleasant ranch home on a hill atop Fishers Hill, Virginia. As he was in the '50s, he continues to be a rather good-natured, somewhat loud, animated, humorous, playful, and outgoing individual who readily bantered with his wife as they recounted information. Robert Peer is deceased.

Bob Dobyns

Dobyns Gets the Fever

Bob "Tilly" Dobyns, a native of Orange, Virginia, began racing in 1950 at the quarter-mile dirt track at Unionville, Virginia. His interest in racing had been ignited when working on a gas pipeline around

Bob Dobyns in the early days at Eastside.

Manassas, Virginia, and he and several co-workers had walked to Longview Speedway. When he returned to Orange, he built his own racecar. He ran in the jalopy division and won his first race at Unionville, pocketing $30 for the win.

From there, Dobyns raced at Douglas Speedway in Ruckersville, Virginia, Eastside, Massanutten Speedway in Keezletown, Virginia, Winchester, Cavalier Speedway in Charlottesville, Virginia, and Hilltop Speedway in Zion's Crossroads, Virginia, in the early 50's.

He then built a 1939 Ford Coupe racer with a Flathead engine and ran in the modified division. By this time, Dobyns had "racing fever" and would race until 1974 when he retired due to medical advice because of a pulmonary embolism. During his 24 years of racing, he prides himself on the fact that he drove at many tracks. Among those include Trenton, New Jersey; Daytona, where he drove in the ARCA division; Natural Bridge, Virginia; Fredricksburg, Virginia; Moyock, North Carolina; Langley, Virginia; Strawberry Hill and Royal Speedways in Richmond, Virginia; Beltsville, Maryland; Martinsville, Virginia; Craigsville, Virginia; Lawrenceville, Virginia; and Southside Speedway outside Richmond, Virginia.

When asked to describe his favorite track, Dobyns replies, "It really didn't matter. I just loved to race."

Most Money for Dobyns

During his career, he garnered 37 trophies. The most money he ever won in a race was $1,200 at a race at Southside. According to Dobyns, "I had never seen that kind of money. I was as happy as a pig in slop!"

Dobyns' Accomplishments

In 1998, Dobyns was elected to the Legends Hall of Fame at Natural Bridge Speedway.

He won track championships at Craigsville Motor Speedway, Manassas' Old Dominion Speedway, and Eastside.

Like many other drivers of the day, Dobyns was especially impressed with the Lawrenceville track, which was a high-banked oval with a clay that allowed for high speeds and good handling. According to Dobyns, "Lawrenceville was one of the best dirt tracks in the world."

His best finish ever at Daytona in the ARCA division was an eleventh. He was running in one race at Daytona and ran out of gas while in fourth place.

Dobyns is quite proud of the fact that he always qualified his own cars. On several occasions driving for other people, he did not qualify.

In 1971, he was selected by fans at Craigsville Motor Speedway as the most popular driver.

Dobyns and Wendell Scott

Dobyns fondly remembers the late Wendell Scott. According to Dobyns, "He was a good man. He towed his car behind an old hearse."

Dobyns relates that at Hilltop Speedway, Scott had broken an axle. Dobyns remembers Scott under the car, in darkness, holding a flashlight in his mouth while he repaired the car, refusing help from Dobyns when offered.

Going to Late Models

In the mid-60's, the modified division was eliminated and Dobyns moved to the late model division, buying his first car, a 1957 Ford, from Elmo Langley, one-time pace car driver for NASCAR.

At Beltsville, Maryland, Dobyns says that he was the winner of four straight late model features. The track promoter paid Junior Donlevy $300 to bring his driver Sonny Hutchins to outrun Dobyns. For reasons that were unknown and protested by Dobyns, Hutchins started on the pole and Dobyns in the rear. Despite this disadvantage, Hutchins only beat Dobyns by several feet at the checkered flag.

Dobyns won two features at Winchester Speedway, the last one on three wheels after having lost his right front wheel.

Rough Driving

Dobyns remembers racing at Southside, however, felt that he received driver's lessons there from Ray Hendricks and Runt Harris, two of the more rougher drivers according to Dobyns and others. According to Dobyns, "I told them, one of these times I'm going to have payback." Indeed, Dobyns did have the pleasure of spinning out Runt Harris after Harris had done this many times to Dobyns.

Dobyns had a number of on-track run-ins with driver Lionel Johnson. One night at Eastside, Johnson was blocking Dobyns. Dobyns bumped him out of the way to take the lead. On the next lap, Dobyns relates that Johnson ran through the infield and intentionally collided with Dobyns' car. According to Dobyns, "My car was all tore up." Dobyns then says that he raced into the pits and ordered his pit crew to replace a tire. At that, Dobyns returned to the track and put Johnson in the fence. According to Dobyns, a large fight ensued, so much so that promoter Al Gore closed the track to further racing that particular evening.

This was not Dobyns' first run-in with Johnson. At Cavalier Speedway in Charlottesville, Dobyns relates that Johnson had bumped him going into the first turn on the start of a heat race. This technique was known as "banking," where an inside car on a turn would slide up the banking into a car on the outside, forcing the outside car to slow down or come close to hitting the outside fence.

During intermission, Dobyns warned Johnson not to "bank" him again. He allegedly told Johnson, "Don't run your wheel up on my door."

In the feature, Dobyns says, "He did the same thing. I ran him in the fence by the grandstand."

To this day (2002), Dobyns relates that he and Johnson, who lives relatively close to him, do not speak.

Dobyns on Cal Johnson

Dobyns was good friends with driver Cal Johnson and remembers him often driving his racecar with one hand and a pipe in his mouth. Dobyns had Johnson repair several of his engines.

INJURIES

Dobyns was never seriously injured. He received a cut over one eye from going over the bank at Douglas Speedway. While being taken to the hospital, he complained that the ambulance driver frightened him worse than driving a racecar!

While racing at Strawberry Hill Speedway in Richmond, he relates a very dusty Sunday afternoon. Dobyns was running well and saw a "flicker" through the dust. Suddenly, he was part of an 18-car pileup. As one car ran into another, several cars caught fire and 11 racecars were completely consumed by fire, including Dobyns' car.

When Dobyns got out of his car, he jumped on a fuel tank and twisted his ankle. He didn't know it at the time, but he had broken his ankle.

When taken to the hospital at Richmond, hospital personnel focused on a blood blister on his back that he had received from the rear impact of the crash. They ignored his ankle despite his pleas to examine it. It wasn't until the following week that his broken ankle was diagnosed.

Dobyns is proud to say that when his ankle healed, "I had another car ready to race."

AGAINST MEDICAL ADVICE

In 1968, Dobyns ignored medical advice and drove a racecar at Eastside on a Saturday night only a day after he had undergone a diagnostic mylogram for a back problem. As a result, at the end of the race he developed severe headaches, so much so that he felt incapable of driving from Waynesboro home to Orange that evening. He and his family searched for vacant motels in Waynesboro to no avail. The next day (Sunday) he raced at Natural Bridge, traveling back to Charlottesville to be admitted that night for back surgery on Monday morning.

RB

During the heydays of the 50's, Dobyns' car "number" was RB. This stood for Roy and Bob, Roy Peyton, who assisted with the car, and Bob Dobyns.

FAVORITE DRIVERS

Dobyns' favorite drivers during his career were Alan Dillard, Gip Gibson, Russ Breeden, Cal Johnson, and Bill Nalley.

TRAGEDY

Dobyns and his wife Joyce had three children. His two daughters live near him. On June 1, 1982, Dobyns' 27-year old son Bobby was killed in a freak welding accident. Bobby had been racing for some time and had experienced some success as a late model driver.

SELECTED EVENTS

On August 15, 1958, Dobyns demolished his car at Lawrenceville and was unable to make the racing show at Eastside.

On August 6, 1957, Dobyns won the amateur feature at Eastside over Harry Lee Rodeffer, Charlie Sipe, Chester Stanley, and Dick Hansberger.

On April 26, 1958, Dobyns won a race-shortened event at Eastside in the amateur division over Charlie Sipe.

On July 5, 1958, Dobyns won the amateur feature at Eastside over Billy Rodeffer, Harry Lee Rodeffer, and Al Grinnan.

When asked about his 24 years of active racing, including his support of his son Bobby's career, Dobyns is quick to describe the amount of time and effort to sustain such an effort. He admits that he often times did not see his wife during the week, saying, "She did her thing and I did mine and we met at the track."

Dobyns was interviewed along with his wife Joyce in their newly remodeled home in a rural setting outside of Gordonsville, Virginia. He continues to work as a millwright, however, as of 2002 is contemplating retirement. He also works diligently at his farm. Dobyns is a very gracious and friendly individual who clearly enjoyed the competition of racing, and gives the impression that he could mix it up with the best of them.

Dobyns sums it up best, "I never had money, but I always enjoyed racing."

Bob Tilly Dobyns in 2002.

Jackie Clore

Jackie Clore was a mechanic and garage owner in Madison, Virginia. He was a competitive racer both in the sportsman and modified divisions and drove from the mid 1950's until 1980.

Clore was noted for his distinctive crossfire engine and is reported to be the first alcohol burner in the Shenandoah Valley. He was an innovative and resourceful racecar builder and was a frequent winner as a driver. His cars were always clean and well painted.

In the early morning of Sunday, May 11, 1980, a crap game was underway at Clore's garage in downtown Madison. A man by the name of William Barbour joined the crap game. After an argument, Barbour was told by Clore to leave his garage.

Barbour left and returned approximately an hour later where again an argument ensued. Clore and Barbour then went into the street where Barbour is alleged to have knocked Clore to the ground with a blow to the head. Barbour was described as "in a rage, mad and cursing." Others tried to restrain Barbour, including Clore's son Mike who had a bad knee from a football injury and fell as Barbour grabbed him. At that, a man by the name of Jack Lam, participant in the crap game and friend of Clore, shot Barbour with a .22 caliber pistol, who fell to the ground and then walked to his apartment across the street. It was at the top of the stairs leading to Barbour's second-floor apartment where he was later found dead.

As the 33-year old Barbour was black and no initial arrests were made, racial tensions grew throughout Madison County and there were threats of protests because of the lack of initial arrests in the case. The Clores received threats and prank phone calls. Clore's garage saw a drop in business. Several days later, John Elmore Lohr was charged with Barbour's shooting, but charges were later dropped. Later, Jack Lam pleaded guilty to voluntary manslaughter and served two years in prison. He was later murdered in an unsolved case.

This altercation left Clore with a head injury and subsequent vertigo, which essentially ended his racing career. Clore then began to serve as a mechanic and mentor for his son Mike who began racing in earnest and was quite successful in the late model division.

Jackie Clore died on January 6, 1993, after a two-year battle with pancreatic cancer at the age of 61.

Tragedy at Winchester

On July 22, 1995, Mike Clore was killed at a Saturday night race at Winchester Speedway. Clore, who was 42 years of age at the time, was dead on arrival at the local hospital after a wreck that occurred on the third lap of the feature race at Winchester.

Clore, who at the time was a 15-year veteran of racing, was the 1994 late model champion at Winchester and also was track champion at Potomac Speedway in Potomac, Maryland.

Clore lost control of his car and hit the end of a guardrail coming off the fourth turn onto the backstretch. It is unsure as to whether or not Clore's car was bumped by another car or if he just lost control; however, it was estimated that his speed was 80 miles per hour when he crashed into the guardrail.

The car then bounced off the guardrail and slid across the track where it was struck on the passenger side by a car driven by Gary Stuhler of Green Castle, Pennsylvania. Stuhler's car was then struck in the rear by Charles Omps of Winchester. It was reported that the crowd of approximately 3,500 remained silent after the accident. The remaining 23 drivers voted against completing the race.

The accident was witnessed by Clore's wife Janice, his two children, and his mother, Marie Clore. His funeral is refuted to be one of the largest ever in the town of Madison. He is buried next to his father in Madison. Both Clores have racecars inscribed on their headstones.

Movies at the Clores

Jackie Clore's wife, Marie Clore, was interviewed related to her husband and son's careers outside her spacious and comfortable home outside Madison. Nearby is a large garage built by her husband to service racecars. It was used by son Mike until his death.

Mrs. Clore produced films taken of her husband's racing career. The films of the old races are interspersed with family remembrances including the Little League baseball participation of her son Mike on a team sponsored by his father's "Clore's Garage." A sadness came over the room. I sympathized with Mrs. Gore as she viewed her deceased husband and son in the films. A tear came to her eye. Seeing the old racers of the past in action at Devil's Bowl and Winchester brought back many fond memories for the author and a sadness for days gone by as well as the fate of Jackie and Mike Clore.

Selected Events

On August 20, 1960, Jackie Clore was the first sportsman across the finish line in the 50-lap feature at Eastside. Both modifieds and sportsmen were running in the same race. Clore received a trophy for being the highest finishing sportsman.

During the summer of 1961, the sportsman and modified cars ran their features together, primarily because of a lack of modified vehicles. In such a race at Eastside, Jackie Clore driving a sportsman car beat Lewis Bocock in a modified car in what was described as a photo finish. It is said, "The two cars were radiator to radiator under the finish line when Clore's vehicle was just inches ahead."

On July 22, 1961, Jackie Clore surprised many fans in attendance at Eastside winning out over Lewis Bocock's modified race in the sportsman/modified heat.

On July 25, 1959, Jackie Clore won the 20-lap amateur feature at Eastside over Jackie Denison and Buck Shipp.

Marie Clore behind the wheel of Jackie Clore's restored coupe.

On September 7, 1959, Jackie Clore won the 100-lap amateur championship feature at Eastside over Jackie Denison and Bob Croson of Winchester.

Avis Wyant

Avis Wyant, a Harrisonburg mechanic and mail carrier in later life, drove in the hobby division at Massanutten, Eastside, and Devil's Bowl. His first race was at Massanutten (Keezletown).

His first car was a 1934 Ford Coupe, followed by a 1941 Hudson Coupe. He ended his career driving a 1948 Nash numbered XM.

Winning at Red Banks

Wyant is unsure as to the number of features he won, but proudly presents a trophy won at Eastside Speedway in a Dr. Pepper Trophy Race. He remembers driving at Red Banks Speedway in 1961 outside Mt. Jackson, Virginia, arriving late for the race. Inexplicably, he was placed on the pole. According to him, the track was not wide enough to pass. According to Wyant, "I started first and finished in first." He says Harry Lee Rodeffer was behind him bumping and pushing but couldn't pass. He remembers Rodeffer as wearing bib overhauls with no shirt while he drove a car.

Extra $ at Devil's Bowl

Avis had the distinction of rolling his car over the third turn at Devil's Bowl. He received an extra $10 for rolling his car.

Innovation

While modern-day NASCAR drivers have nets over the driver's side windows as a safety measure, Wyant placed chicken wire on his driver's side window in the early 50's. While recognizing later that this may be a safety factor, he initially installed the chicken wire to keep large "mud balls" from hitting him, which would be kicked up by other cars.

Wyant on Jackie Clore

Wyant remembers the crossfire engine of Jackie Clore, as well as the smell of burnt alcohol emitted from the car. According to Wyant, "Your eyes would run when you walked around Clore's car."

Avis Remembers

Wyant's most respected drivers were Lewis Bocock, Bill Nalley, Buddy Stinespring, and Jackie Clore.

Wyant remembers a driver by the name of Bubby Strickler, who according to him was "always in trouble." Wyant says that he's the first man to have the distinction of running a full face helmet at local tracks. He also says that Strickler, who was often afoul of the law, had finished a race at Eastside when law enforcement officers came on the track at Eastside to arrest him. Strickler was alleged to have abandoned his car on the speedway and run off into the local woods, escaping from the police.

Wyant also remembers a driver by the name of Bobby Whitmire who drove the Car PG, which stood for Pineville Grocery. He said that the car was nicknamed "Paregoric."

According to Wyant, Whitmire had difficulty towing his car away from Devil's Bowl after a night of racing and left the car at the track to race the next week. When he arrived seven days later, someone had stolen all four wheels and the battery from the car.

Wyant's wife Evelyn raced in one powder puff derby and finished in second place at Eastside.

Wyant cannot remember the exact year he retired, but recounts an incident where he was towing his racecar home from Eastside to Harrisonburg when his racecar blew a tire. The racecar, towed by the family car which was occupied by Wyant, his wife, and children, went wildly out of control and jackknifed. It was this event that prompted Wyant's wife Evelyn to ask Avis to quit racing.

Avis is a friendly and talkative gentleman, who clearly loved racing and becomes somewhat emotional when talking of the sense of loss he feels when he reflects on the days of racing. He is a family man. On the day of the interview, he was surrounded by affectionate children and grandchildren.

Avis Wyant in his shop in Harrisonburg showing a seatbelt used in his first race car. circa. 2002

Short (Track) Stories

Entertainment at Valley Speedway

On September 19, 1959, Valley Speedway in Staunton featured Buddy Starcher and his all-star band who provided between race entertainment. Starcher was described at the time as a "well-known TV and radio personality."

In addition, on this day Valley Speedway boasted that Smokey Stover and his wife Ruby drove in open competition.

Stunts at Winchester

In September 1956 at Winchester Airport Speedway, Charlie Armel, the flamboyant flagman at Winchester, was prohibited by Commonwealth Attorney Joe Massie of Fredrick County, Virginia, from performing stunts without a "stunt license." Armel was known for jumping from the floorboard of one car to another while they sped down the speedway at approximately 70 miles an hour.

In July 1957, the clown Flywheel appeared at Winchester Speedway. Armel transferred from the running board of Lewis Bocock's car to Doug Bailey's car, passing over Flywheel who sat in the middle of the track at over 70 miles an hour.

Charlie Armel Rescues Patsy

Armel, a part-time guitar player and car salesman at Kern Motors in Winchester, came to the aid of Patsy Cline in the 1958 Apple Blossom Festival Parade by borrowing a black Edsel convertible from Henry Kern and driving Patsy in the parade. Cline had been told there were no other convertibles in Winchester available for her. Armel decorated the car and made a sign: "Winchester's Own Home-Grown Star, Miss Patsy Cline--TV and Decca Records Star."

Armel drove to the parade lineup and squeezed into the parade, even though there was no formal place for Patsy in the lineup, driving the entire parade route.

Patsy Cline at Winchester Speedway

On May 13, 1956, Patsy Cline appeared at Winchester Speedway. The Winchester Star had this account:

For their entertainment, the crowd had a first-rate country singing lesson from TV's Pasty Cline, a Winchester girl who currently appears with Jimmy Dean and the Texas Wildcats in Washington. Music for the show was presented by announcer Ralph Lamp's Kountry Krackers.

Tragedy at Fort Ashby

On April 25, 1959, Al Gatto, a 42-year old flagman, was killed at Fort Ashby's Potomac Valley Speedway.

According to accounts, Kenneth Jeffries lost control of his car coming out of the number four turn and swerved down the track. Seeing it headed in his direction, Gatto jumped for safety but the erratic path of the car met him head on. Approximately 750 fans watched in disbelief.

This was Gatto's first attempt at being a flagman. Until then, he had been a regular participant in stock car races at Winchester Airport Speedway, but had quit racing and had become an official at the newly purchased and renamed track at Fort Ashby.

Cutting Costs at Winchester

In April 1953, Kermit Batt, owner of the Winchester Airport Speedway, ruled that cars racing there could not exceed a cost of $500 each.

New Cars on Parade

In April 1953, at the Douglas Speedway in Ruckersville, Virginia, the event was known as the Futuramic Parade of Motor Travel and was held on a Sunday afternoon.

The News Virginian had this account:

The pace car will be the beautiful gold and white Ford custom convertible that will serve as the pace car at the Indianapolis 500 Classic on Memorial Day. Represented in the Futuramic Parade will be new Fords, Plymouths, Chevrolets, Hudsons, Cadillacs, Studebakers, Dodges, Pontiacs, and all the traditional American cars.

The American Legion Color Guard of Charlottesville will open the ceremonies with a flag raising at approximately 2:30 p.m.

Tragedy in Saluda

Gip Gibson had been one of the earlier drivers to drive at Eastside Speedway and other early tracks. From the early 50's to 1974 he had been a regular racer at a variety of tracks.

On July 15, 1974, driving in the late model division in Saluda, Virginia, approximately 26 miles south of Tappahannock, Virginia, Gibson was fatally injured on the 18th lap of the 50-lap feature. His 1971 Ford Torino was involved in a 3-car pileup with Ernest Snider and Charlie Johnson. Snider spun. Gibson hit Snider, and then Johnson plowed broadside into Gibson.

Gibson was pronounced dead on arrival at Tappahannock Hospital.

After the race, drivers voted to give their winnings totaling approximately $1,000 to Gibson's family.

At the time of his death, Reasel "Gip" Gibson was the superintendent of the grounds at the Boar's Head Inn outside Charlottesville. He was 46 years old.

Gip Gibson wins at Eastside in 1955.

Kuda Bux at Winchester

The Winchester Star had this account:

It was quite a day for the fans, particularly with the all-new Kuda Bux show. The Hindu performed tricks of magic as well as demonstrating his ability to act normally with his eyes heavily bandaged over.

His most amazing trick was the old favorite of a pretty girl in a box with a sharp pointed rod going through it from every angle. His model was New York ballerina, Doris Lee.

\Kuda Bux is known that day for driving around the track in a convertible blindfolded. This event was witnessed by the author as a young boy.

Modifieds Out at Devil's Bowl

In June 1960, Devil's Bowl discontinued the modified position as only six cars were on hand.

Jalopy Cars

During the 50's and 60's, jalopy cars, eventually known as hobby cars, were essentially stock automobiles with minimal safety equipment. The dominant drivers of the day in the jalopy division were Charlie Almond of Staunton, Carol Bridgeforth of Winchester, Avis Wyant of Harrisonburg, and Harry Lee Rodeffer of Mt. Jackson.

Go Carts and Stock Car Tracks

Go carts were regularly raced at Winchester Speedway on Friday nights during the early 60's.

In July 1960, Homer Weaver, owner of Devil's Bowl, utilized the first and second turns of the stock car track and a straightaway across the infield to make a triangular go cart track. Go cart events became a regular part of the racing evening at Devil's Bowl.

Injunctions Against Devil's Bowl

In May 1961, one of the many injunctions was obtained against Devil's Bowl. The News Virginian had this account:

Devil's Bowl Speedway here has been closed at least temporarily due to an injunction obtained by residents of the area.

It is understood that property owners near the track objected to the noise and dust and, as a result, obtained an injunction closing the oval.

A spokesman for the speedway indicated racing may resume there in the near future.

Patsy Cline's Funeral

On Sunday, March 10, 1963, 30-year-old Patsy Cline was buried at Shenandoah Memorial Park within three miles of the Winchester Airport Speedway. Over 25,000 persons were on hand. Cline had been killed with two other Grand Old Opry stars, Hawkshaw Hawkins and Cowboy Copus, in a light plane crash in Tennessee earlier in the week.

Wendell Scott in Lynchburg

It is alleged that one night at Shrader's Field in Lynchburg, a wheel came off of Wendell Scott's car and flew into the grandstands, injuring several fans. A mob of whites gathered to attack Scott, who was black, but Earl Brooks, who periodically drove at Eastside, intervened. Brooks is alleged to have stood on top of a racecar swinging a metal pipe and saying, "Y'all got to come through me." The crowd dispersed.

Tragedy at Manassas

On August 11, 1956, 24-year old Ivan Breighner became the first fatality at Al Gore's Old Dominion Speedway when he was killed on the fourth lap of a 25-lap sportsman stock car event.

Massanutten (Keezletown) Speedway

Massanutten Speedway near the small village of Keezletown outside of Harrisonburg, Virginia, was a three-eighth mile dirt oval that operated only for several years. During that time, however, it drew very large crowds. Racing occurred on Sunday afternoons.

The track was located on farmland owned by Bill Wright. The track was operated by Bill Rodeffer, Sr., mechanic, garage and junkyard owner, and Gus Julius, a Harrisonburg restaurant owner.

Although racing drew large crowds there, the track, located in somewhat of a valley, was an easy mark for rainwater drainage. On several occasions, the entire third and fourth turns and backstretch were severely eroded due to heavy rains.

After the decision was made to close the track, the cinder block tower in the infield of the track as well as the grandstand was dismantled. Wood from the grandstand served as floor joists for the newly built home of Bill Rodeffer, Jr., and his wife Betty. Cinder block from the tower was also used in the construction of the home.

An interview was held with Donny Rodeffer, grandson of Bill Rodeffer, Sr. He was a child when the track was operating, yet has vivid memories of the track. He relates that his father, Bill Rodeffer, Jr., drove regularly at local tracks including Massanutten. An uncle, Harry Lee Rodeffer, was also a regular at local tracks.

Donny Rodeffer remembers Earl Brooks and Wendell Scott both racing at Massanutten and visiting his parents' home. Other notables who ran at Massanutten include Bill Nalley, Smokey Stover, and Ray Dovel.

In those days, he remembers Smokey Stover as an extremely aggressive driver at Massanutten and says that Stover and his mother "didn't like each other." According to Rodeffer, Stover allegedly said to his mother, "I'll win a race if I have to spin out everybody."

On one occasion, he remembers vividly that Smokey Stover spun out his father, Bill. On the next lap, Uncle Harry Rodeffer waited for Stover to round the track and ran him over the bank. According to Rodeffer, a fight ensued.

He also remembers a driver by the name of C. P. Foley, who had a car that was prone to overheat. In those days, drivers lacked the sophistication to be concerned about matters related to weight, and as such, Foley is alleged to have had a 55-gallon drum of water in his car to curtail overheating.

While the names of the parties are not remembered, a flagman at Massanutten Speedway apparently was hit by a car as he flagged from the track. While the injuries were not serious, flagging was then done from the infield behind a fence. When another close call happened with this flagman, the flagman then stood in the judges' stand, which was on top of the cinder block tower in the infield. This was unusual because drivers had to eye the middle of the pits to see the flagman.

FREAK INJURIES AT EASTSIDE

Donny Rodeffer also remembers as a child an incident that occurred at Eastside when the rear axle and tires came off of a car driven by Ernie Alders. The axle with the tires attached flew over the guardrail and into the pits, hitting a driver standing there by the name of Doug Stout. The impact literally knocked Stout out from his boots and broke both legs, according to Rodeffer.

WENDELL SCOTT AT WINCHESTER

The August 12, 1957 edition of The Winchester Evening Star had this account of Wendell Scott participating at Winchester Speedway:

Scott is the best Negro driver in the Old Dominion, making his home way down in Danville. He's going to give the fans something to think about when he gets to the Winchester track.

MISS AIRPORT SPEEDWAY

On September 5, 1959, Kaye McKean of Winchester was named Miss Airport Speedway. She was crowned by the 1958 Miss Airport Speedway, Gail Dean.

FANS INJURED AT WINCHESTER

In September 1964, a stock car crashed through a fence at Winchester Speedway, injuring seven spectators. The crash came on the first lap of the 25-lap sportsman feature trophy race when a car driven by Harold Shepherd of Springfield, Virginia, plunged through the fence and landed atop two automobiles.

Most seriously hurt was Irwin Frank Dixon, 30, of Leesburg, who fractured his skull. He was listed in critical condition but survived.

Miss Virginia at Devil's Bowl

In July 1960 at Devil's Bowl Speedway, Cathy Birch, Miss Virginia 1960, presented the Pepsi Cola trophy to Bill Nalley, who the week before had won a 50-lap feature at Devil's Bowl.

Lash LaRue at Winchester

On August 5, 1956, Lash LaRue, a popular western movie and TV actor, signed autographs and put on a bullwhip demonstration for fans at Winchester Speedway.

Summary of Personalities

Kermit Batt
Original owner and promoter of Winchester Airport Speedway. Deceased.

Charlie Beeler
Winchester, Virginia, based mechanic who drove primarily in the amateur and hobby divisions from 1956 to 1979. He is noted for driving four years for noted owner/mechanic Lee Stultz from 1961 to 1965.

Lewis Bocock
Staunton, Virginia, based modified driver of Car 500. He was a tile setter who raced regularly at Eastside and Winchester from 1953 to 1963.

Junior Bowers
Staunton, Virginia, based modified driver, killed in a racing accident in Winchester in 1960.

Shorty Bowers
Controversial Hagerstown, Maryland, driver, a regular at Winchester. Deceased.

Kuda Bux
"The man with x-ray eyes." Appeared at speedways performing stunts blindfolded.

Bobby Campbell
Staunton, Virginia, based pipe fitter who was co-owner and mechanic/painter of the famous 306 car driven by Smokey Stover.

Tommy Campbell
Staunton, Virginia, based pipe fitter who was co-owner and engine builder for the #306 car driven by Smokey Stover.

L. P. Claytor
Owner of Eastside Speedway from 1954 until April 1956, when he died at Eastside during a race.

Jackie Clore
Madison, Virginia, based mechanic/garage owner who drove extensively in the sportsman and modified divisions. He is noted for innovation in the building of his cars. His racing career ended in 1980 after suffering a head injury in a fight at his garage. Son Mike Clore killed in a racing accident at Winchester in 1995. Deceased.

Chuck Dedrick
Waynesboro, Virginia, based mechanic who owned Car 555, a prominent car at Eastside and Valley Speedway during the mid to late 50's.

Bob Dobyns
Orange, Virginia, based millwright/farmer/mechanic who drove throughout the Shenandoah Valley and beyond from 1950 to 1974. Son Bobby Dobyns, who had succeeded Dobyns with a racing career, killed in a freak welding accident in 1982.

Ray Dovel
Elkton, Virginia, based mechanic/garage owner who drove extensively throughout the Shenandoah Valley from the early 50's to 1980. Notable for having driven the Car S3 owned by Lee Stultz during the mid-60's.

Willie Wayne Gearheart
Pilot, Virginia, based mechanic/garage owner who opened and operated Pilot Speedway from 1958 to 1970.

Gip Gibson
Charlottesville, Virginia, driver of the early 50's in the Shenandoah Valley until his death in a racing accident in Saluda, Virginia, in 1974.

Al Gore
Northern Virginia based construction worker who came to be the owner of Old Dominion Speedway in Manassas, Virginia, and Eastside Speedway in Waynesboro, Virginia. He purchased both in the 50's and the tracks operate to this day managed by his sons.

Al Grinnan
Fredricksburg, Virginia, tire salesman who drove extensively throughout the Shenandoah Valley and beyond from the early 50's to late 70's. Winner of over 400 feature races.

Dick Pappy Hansberger
Mt. Jackson, Virginia, based truck driver/Virginia Game Commission employee who drove extensively throughout the Shenandoah Valley from the early 50's to 1979. Known as Pappy because he was older than most drivers of the time. Deceased.

Clyde Harris
Staunton, Virginia, based auto-body shop owner who was a scorer at Eastside, Winchester, and Devil's Bowl, as well as car owner. Operated Craigsville Motor Speedway from 1970 to 1975.

Tommy Irwin
Purcellville, Virginia, based mechanic who drove extensively during the 50's in the Shenandoah Valley of Virginia. A very successful driver, in 1958 began driving in the NASCAR Grand National circuit. Ceased driving in 1963 after sustaining severe injuries in Spartansburg, South Carolina.

Cal Johnson
Ashland, Virginia, based machinist who drove extensively throughout the Shenandoah Valley and beyond from 1949 to the mid-70's. Severely burned in an accident at Eastside in July 1955.

Clem Lamaster
Winchester, Virginia, based mobile home dealer who raced from 1952 to 1965 throughout the Shenandoah Valley of Virginia. Racing career ended in April 1965 as a result of a severe accident at Winchester. Later, Lamaster became promoter of the Winchester Speedway from 1968 to 1982.

Earl Moran
Verona, Virginia, based service station owner, Moran raced extensively throughout the Shenandoah Valley of Virginia from 1953 to 1970.

Bill Nalley
Brunswick, Maryland, based railroad foreman who dominated stock car racing throughout the 50's until 1964, mostly driving for Lee Stultz in the Car S3.

Roy Neff
Toms Brook, Virginia, based heavy equipment operator who owned and drove cars in the modified and sportsman divisions through the mid to late 50's. His Car Z01 was often driven by the late Robert Peer.

Red Ninninger
Brunswick, Maryland, based mechanic who raced throughout the Shenandoah Valley and beyond from 1951 until 1987. Still involved with racing with his son and grandson as of 2002.

Robert Peer
Star Tannery, Virginia, based huckster who drove Cars P-38 and Z01 for Roy Neff. Deceased.

Wendell Scott
One of the first black drivers to race in the 1950's. Later, he raced at the Grand National level as the first black driver. Deceased.

Chester Stanley
Staunton, Virginia, based meat cutter who drove extensively throughout the 50's and 60's in the Shenandoah Valley of Virginia, being quite dominant at Valley Speedway. Deceased.

Buddy Stinespring
Staunton, Virginia, based service station operator who was a dominant driver in the amateur and sportsman divisions, driving the Car 501 from 1955 until the late 60's. Noted for almost complete dominance for a 3-year period at a track in Pilot, Virginia. Also served as a flagman after retirement from racing.

Smokey Stover
Staunton, Virginia, based machinist who was a dominant driver in the modified division from 1958 to 1963 driving the famous 306 car. After 1963, he was involved in two serious accidents, sustaining severe leg injuries in 1964 and severe burns in 1968. The latter accident ended his career. Later served as a flagman at various speedways until his death in 1988.

Lee Stultz
Winchester, Virginia, based mechanic noted for producing fast and durable cars for Bill Nalley, Ray Dovel, and Buddy Armel in the S3 car driving in the modified division, and for Charlie Beeler driving in the amateur division. Deceased.

Avis Wyant
Harrisonburg, Virginia, based mechanic who drove extensively in the hobby division from the early 50's to late 60's.

Glossary of Terms

Airport Speedway - One-third mile dirt oval located outside Winchester, Virginia. Still operates as Winchester Speedway.

Amateur Division - Racers primarily operating with 6-cylinder engines with limited modifications. This division eventually became the sportsman division.

Bounty - An amount of money offered by a track promoter to any racer who could defeat a dominant driver who may have been winning regularly at that track.

Cavalier Speedway - Defunct dirt track oval which operated in Charlottesville, Virginia during the 50's.

Coupe - A 2-door passenger car with no back seat. These models were used extensively in building racecars during the 50's and 60's for the modified division.

Craigsville Motor Speedway - Initially opened as John's Speedway in the early 50's and later reopened by Clyde Harris in 1970 as Craigsville Motor Speedway. This is a defunct three-eighth mile tri-oval track located outside Craigsville, Virginia.

Demolition Derby - Contest where cars intentionally wreck into each other. The winner is that last car able to move.

Devil's Bowl Speedway - Opened as Valley Speedway in 1953, giving way to the name Devil's Bowl Speedway in 1960. The track closed in 1962 because of complaints from surrounding residents.

Douglas Speedway - Defunct dirt track oval located in Ruckersville, Virginia.

Eastside Speedway - Four-tenths of a mile dirt oval located outside Waynesboro, Virginia. Still in operation under the leadership of the Gore family.

Feature Race - The last race for each division in a racing show. These races usually are 25 to 50 laps in length, earning the top money of the event and at times a trophy.

Flathead - An engine no longer produced, but produced extensively during the 40's and 50's in which the valves are located in a block of engine as opposed to the overhead valve configuration used widely today.

Fort Ashby Speedway - Defunct dirt oval located in Fort Ashby, West Virginia.

Hagerstown Raceway - One-half mile dirt track still in operation outside of Hagerstown, Maryland.

Heat - Short races usually 8 to 10 laps in each division held to qualify for a position in the feature race.

Hilltop Speedway - Initially a fourth of a mile dirt oval, it was eventually paved. Now defunct in the Zion's

Crossroads, Virginia, area.

Hobby Division - Stock automobiles equipped with minimal safety features. No modifications are allowed with regard to preparation for racing. Also see Jalopy Division.

Jalopy Division - See Hobby Division.

Late Model - A division which developed after the demise of the modified division in the mid-60's. It started with mostly full-size sedans with modified drive trains.

Lawrenceville Speedway- Defunct dirt track oval outside Lawrenceville, Virginia. Noted as the favorite of many drivers during the 50's. It was eventually turned into a figure-eight raceway before it permanently closed.

Massanutten Speedway - Also known as Keezletown Speedway, this defunct track operated for several years outside of Harrisonburg, Virginia, in the early 50's.

Modified Division - Racecars with V-8 engines with multiple modifications. Modified engines were usually placed in 1930's and 40's vintage coupes. This division was the fastest division during the 50's and 60's.

Natural Bridge Speedway - One-half mile dirt oval still in operation outside Natural Bridge, Virginia.

Old Dominion Speedway - Three-eighths mile asphalt oval still in operation near Manassas, Virginia, under the operation of the Gore family.

Pilot Speedway - Defunct one-fourth mile dirt oval speedway outside Pilot, Virginia, which operated from 1958 to 1970.

Pole Position - The most coveted position in starting a race. The pole sitter occupies the inside position of the first row of racers beginning a race.

Powder Puff - A race with all female drivers.

Protest - A situation where a driver alleges that another driver may have an illegal engine. The protesting driver places a certain amount of money to initiate the protest. If the engine is found to be legal, the driver being protested keeps the money. If the engine is illegal, the defending driver loses position and all winnings.

Purse - The total amount of money distributed to drivers based on position at a racing event.

Red Banks Speedway - Defunct dirt oval located outside Mt. Jackson, Virginia, which operated for a short period of time during 1961.

Royal Speedway - Defunct dirt oval located outside Richmond, Virginia.

Scratch Position - The car starting in the outside position of the last row when beginning a race.

Sportsman Division - Initially, the fastest division of local racetracks. After the division was renamed modified, the sportsman division was known for 6-cylinder engines with limited modifications.

Sprint Cars - Small, specially built racers similar to, but smaller than, a Coupe. Designed for relatively short races. Noted for large air [scopes] on their roofs to enhance handling.

Strawberry Hill Speedway - Defunct dirt oval located outside Richmond, Virginia. The current Richmond International Raceway sits on these grounds.

Torn Down - See Protest.

Unionville Speedway - Defunct dirt oval located outside Orange, Virginia, which operated in the early 50's.

Valley Speedway - See Devil's Bowl Speedway.

INDEX

Alders, Ernie - 147

Alford, Ward - 6

Alfred, Otis - 2, 28

Allison, Bobby - 31

Ard, Sam - 113

Armel, Buddy - 42, 129

Armel, Charlie - 38, 41, 120, 124, 144

Bailey, Doug - 46, 76, 144

Baker, Buck - 31, 81, 83, 86

Baldwin, Claude - 10, 12, 49, 87, 101

Barbour, William - 140

Batt, Kermit - 42, 80, 103, 109, 125, 128, 129, 144

Bouchamp, Johnny - 82

Bear, Tommy - 68, 125

Beeler, Charlie - 16, 17, 19, 68, 91, 94, 105, 107, 109 - 111, 129

Bonbrake, Denny - 126

Bocock, Jean - 66, 95, 97, 99 100, 101

Bocock, Lewis - 10, 11, 12, 14, 16, 17, 21, 29, 42, 44, 45, 49, 51, 57, 60, 61, 62, 63, 78, 79, 85, 86, 87, 95 - 102, 114, 121, 125, 130, 131, 141, 142, 144

Bowers, Cindy - 49, 50, 53

Bowers, Diane - 49, 50, 53

Bowers, Junior - 10, 28, 43, 44, 46, 48 - 53, 55, 59, 63, 85, 86, 87, 91, 90, 100, 117

Bowers, Helen - 11, 49, 50, 52, 53, 55, 100

Bowers, Shorty - 42, 95, 97, 121, 127, 132, 134, 135

Brannon, Chuck - 45, 118, 121

Breighner, Ivan - 146

Breedon, Russ - 151, 138

Bridgeforth, Carol - 49, 146

Brooks, Earl - 10, 146, 147

Bux, Kuda - 11, 85, 129, 145

Campbell, Bobby - 49, 54, 55, 56, 57, 58, 59, 60, 61, 63, 64, 116, 125

Campbell, Tommy - 54 - 61, 63, 64, 91, 115, 117, 125

Cauly, Paul - 10, 11, 12

Cavalier Speedway - 54, 74, 76, 77, 112, 136, 137

Charles, Al - 6, 58

Chitwood, Joey - 6, 85

Claytor, Ernest - 7, 8, 9

Claytor, Mary - 9

Claytor, L. P. - 6 - 9, 11, 27, 43, 48, 51, 58

Clayor, Yortha - 66

Cline, Patsy - 40, 78, 113, 120, 129, 144, 146

Clore, Jackie - 14 42, 45, 60, 91, 92, 93, 100, 101, 121, 125, 140 - 141, 142

Clore, Marie - 92, 141

Clore, Mike - 140 - 141

Cook, Bob - 9, 15, 30

Craigsville Motor Speedway - 29, 54, 67, 68, 69, 105, 106, 136, 137

Crosen, Bob - 12, 86, 107, 108, 141

Crum, Johnny - 55, 119, 125

Daytona - 40, 47, 81, 82, 83, 136

Dedrick, Chuck - 2, 3, 14, 71, 125

Denison, Jackie - 13, 118, 121, 141

Devil's Bowl Speedway - 14, 20 - 21, 48, 56, 68, 101, 104 - 105, 108, 112, 116, 118, 141, 142, 145, 146, 148

Dobyns, Bob - 10, 28, 68, 100, 106, 136 - 139

Dobbins, Bobby - 138, 139

Douglas Speedway - 74, 76, 136, 138, 145

Dovel, Ray - 13, 29, 39, 44, 45, 46, 52, 57, 58, 68, 86, 99, 101, 123 - 126, 147

Earnhardt , Sr., Dale - 3, 113, 116

Eastside Speedway - 2, 3, 6 - 19, 20, 21, 27, 28, 29, 30, 32, 39, 43, 44, 45, 46, 47, 48, 51, 55, 56, 58, 59, 60, 61, 62, 63, 64, 65, 67, 71, 72, 76, 77, 80, 81, 85, 86, 87, 88, 92, 93, 94, 98, 99, 101, 108, 110, 111, 112, 114, 115, 116, 117, 118, 119, 121, 123, 124, 129, 130, 131, 136, 138, 141, 142, 147

Fauble, Fudgie - 107

Flock, Fonty - 31

Fort Ashby Speedway - 75, 103, 104, 119, 144

Garlits, Don - 29

Gatto, Al - 144

Gearhart, W. W. - 33 - 37, 88

Gibson, Gip - 8, 10, 11, 13, 29, 43, 51, 57, 68, 74, 75, 101, 114, 138, 145

Gore, Al - 12, 14, 17, 27 - 32, 49, 50, 57, 59, 61, 64, 65, 67, 101, 120, 137, 146 153

Gore, Dicky - 31

Gore, Gary - 31 - 32

Grinnan, Al - 8, 15, 16, 43, 46, 48, 51, 57, 77, 79, 85, 86, 91, 93, 112 - 114, 125, 138

Hagerstown Raceway - 54, 58, 80, 111, 115, 116, 117, 119, 123, 124, 125, 127, 128

Hansberger, Delores - 103, 105, 108

Hansberger, Dick - 12, 17, 68, 69, 93, 103 - 108, 125, 138

Hansberger, P. C. - 103, 104 - 108

Harris, Clyde - 18, 19, 29, 30, 58 - 70

Harris, Runt - 78, 137

Hite, Bobby - 17, 19, 94, 111

Irwin, Tommy - 8, 12, 43, 44, 45, 51, 77, 79, 80 - 86, 101, 105, 109, 114, 127, 134

Jarrett, Ned - 31, 84

Johnson, Cal - 2, 3, 8, 10, 11, 12, 43, 44, 71 - 79, 86, 96, 100, 137

Johnson, Junior - 31, 84

Johnson, Lionel - 28, 137

Kirby, Eugene - 6

Lam, Jack - 140

Lamaster, Clem - 42, 45, 62, 63, 125, 127 - 131

Larue, Lash - 148

Lawrenceville Speedway - 54, 56, 57, 74, 96, 112, 123, 136, 138

Lund, Tiny - 31

Lydell, Bill - 66

Mader, Dave - 42 - 43

Massanutten Speedway - 26, 80, 103, 123, 136, 142, 146 - 147

McNeal, Bob - 66

Mast, Rick - 56, 113

Matthews, Red - 41, 120

McCrary - Earl - 16, 17, 19, 65, 66, 67, 69

Moran, Earl - 9, 10, 11, 12, 16, 29, 36, 45, 49, 57, 61, 62, 68, 87, 93, 107 - 118, 121, 130

Nalley, Bill - 8, 10, 11, 12, 13, 14, 15, 16, 17, 18, 19, 29, 38 - 47, 57, 61, 75, 77, 79, 85, 86, 91, 92, 93, 98, 99, 101, 105, 107, 109, 118, 123, 124, 125, 130, 131, 138, 142, 147, 148

Nalley Lorraine - 39, 40, 43

Nalley, Sam - 39, 46, 47, 125

Natural Bridge Speedway - 21, 30, 54, 65, 136

Neff, Roy - 12, 42, 49, 55, 93, 105, 121, 132 135

Nesbeth, Harold - 27, 28

Newland, Louie - 19, 111, 130

Ninninger, Red - 14, 38, 39, 45, 63, 86, 105, 119 - 122, 127

Old Dominion Speedway - 27, 28, 31, 115, 136, 147

Panch, Marvin - 31

Peer, Robert - 8, 12, 43, 45, 79, 107, 121, 132, 133, 134, 135

Petty, Lee - 31, 83, 84

Petty, Richard - 31, 84, 112

Pilot Speedway - 33 - 37, 88, 89, 91, 103, 92, 112

Props, Charlie - 10, 49, 95, 96

Pulaski Speedway - 35, 89, 90, 112

Radford, Leroy - 6, 9, 52

Red Banks Speedway - 21, 103, 142

Repass, David - 30, 68

Roberts, Fireball - 31, 84

Rodeffer, Jr., Bill - 93, 138

Rodeffer, Sr., Bill - 146, 147

Rodeffer, Donnie - 147

Rodeffer, Harry Lee - 8, 10, 138, 142, 146, 147

Royal Speedway - 73, 78, 136

Scott, Wendell - 2, 10, 12, 14, 31, 40, 44, 66, 86, 103, 104, 112, 116, 133, 134, 137, 146, 147

Shifflett, Cotton - 10, 12, 113

Shipe, Bobby - 18

Shipp, Buck - 16, 19, 110, 141

South Boston Speedway - 41, 77, 112

Shuman, Buddy - 73 - 74

Shull, Leonard - 66

Sipe, Charlie - 8, 118, 138

Stanley, Chester - 9, 25, 49, 61, 138

Stinespring, Buddy - 13, 15, 16, 17, 36 - 37, 42, 49, 61, 62, 69, 87 - 94, 100, 101, 105, 110, 111, 118, 121, 125, 142

Stinespring, Pop - 36 - 37, 87, 88, 89, 90, 92, 94, 110

Strickland, John - 10, 11, 12, 43, 51

Stover, Don - 49, 54

Stover, Ruby - 10, 11, 59, 60, 67, 119, 144

Stover, Smokey - 8, 9, 10, 12, 13, 14, 15, 16, 17, 18, 29, 29, 39, 40, 44, 45, 46, 47, 49, 51, 54 - 64, 67, 68, 69, 75, 85, 86, 87, 91, 97, 98, 99, 100, 101, 117, 118, 119, 121, 127, 130, 131, 144, 147

Strickler, Bubby - 142

Stultz, Lee - 39, 41, 43, 46, 47, 49, 109, 111, 123, 129

Turner, Curtis - 31, 112

Trenary, Clyde - 17, 27

Unionville Speedway - 38, 75, 76, 112, 113, 119, 136

Valley Speedway - 6, 24 - 25, 54, 55, 76, 78, 80, 81, 88, 95, 96, 97, 115, 144

Weatherly, Joe - 31

Weaver, Homer - 66, 146

Weaver, Jesse - 66

Winchester Speedway - 14, 20, 21, 26, 28, 38, 39, 41, 42, 43, 45, 46, 48, 49, 50, 51, 52, 54, 59, 63, 65, 72, 74, 76, 77, 80, 81, 85, 91, 95, 109, 111, 112, 115, 116, 118, 119, 120, 125, 127, 128, 129, 133, 134, 135, 136, 140, 141, 144, 146, 148

Wyant, Avis - 16, 142 - 143, 146

Zion's Crossroads (Hilltop) Speedway - 20, 21, 54, 74, 75, 76, 117, 136, 137

Made in the USA
Lexington, KY
17 November 2013